Against the American Dream
ESSAYS ON CHARLES BUKOWSKI

Russell Harrison has a Ph.D. in English from SUNY Buffalo. He has taught American literature at St. Peter's College, Hudson County Community College and Hofstra University. From 1987 to 1989 he was a Fulbright Lecturer in American literature at Palacky University in Olomouc, Czech Republic.

Against the American Dream

Essays on Charles Bukowski

Dream

RUSSELL HARRISON

REBEL inc.

First published in the United States of America
in 1994 by Black Sparrow Press

This edition published in Great Britain in 2001
by Rebel Inc, an imprint of
Canongate Books Ltd, 14 High Street,
Edinburgh EH1 1TE

10 9 8 7 6 5 4 3 2 1

ACKNOWLEDGMENTS
The excursus "Gleason" appeared in slightly different form in
sure the charles bukowski newsletter

Rebel Inc series editor: Kevin Williamson
www.rebelinc.net

British Library Cataloguing-in-Publication Data
A catalogue record for this book is available on request
from the British Library

ISBN 1 84195 097 1

Typeset in the United States of America
Printed and bound by CPD, Ebbw Vale, Wales

for David Friedkin and Nancy Kennedy

PREFACE

Having a somewhat less jaundiced view of contemporary literature than the subject of these essays, I can't say that my discovery of Bukowski's work was like "finding gold in the city dump"
(Bukowski's description of his discovery of John Fante's work),
but it was a revelation nonetheless. My discovery was the first
chapter of *Post Office* (in the anthology *On the Job*) and such
a work had special meaning for me because I had—briefly—
worked in the Post Office. In my twenty-four weeks of work as
a substitute clerk-carrier, however, I had been absent thirty-eight
times. (While not a promising beginning to a working career, it
did reveal a minor talent for refusing work, at least work of a
certain kind.) And the sentence in *Post Office*: "Although each
night had been long, the years had gone fast," while thankfully
only in part applicable to me, nonetheless resonated. In any event,
I was impressed to see someone writing about work, a subject
that for a reason I still cannot fathom seems to leave many writers
and most literature professors cold.

   Imagine my surprise, then, when not too much later I dis-
covered that my view of most substantial gainful activity was
shared by *some* academics and that, indeed, a substantial amount
of *their* gainful activity was devoted to theorizing that refusal.
That was a discovery. At that time I thought the writings of
the Italian Autonomy Movement and its American offshoot,
the members of the *Zerowork* collective, had much that might
prove useful for literary analysis, and I still do. Along with
traditional marxist concepts, they seem more and more applicable to the situation in which capital finds itself these days—
less and less able to provide secure lives for more and more people. Those scarce twenty years between the end of World War

II and the Vietnam War when people thought capitalism a benign phenomenon, capable of gradually raising all boats (though some boats were nicer and raised higher than others, naturally) now seem more and more like a statistical "outlier" which any competent interpreter disregards as irrelevant. Bukowski's work, or so it seems to me, is valuable evidence of the fact that not everyone was of that mind.

No reader of this preface, however, should be scared off in the belief that the following essays all strike this note. They are much broader than that, as befits a body of work as wide-ranging as that of any American writer.

☆

I would like to thank George Caffentzis, Neil Donahue, Silvia Federici, David Friedkin, Birgit Funk, Nancy Kennedy, Minette Marcroft, Carey McIntosh, Rhoda Nathan and Shari Zimmerman for having read parts of the manuscript and for their useful comments and suggestions.

I would like, as well, to express my gratitude to Neil Donahue for his timely and sensible professional advice.

I also want to acknowledge, with much gratitude, the intellectual aid that George Caffentzis and Silvia Federici have given me over the years.

I also wish to express my gratitude to Seamus Cooney for the large amounts of time and effort he gave in editing the manuscript and to thank him for his extraordinarily helpful and careful editorial assistance. Without his consistently intelligent suggestions the finished product would certainly have far less value than it does.

Finally, I want to thank John Martin of Black Sparrow Press for his willingness to publish a scholarly-critical study of Charles Bukowski's work.

TABLE OF CONTENTS

Introduction   11
Abbreviations Used in the Text   23

THE POETRY

Poetry and Class   29
The Individual and the Social in Bukowski's Poetry
       of the '80s   47
Poetry and the Working Class   69
Metonymy   95
Excursus: Brecht   115

THE FICTION

Work, Refusal of Work and the Job in *Post Office*
       and *Factotum*   123
Excursus: Miller   153
Politics, Class and the Plebeian Tradition   159
Sex, Women and Irony   183
Connections: Fante—Hamsun—Mahler   217
Excursus: Gleason   243
The Fascination of the (Extra)Ordinary: The Short Stories
       of Charles Bukowski   249
Notes   281
Works Cited   309
Index to the Text   319

INTRODUCTION

The writing of Charles Bukowski and the strained reception it has received constitute one of the most intriguing and revealing aspects of the American literary scene of the last twenty years. After a steady progression through the little magazines and small presses in the 1950s and 1960s, Bukowski has produced in the subsequent two decades a body of work (ten collections of poetry, five novels and five short-story collections) that by virtue of its volume, its quality, and its uniquely representative character should have made him a recognized and critically appreciated writer in all three genres. Furthermore, he had also achieved, by the late 1970s, a significant European reputation, indeed, had become in Germany at the end of the 1980s possibly the most-published and most-read contemporary American author. Yet a serious critical scholarly response has been denied him in the United States and this omission is not the least intriguing aspect of this quintessential American writer. Indeed, because Bukowski is so unmistakably American (a number of the essays in this book reveal how truly his work reflects American society), the lack of a critical response in this country is all the more striking.°
The aims of this introduction are to emphasize the salient features of Bukowski's writing, all of which were factors in the lack of a critical response to his work: the issue of social class, the critique of the American Dream and the critical analysis of work, as well as to note some important aspects of his career.

The content of Bukowski's writing has been close to everyday life. However, one person's everyday life may not be another's

---

Notes are signalled by a superscript ° and begin on p. 281. A list of abbreviations used in the source references is on p. 23.

and thus the phrase, for all its familiarity, embodies a vague concept and undoubtedly owes its easy currency to this vagueness. With respect to much of Bukowski's writing, we can substitute "working-class life" for "everyday life" and better capture that content as well as the reason for his appeal to those readers who are not usually viewed as part of the audience for serious literature. This content has sometimes been dismissed as "banal" (a word that originally meant "common to all"). I think it is the working-class content of much of Bukowski's work, rather than any so-called "banality," that is the sticking point for many academic critics as well as for others. Writers who treat such experience find it rough sledding in the United States. Their work may even be critically acclaimed, as was, for example, the work of Nelson Algren, and yet real acceptance will elude them.°

The rejection and ignoring of Bukowski is a result of many Americans' reluctance to acknowledge the fact that ours is a class society, something Bukowski's work constantly reminds us of. That ours was a rapidly expanding economy, a society with a great deal of mobility (especially in comparison to Europe), a relatively homogenous culture and relatively low class barriers was—always excepting the slaves—true before the Civil War and the great industrialization that followed it; but since that time, and especially in the 20th century, and most especially in the last twenty years, class barriers have risen and (upward) mobility has decreased. Americans don't like to be reminded of the barriers of social class, nor that the middle class has decreased in both relative and absolute terms since the early 1970s because it leaves our system without the distinguishing moral cachet that had accompanied its birth and remained for many years thereafter.° There remains only the possibility of material affluence for a decreasing proportion of the population; and while material affluence is, in fact, an adequate raison d'être for most Americans (as perhaps for most people in the West, generally), however elusive or chimeric it may be for the vast majority of them, it is not one that has any great intellectual or moral appeal. Moreover, with the increasing uncompetitiveness of the American economy, the decrease of our standard of living in the last two decades, and the redistribution of wealth upward of the last fifteen years, for an increasing number of Americans material affluence is no longer as assured as it once was. While the significance of social class in the United States has always been recognized by Bukowski, it has become more prominent in his recent work.

Bukowski is the only major post-War American writer who has denied the efficacy of the American Dream (a phenomenon based on a class society). He has done this in two ways: first, by his unrelenting assault on deadening, routinized work as it exists for the vast majority of Americans—this is the most important political feature of Bukowski's work and one of the linchpins of my analysis of much of his writing; second, by his decidedly anti-consumerist trait, the most consistent symbol of which may be the small radio that seems to follow Henry Chinaski through all his vicissitudes so that even as a successful writer, living "behind a six-foot hedge with a long driveway leading / to a two car garage, rose garden, fruit trees. . . ." (D 270), the strains of Mahler and Shostakovich seem still to reach him through that radio which, as a young man, he would repeatedly hurl through windows but which would never fail to function (something confirmed by a recent poem: "I have continued to listen to / classical music via the radio / for decades" [R 55]). The late accumulation to the contrary notwithstanding, the Chinaskian ethos embodies a rejection of clothes, gadgets and a new car every other year and the refusal to live on credit—of consumption for the sake of consumption (really increased consumption for the sake of increased consumption). This is a decidedly different ethos from that on which American society and (to a lesser extent) other capitalist societies are based. And Bukowski's rejection possesses an unusual authority because it comes from someone of a working-class background. Moreover, it is a refusal that is positive in its implicit demand for something more than material affluence. Consumption and accumulation as ends in themselves were never a part of the Chinaskian project. Use-value takes precedence over exchange-value in Bukowski's work.

Benjamin Franklin's *Autobiography* gave us the classic definition of the American Dream; indeed, as one scholar put it, "it is because Franklin gave us the definitive formulation of the American Dream that [the *Autobiography*] has become a classic of American literature."° In Franklin, the American Dream has three principal features: economic success (the rise from rags to riches); the "rise from impotence to importance, from dependence to independence, from helplessness to power," i.e., personal fulfillment; and "the philosophy of individualism," "the recognition of the free will of the individual as opposed to his determination by forces larger than himself," all of which, finally, support a "philosophy of hope, even of optimism."

I have mentioned the critique of consumerism; but Bukowski's writings directly contradict each of these principal features. Bukowski's work everywhere embodies, explicitly or implicitly, a rejection of the ideology of success and power and though it is not often acknowledged, his work has increasingly critiqued traditional individualism. One may be fooled by his protagonists' frequent reference to their need to be alone, their scorn for "the crowd," their assertion of their individuality. Such assertions are almost always suspect and often undercut themselves: Henry Chinaski's response to John Handler in *Factotum*—"All I want to do is get that check and get drunk. That may not sound noble but it's my choice"—is a less than satisfying defense of individualism (and surely not what Franklin had in mind). An analysis of Chinaski's decision-making, there and elsewhere, hardly leads to the conclusion that Bukowski's work asserts the free will of the individual in our society.°

Indeed, quite the opposite is the case. Bukowski's work represents the late-twentieth century American response to the Franklin mythology and arrives at an almost diametrically opposed view regarding the relationship between the individual and society. Just as Franklin's work holds an "archetypal appeal" for many readers, so, too, does Bukowski's. The realm of individual autonomy has been narrowly circumscribed by the historical changes of the intervening two centuries and it would be silly to deny that the individual's place in the 20th-century United States is qualitatively different from what it was in the Colonies of Franklin's time. Yet ideology lags behind reality and Bukowski's writings constitute one of the few attempts by a contemporary American writer to produce a body of work consonant with the contemporary United States in any fundamental sense, and he succeeds because his is— with all the adjustments that have to be made for a writer's work in relation to society—a working-class point of view. The following essays are an attempt to make this, along with much else, clear.

14

2

Bukowski has emphasized the most important feature of the American class system: the individual's role in the relations of production; and he has emphasized it more consistently and to greater effect than any American writer in three-quarters of a century. He has done this through the prominence he has given to the role of the job and of work in American life. One has to go back to the pages in Jack London's *John Barleycorn* describing the protagonist's hiring and work at the power plant of the Oakland Street Railway, for example, or the eponymous hero's job at the machine laundry in London's *Martin Eden* for passages about work of power comparable to those in *Factotum*, *Post Office* and many of the poems. If something is banal by virtue of being common to all then for most people the most banal (in both root and contemporary senses of the word) aspect of life is the job. I think it is a fact, obvious to some and denied by many, that the banality of this activity holds for the vast majority of workers in the United States. Though the job can provide emotional rewards, including a social life and a feeling of solidarity with others, the activity itself is, for this vast majority, boring and routine, a banal, trivial, pointless thing. As Bukowski put it in "The Life of a Bum," his finest short story: "People were caught in traps. . . . They felt as if their lives were being wasted. And they were right."

But although this holds for most people, it is significantly less true for readers of serious literature. Such readers are confronted in Bukowski's writings with a world that is very different from their own and probably at odds with their conception of the world Bukowski depicts. This representation is so jarring, jibes so little with their conception (if they do conceive of it) of work as it exists for most people that an uneasiness, almost a cognitive dissonance results. Things can't be *that* routine, we think, *that* boring, that *bad*, because if they were then people would . . . . Bukowski is then dismissed as a cynic, a chronic malcontent, an individual who has failed to "adjust." He may well be all these things, but that does not detract from the reality he depicts which does exist for most people, people who are neither cynics nor malcontents nor failures in adjustment. It is a world no one has caught better, where "although the nights were long, the years went by fast"; where

> sitting on those stools
> eleven-and-one-half hours a night
> every bit of outside news
> was greeted by us
> much like the inmates of a prison camp. . . .
>
> (WT 162)

where, finally, "Time stood still while existence was a throbbing unbearable thing."

There is, however, another tack taken in response to these undeniable realities by those who recognize the truth of what Bukowski is saying about most people's work (though not theirs). This is to acknowledge the imperfections, the dissonances, in their own jobs and aver, "Well, no job is perfect; we've all got problems with our jobs. That's life," i.e., so to abstract the experience as to rob it of all meaningful content. But while it is true that work has an inherent problematic, it is certainly not true that the problems are of an equal seriousness, equally destructive to a humane existence, or suffered equally by all.

It might be noted that Bukowski's critique of American society is one reason for his greater acceptance in Europe, especially in Germany. With class a more acknowledged phenomenon in Europe, the realities of Bukowski's representations are in no way seen as distorting reality, as evidence of a warped subjective perception, and hence denied out of hand. The more general critique of the status quo implicit in such a representation of work has, over the years, again especially in Germany, made Bukowski popular with the left and with social alternativists, an acceptance more difficult to achieve in American society, whose legitimacy is based on a broad, shallow consensus and an extremely narrow band of acceptable political opinion.°

Indeed, Henry Chinaski's polemics against everyday life, the family and the nine-to-five routine have a political dimension. To a contemporary reader, his railing against conventional lifestyles may be seen as fighting a straw man, or as passé, an anachronism, overtaken by the events of the 1960s and later. However, the ideology of work that prevailed in the U.S. up until the 1960s and the milieu in which Bukowski was shaped make it clear that it is no straw man that is being set up, nor in fact, that it was passé. Through the entire post-War era, the ideology of Frederick Taylor's *Scientific Management* was still potent in many areas of work. Indeed, it seems to have gained a new lease on life in the 1980s and 1990s.

3

While Bukowski has been critical of conventional American social values, his criticism has rarely been overtly political and he might well disagree with the claim I make in this book for the political content of much of his work. This claim, however, is based on his focus on the refusal of work, on the working-class consciousness, and on his critique of hierarchic society with its inevitable exploitation. This is the significant political under-pinning of *Post Office, Factotum, Ham on Rye* and much else he has written.

In his own terms Bukowski does see himself as "apolitical." But his brand of apolitics bears a closer analysis than it has received. The point I make in this book is that much of his best work (especially from the early 1970s on) expresses in fictional and poetic terms a critique of late capitalist society from a working-class point of view, at times suggesting the need for the kind of change that many on the left were demanding in the 1960s and 1970s.

Moreover, politics is sometimes a strong presence in his writings, if at times manifesting itself through a violent rejection of politics.° Bukowski's overt political stance has ranged from the New Leftish views of the newspaper columns of the late 1960s and early 1970s, in which the vast social, and briefly, political changes of the 1960s were reflected, through the welfare state liberalism of *Ham on Rye* to the poems of the 1980s with their criticism of the Reagan-era roll-backs. Moreover, his virtually complete drop-out from writing or any intellectual engagement with society in the decade immediately following World War II, the renewed spur to his writing that the social movement of the late 1960s and early 1970s provided and its positive reception within that movement taken in conjunction with his positive valuation of the social relations obtaining in the 1930s are evidence of the close relationship between his writing and the political left, if not of politics in the narrowest sense.

One of the points I make in this book is that Bukowski began to identify more and more with a working-class perspective from the early 1970s on and that his most successful works (*Factotum*, *Ham on Rye* and the poetry collection *War All the Time*) receive their power from this identification. Having left the world of conventional work, he was able to view his experience more objectively and this facilitated a proletarian identification previously lacking. Bukowski's attitude towards the working class has changed markedly in the later poems. Poems such as "Sparks," "transformation and disfiguration," and "sometimes it's hard to know what to do" are fundamentally different from poems like "the workers," "$$$$$$," and "Yankee Doodle" in their attitude toward the working class. Clearly, with a writer as productive as Bukowski, a different selection, emphasizing the earlier poetry and short stories, might support a different interpretation. It should, however, be understood that when I claim Bukowski as a proletarian writer it is in no simple or prescriptive sense as sometimes informed the debate on that term in the *New Masses* in the 1930s. One of the premises underlying much of my discussion of this issue is that post-industrial capitalism produces a "postmodern proletarian" literature. Work and the working-class have changed in the last half century and it is only to be expected that the creative literature reflecting that change will be different.

4

For roughly a decade, from 1945 to 1955, Bukowski published very little, indeed, nothing at all in the second half of that period. This gap has played a significant role in his career. Though born in 1920, Bukowski didn't begin to publish seriously (after a false start in the mid-1940s) until the late 1950s (his late thirties), did not achieve significant recognition until almost a decade later and did not achieve a mastery of his medium until he was in his fifties. When this progression is combined with the fact that often enough he has taken his material (this is especially true of his novels) from the events of his childhood, youth and early manhood, i.e., the 1920s through the 1940s, his writing can seem out of step. Hence, as is most evident in *Love Is a Dog from Hell* (1977) and *Women* (1978), we have the phenomenon of a man whose deepest attitudes to women were shaped almost a half-century earlier than the era in which they were being given artistic expression. This has had two results: first, chauvinistic traits were more likely to be perceived as salient and to evoke stronger reactions in the context of the raised and rising consciousnesses of the 1970s and 1980s than even more chauvinist books of his contemporaries which had, however, been published earlier. Secondly, the fact that Bukowski's books were being written well after the start of the women's movement meant that that movement affected them as it hadn't others.

Another effect of Bukowski's ten-year withdrawal from writing was that he did not achieve mastery of the medium until he was into his fifties.° I realize that this is a controversial statement because many readers favor his earlier poetry over that published during the 1980s and *Post Office* over some of the later novels. Yet to me *Factotum* (1975), the poetry collection *Dangling in the Tournefortia* (1981) and the short-story collection *Hot Water Music* (1983) are the generic watersheds in Bukowski's oeuvre, the books in which he finally found himself as a writer.°

Two related events occurred which contributed to the marked change in Bukowski's writing that began in the early 1970s and came to fruition in the course of the decade. The first was the prospect that John Martin, his publisher at Black Sparrow Press, revealed to him with his promise of a stipend that would enable him to quit the Post Office and devote himself to his writing.° The significance of this offer, both for what such faith meant for Bukowski's self-confidence as well as for the money (and time) itself, should not be underestimated.° It was a significance recognized by the writer himself, as a recent poem, "the good old machine," attests where he tells of Martin's financial and emotional support that enable him to quit the Post Office and devote himself full time to writing, noting, indeed, that it wasn't the money alone that was appreciated, but also

```
. . . his encouragement
since I hadn't had much of that
surely was a hell of a
lift
especially since he was an
editor-publisher.
```
                                        (SS 251)

The other, related, event that affected his writing was the decision to write a novel. According to Neeli Cherkovski, his biographer, Bukowski "feared that he might not really make enough money as a writer if he did not concentrate on a long prose work, and for that he needed hours of isolation each day" (208). The need for money may have played a part, but it can hardly have been the primary reason for the decision. Well into middle-age, Bukowski had achieved a distance from the events of his life which enabled him to place them in perspective and see them as objectively meaningful. The impulse had been there as early as the 1965 story "Confessions of a Man Insane Enough to Live with Beasts." Indeed, the greater the distance in time from the events he writes about (as in *Factotum* and *Ham on Rye*) the more sure the handling. I don't think this is an accident. By the nature of the form, the novel, especially as practiced by Bukowski, demands a broader perspective on its material than does the poem or the short story. The part that time plays in the novel is one of the most significant aspects of the form. Bukowski was forced by the form of the novel to view his life more objectively—to shape it—than had been his wont or than had been necessary while working in shorter forms. This resulted in the loss of that "immediacy" which constituted a problem in much of his early work, both poetry and short fiction. The exigencies of the novel form—the constraints of plot, character, the inevitable demands of the objective world of the realist novel—forced Bukowski to adapt his prose, and his poetry followed suit.

If one had to sum up the salient formal feature of this new style, one could say it was the shorter sentence, which in turn allowed a more careful control of the text as a whole. The effect of such formal demands is evident in *Factotum*, in all respects the watershed book in Bukowski's career. Here the short(er) sentence becomes the dominating syntactic structure, as the short chapter dominates the work as a whole. Along with shorter sentences there are, in a sense, fewer of them. The repetitions and redundancies—signs of a lack of confidence—which are present in *Post Office* are nowhere in evidence in *Factotum* where redundancy yields to ellipsis and implication, producing a subtler and more complex work. Similar effects are to be seen in the poetry that followed *Factotum* with the added change that a figurative, at times surrealistic language yielded to a poetry that is among the most non-metaphorical in English. Metaphor substitutes and Bukowski did not want a substitute, though he did want to make vivid the object being described and this accounts for his reliance on metonymy. He did not see that "unity behind the apparent diversity of phenomena" which M. H. Abrams felt metaphor "discloses" (357). Indeed, metonymy, the partializing figure, was the perfect poetic vehicle for a body of work which, from beginning to end refuses a specious unity designed only to paper over the splits in a society fragmented by class.

5

A word is in order concerning the texts chosen and the topics of the essays in this volume. Bukowski is so prolific a writer that any treatment of his work, especially his poetry and stories, can only deal with a very small percentage of the whole. Therefore, selection plays an especially important role. As I have made clear, I feel that Bukowski's work of the last two decades includes most of his best writing. Hence, the most obvious omission in these essays is an extended discussion of the poetry of the 1950s and 1960s. The same holds for the shorter prose, fictional and otherwise, of that period. Furthermore, my reason for ignoring that work is tied to the topics of my essays: in one way or another all of the essays on the poetry take as their premise the fact that there was a significant change in his writing in the 1970s and that that change had, broadly speaking, to do with the political. The issue of politics and social change also informs my essays on the novels, not only in the essays on the refusal of work and the plebeian worldview but also in my analysis of Bukowski's relationship to Fante, Hamsun and Orwell. Moreover, any thorough analysis of Bukowski's work has to discuss its portrayal of women.

In view of the misunderstandings and misinterpretations that have arisen in this area, a careful analysis of Bukowski's representations of women and of relations between the sexes should prove useful. The essay on the short stories embodies to some extent aspects of the essays on the poetry and the novels: the misreadings of the later works in terms of the earlier and the radical change his efforts in the form underwent in the middle of his career. Finally, for several reasons, it didn't prove feasible to discuss the late poetry and the novel *Hollywood.* I hope to treat them in subsequent essays on Bukowski.

ABBREVIATIONS
USED IN THE TEXT

B   Burning in Water, Drowning in Flame (1974)
D   Dangling in the Tournefortia (1981)
E   Erections, Ejaculations, Exhibitions and General Tales of Ordinary Madness (1972)
F   Factotum (1975)
H   Ham on Rye (1982)
HP   Horses Don't Bet on People & Neither Do I (1984)
HW   Hot Water Music (1983)
L   Love Is a Dog from Hell: Poems 1974–1977 (1977)
N   Notes of a Dirty Old Man (1969)
P   Post Office (1971, 1992)
PP   Play the Piano Drunk/Like a Percussion Instrument/Until the Fingers Begin to Bleed a Bit (1979)
R   In the Shadow of the Rose (1991)
S   South of No North (1973)
SS   Septuagenarian Stew: Stories and Poems (1990)
W   Women (1978)
WT   War All the Time: Poems 1981–1984 (1984)
Y   You Get So Alone at Times That It Just Makes Sense (1986)

Against the American Dream

ESSAYS ON CHARLES BUKOWSKI

T H E   P O E T R Y

CHAPTER ONE:
POETRY AND CLASS

As noted, Charles Bukowski's poetry has not received much of a critical response in the United States. In light of his popular success in the United States (the more impressive since it has been achieved exclusively through small presses) and his resounding success in Europe (above all in Germany where, by 1990, 2,200,000 copies of his books had been sold) the absence of such a response is striking.° To take just one example: Robert von Hallberg in his otherwise excellent book, *American Poetry 1945–1980*, does not mention Bukowski, even though a section of the book discusses poems on working-class life. Moreover, the fact that Bukowski has not appeared in any of the large mainstream anthologies that include American poetry of the last 30 years is remarkable.

There are a number of reasons for this lack of a critical response, but two are noteworthy. The first is the sheer volume of his poetry and the attitude such a production bespeaks, an attitude sharpened by some of Bukowski's comments on his own poetic practice; the second, subtler and more important reason arises out of a failure to appreciate the significance of, or to react against, the class content of Bukowski's poetry. Superficially, Bukowski may be seen as a late-blooming confessional or a late-blooming Beat or even as a poet of the counter-culture. But Bukowski is neither a confessional nor a Beat/counter-cultural poet in any of the conventional senses of those terms. More than anything else, he is a proletarian poet, but a proletarian poet of a special sensibility, whose poetry owes something to the Confessionals, the Beats and to the counter-culture of the 1960s.

Bukowski has brought into contemporary American poetry an experience which is neither elitist, bohemian nor overtly political, but working-class. He has done this, in part, by depicting as class experience what might otherwise be viewed as confessional material. Were it the latter, it would lead to a privileging of such experience in a way that is antithetical to Bukowski's class ethos, as did the Confessional Poets' treatment of similar material. By mainstreaming such experience, by stripping it of its privileged status, Bukowski has performed a cultural and, in the broader sense of the word, political service and this in part constitutes his significance and for this reason it is important to distinguish his poetry from the Confessionals'. In a sense, Bukowski has incorporated the achievements of the earlier poets and gone on to produce a body of poetry treating a wide variety of subject matter with a freedom and frankness vis-à-vis its material that earlier poets did not have.° In sum, he has been able to present in his poetry a picture of life in the United States in the second half of the 20th Century that is unique in its range, its detail and its perspective.

Bukowski's poetry can be difficult to assess in terms of the 20th-century modernist tradition; its very volume works against easily getting a handle on it. Indeed, the amount of poetry Bukowski has published and the apparent ease with which he has produced it offend against certain tenets of modernism and his work provides a sharp contrast to the production of many 20th-century poets.° Eliot's collected poems, for example, total fewer pages than some individual collections of Bukowski's, and in roughly the last two decades alone Bukowski has published as much poetry as did Pound or Williams in much greater spans of time. The major Black Sparrow publications which collect the poems of that period run to almost 1,100 poems, 2,200 pages of poetry.° "A dry period for me," Bukowski told William Packard, "means perhaps going two or three nights without writing." Such production is the result of a different aesthetic from that of many of his contemporaries.

Since Flaubert there has been an aesthetic—one might even call it an ethic—which prized a craft that might restrict production to three or four lines a day for a novelist, and a similar intensity brought to bear on the poem had almost become the norm in the intervening century. While there have been others who have produced substantial poetic oeuvres (Lawrence, Ginsberg and Brecht—the one who has perhaps come closest to equaling Bukowski in output—come to mind) it is not sheer bulk alone that is the issue. Rather it is the combination of his absolute reliance on a free verse of the most varied sort: long lines in the tradition of Whitman as in "I didn't want to" (D 35-38), one of his finest poems (though diametrically opposed to Whitman in content), as well as—and this seems to have increased recently—lines of just a few syllables (many of the poems in *You Get So Alone at Times That It Just Makes Sense* and *Septuagenarian Stew*). Bukowski has no single, preferred form as (even within the greater freedom of free verse) poets often do: neither long nor short poems, neither long nor short stanzas, neither long nor short lines. This variety has contributed to the feeling that there really is no form, and therefore no craft, no underlying aesthetic of *some sort*, at least, to Bukowski's poetry, the feeling (even at this late date) that it isn't even, really, poetry.°

After the achievements of Flaubert and James, Pound had charged poetry to be as well written as prose. Such an attitude was, of course, a reaction against the Romantic emphasis on individual genius and its concomitant disregard for formal and generic limits, as well as against the voluminous productions of the Victorians. Flaubert, indeed, became the locus classicus for such an attitude towards the artist's work. In his essay "Flaubert and the Sentence," Roland Barthes captured the aura of this attitude well:

> the labor of style is for him an unspeakable suffering (even if he speaks it quite often), an almost expiatory ordeal for which he acknowledges no compensation of a magical (i.e., aleatory) order, as the sentiment of inspiration might be for many writers: style, for Flaubert, is absolute suffering, infinite suffering, useless suffering. Writing is disproportionately slow (*"four pages this week," "five days for a page," "two days to reach the end of two lines"*); it requires an "irrevocable farewell to life," a pitiless sequestration. (296)

While Flaubert, and those he influenced, were prospectors sifting the stream for that nugget containing the *mot juste*, Bukowski was strip-mining a much wider territory.

Yet there is another attitude toward literary production manifested both in what is produced and in the conditions under which it is produced, a more specifically American attitude of the modern period (though it expresses a tendency which has been present throughout much of the history of poetry). This line, beginning with Whitman and extending through Williams, had broad sympathies and generous ideas as to what constituted proper poetic content and did not fetishize its mode of production. The conditions under which one writes are not always the quasi-monastic ones suggested by Flaubert. For Bukowski, far from being "a pitiless sequestration," they are markedly casual. As he told Packard, he "usually [writes] late at night, while drinking wine and listening to classical music on the radio and smoking. . . ."° And he told Robert Wennersten:

> You get a bit dramatic when you're drunk, a bit corny. It feels good. The symphony music is on, and you're smoking a cigar. You lift the beer, and you're going to tap out these five or six or fifteen or thirty great lines. You start drinking and write poems all night. You find them on the floor in the morning. You take out all the bad lines, and you have poems. About sixty percent of the lines are bad; but it seems like the remaining lines, when you drop them together, make a poem.°

Here a craft view of poetry is replaced by a more casual stance. At the same time, such an attitude was not likely to result in the type of poem that most of Bukowski's contemporaries were learning to write, whether it was in the 1950s what W. D. Snodgrass described as "a densely textured lyric, crammed with learned allusions, witty metaphors, startling changes of tones, verbal ambiguities—all packed tightly into the hermetically sealed space of the autonomous symbolist poem" (Breslin 17) or the dominant-mode "scenic poem" of the 1970s.°

Just as the emphasis on craft suggests an ethic, so, too, does Bukowski's massive—almost industrial—production. As with Whitman, it is a clear statement that poetry is not to be restricted to certain subject matter. In fact, it easily enough becomes a statement that poetry should include everything and that everything should be included in poetry. And for this there exists a long and respected tradition which has always had its adherents, though it has not been dominant in modern Western literature. Introducing the poems of Tu Fu, David Hinton wrote:

> He brought every aspect of public and private experience into
> the domain of poetry, including life's more unpleasant aspects,
> which traditional decorum had frowned upon. And the spirit of
> Tu Fu's engagement with this unexplored terrain was profound
> in its implications: he conceived experience in the precise terms
> of concrete detail. As a result, the very texture of his poetry is
> an act of praise for existence itself. . . . Tu Fu was the first poet
> to write extensively about real, immediate social concerns.
> . . . Tu found poetry in the most pedestrian experience. (viii.)

Thus this broadly sympathetic poetic stance ranges across centuries and cultures: it is apparent in Tu Fu's revolution in the
poetry of the High T'ang, in Wordsworth's *Lyrical Ballads* and
1802 Preface and Whitman's *Leaves of Grass* with its Preface of
1855. It also includes Brecht (whose "Lyric Competition" essay
of 1927 may be added to the list) and Williams as its most important 20th-century Western practitioners. Bukowski, some
1200 years after Tu Fu, described it as "The Poetic Revolution"
(beginning, in his view, around 1955), when poetry had "turned
from a diffuse and careful voice of formula and studied ineffec-
tiveness to a voice of clarity and burnt toast and spilled olives
and me and you and the spider in the corner."°

However, it was not only content that Bukowski objected to,
but form and language as well; certainly Eliot and others had
incorporated "burnt toast" into their poetry. As he put it in "A
Rambling Essay": "I was aware of the glass-prison terminology:
that fancy, long, and twisted words were evasions, crutches,
weaknesses" (11). It was rather the high modernists' emphasis on
irony and the impersonal stance, reflected in their language, that
Bukowski reacted against strongly, the specious objectivity of
such a stance. The emphasis on the "organic" quality of a poem
and the concomitant irony—either as effect or cause—were
anathema to Bukowski. For Cleanth Brooks, perhaps the foremost New Critical proponent of such an attitude, "the poem is
like a little drama. The total effect proceeds from all the elements
in the drama, and in a good poem, as in a good drama, there
is no waste motion and there are no superfluous parts" (800).
(This emphasis on value, a kind of Tayloristic abhorrence of
"wasted motion" and superfluity, is something Bukowski's poetry
profoundly reacts against and it will be discussed in more detail
at the end of this essay.) The organic quality that the New Critics

33

and the poets influenced by them (and several of the New Critics were important poets) demanded is something to which Bukowski's poetic ethos is diametrically opposed. Indeed, the organizing principle of so much of his poetry, the subjectivity that structures everything, flies in the face of the New Critical demand for "the poet as impersonal craftsman, who refuses to reduce the full complexity of human experience by thrusting his private vision upon it" (Breslin 18) and thus in the face of the concomitant formal restraints. There are no *personae* in Bukowski's poetry, only the one *persona,* "Bukowski."°

That Bukowski felt this impersonal, "objective" attitude was an evasion is clear from his poem "*Kenyon Review,* After the Sandstorm," where, commenting on the writing of that magazine's contributors, he

> . . . marvel[ed] at the most brilliant way those
> professors used the language to criticize each
> other for the way they criticized literature.
> I even felt that they were humorous about it,
> but not quite: the bitterness was rancid and
> red steel hot, but at the same time I felt the
> leisurely and safe lives that language had
> evolved from: places and cultures centuries
> soft and institutionalized.
> I knew that I would never be able to write
> in that manner, yet I almost wanted to be
> one of them or any of them: being guarded,
> fierce and witty, having fun in that way.
>
> (HP 121)

Artistic distance—"being guarded"—is an important target of Bukowski's critique here and this stance is directly related to the irony and "impersonalism" of the New Critical tradition. It is also important to note that Bukowski is writing here not about poets, but critics and not even critics of literature but rather critics of critics so that one source of his critique is the tremendous distance that has removed literature and culture from living. Clearly such a critique carries with it a critique of content as well: people this far removed from life are surely going to be writing about something else than would a proletarian rudely experiencing the relations of production. It is also clear that the craft ethos that produced the poem prized by the New Critics

34

militated against the extensive production that Bukowski favored.

This production is a result of three factors. The first can be characterized as an aesthetic of the little event. There is nothing so trivial or mundane in either the subjective or the objective world that it cannot be transformed into poetry. Like Tu, Bukowski "conceived experience in the precise terms of concrete detail." And Bukowski, finally and completely, lays to rest the idea that there is such a thing as "fit" (or "unfit") subject matter for poetry and he does so simply by ignoring such a possibility. In the course of the 20th century this issue had been resolved with respect to fiction, and certainly the possibility of a similar freedom for poetry had been broached by Whitman and furthered by Williams and others. As Williams wrote in his letter to Moore: "Always, to me, poetry seems limitless in its application to life. If a man were able there is no subject or material which can rightly be denied him. But if he fails, he fails through the lack of power not through the material he develops." But the issue of "appropriate" material had not been irrevocably laid to rest in poetry, as it had in fiction by Joyce, Miller, Burroughs and others.° This emphasis on the mundane as fit, perhaps even necessary, material for poetry leads, naturally enough, to an extensive production because there is a lot of the mundane to write about. With Bukowski one doesn't even have to leave one's house or apartment (and one almost never leaves the city).

A second factor in his voluminous production is Bukowski's use of the narrative as his primary formal structure. Whether a recollection of a past event, a present-tense narrative, something experienced first-hand or something told to the narrator by another person, the overwhelming majority of his poems are narratives of one sort or another and telling a story takes time: the scene has to be set, characters delineated and (sometimes) a plot developed.

The final factor (whether as cause or effect) and an aspect of Bukowski's poetry that must strike even the most casual reader, is its extensive (though not intensive) subjectivity. The self—our self—is something that many of us believe we know something about, certainly more than anyone else. Yet Bukowski's subject— the agent of that self—is firmly rooted in the objective world. (One proof of this is the large amount of conversation in his poetry.) Bukowski does not suggest that the self creates its own, or a "truer" reality. There is, however, an assumption that the self, through its reflection in subjectivity, i.e., as agent, is something the individual has a firm grasp on and that through the presentation of this one complete (though circumscribed) piece of the world we achieve a limited objectivity. Intense self-consciousness is not the principal factor here. The narrator of "let nothing ever happen" reveals this view of self as defined through activity in his reply to a couple of road workers who have questioned his driving in a lane that has been closed to traffic:

> "who the fuck do you think you are?" asked the
> blond.
> "I don't know who I am, but I'm going to get into
> my car now and make a right turn from this lane."
>
> (D 214)

By avoiding an emphasis on consciousness, per se, Bukowski has avoided the pitfalls of a characterization where "extreme individualization annuls all individuality" through "the description of all fleeting thoughts and feelings, all transitory associations that occur to [characters] in their contact with the outside world, with the greatest detail and exactness."° Bukowski does not emphasize the psychological factor at the cost of the objective world and often there is little psychological detail. It is most frequently the subject's concrete perceptions of, and actions in the objective world that fill the poem. Moreover, the form and the dynamic of the poetic narrative preclude its presentation being overwhelmed by detail because they preclude the abstract consideration of such detail.

We are never in doubt of the objective world in which the narrator is placed; indeed the narrator's subjectivity is severely constrained by that world, a constraint which helps produce the heightened subjectivity: the pressures of the world are so great that constant self-assertion is necessary to the subject's survival. But again, this results not so much in its own endless cogitations as in the narrative registration of the subject's environment. The absence of metaphor and the relentless metonymy further emphasize both the extent to which the physical world impinges on the threatened subject and the extent to which the subject is a part of that world: the subject becomes defined in narrative and

36

through its contiguous relations to objects. Hence, both as a result of and a defence against this objective world we have the mass of Bukowski's poems, poems delineating the narrator amidst and through the contingent phenomena of his world.

This inextricability, the "object-in-subject" quality of Bukowski's poetry is reflected formally in the way many of his poems have of starting off as third-person narratives (or apparent third-person narratives) and then shifting to reveal themselves as first-person narratives. It is as if the poem cannot resist the underlying subjective dynamic that is always there but at the same time cannot escape its environment. It is not that an identity is being set up à la Hegel but neither is it quite the sharp categorical distinction between the self and the other that it might seem. The poem "out of the mainstream" is a good example of this:

out of the mainstream

after Mickey's wife goes to work
he walks to the back of the court and starts smoking dope
with Harry the house painter.
Harry the house painter has a cowed dog named
"Pluto"
who whines away the day
at the end of a long rope.

I can't blame anybody: people get tired of the
mainstream

I sit inside my place
reading the daily newspaper over and over
again.

then I turn on the tv to the
morning soap operas
and I am glad that I don't live
with any of those women
they are always getting pregnant and are
always unhappy
with their doctors and lawyers.

I snap the set off
consider masturbating
reject that and
take a bath instead.

37

the phone rings, it's my
girlfriend: "what are you
doing?"

"nothing."

"what do you mean, 'nothing'?"

"I'm in bed."

"in bed? it's almost noon."

"I know."

"why don't you take a walk?"

"all right."

                *

I get up, get dressed and go outside.
I walk south down Western
I walk all the way to Santa Monica Boulevard
go into Sears Roebuck.

there's a blue jean sale on.
I purchase a pair for under $10.
I take the escalator down
and in the candy section
I buy a large bag of popcorn.

then I stroll through the hardware section
looking at tools that I have no interest in,
then to the electrical section
where I stand looking at a series of
sun lamps,
jamming the popcorn into my mouth
and feeling like a total
asshole.

                                    (D 87-88)

This is an impressive poem. Out of "doing nothing" Bukowski
weaves a poem that is both richly detailed social commentary
and accurate depiction of a certain psychological state of mind,
though there is, strictly speaking, very little of "the psychological factor" in the poem. Only in the last line does the narrator

even tell us how he feels, although it's clear from what he's doing. The subtle (and less subtle) connections between the narrator and his world, the low-level pressure of the social world, personal and impersonal, are done with tremendous skill: he reads the newspaper again and again; he watches tv; he takes a walk because his girlfriend suggests it. There is a rejection of absolute solipsism—he decides not to masturbate—yet here, too, there is a hint of the outside world in that there's a good probability that the impetus for masturbating (and in all likelihood what would constitute the fantasized content) was seeing the—unhappy—women on the soap operas, women whom he immediate brings into his (fantasy) life. His *flaneur*-like amble through the Sears appliance section suggests his rejection of society's general resolution to such feelings of anomie: consumption. He rejects the "tools that [he has] no interest in" just as he had ultimately rejected masturbation (a tool he had no interest in) as a solution, the linking of consumption with masturbation subtly suggesting the role of consumption in keeping us in our own private masturbatory world. These rejections are both ultimately a rejection of solipsism as mindless though popular (cp. "the mainstream") "ways out," in that many people use them to escape from personal dilemmas. The narrator sensibly restricts *his* consumption to food and clothing, yet is rightfully irritated because he realizes that he's only buying these things to "justify" his long walk, forced as he is in spite of himself to confess the meaninglessness that would result without the consumption, the irritation nicely expressed in the angry consumption of the popcorn. What is impressive about such a poem, and perhaps easily overlooked, is both the skill with which Bukowski gets absolutely right a mood and feeling through his selection of detail, with very little subjective comment, and the extremely effective social criticism.

Thus subjectivity, the narrative with its privileging of events in duration and the incorporation of the seemingly inconsequential details of the subject's everyday life have combined to produce Bukowski's massive oeuvre and it is possibly all three aspects (and certainly the mundane details and the extensive oeuvre) that have militated against Bukowski's receiving the serious critical attention he deserves.

☆

The early reception of Bukowski's poetry often used the "outsider" epithet that had, with some justification, been affixed to Bukowski the poet, to characterize the individuals who appeared in the poetry. This was accomplished by overemphasizing the extent to which Bukowski's poetry had been about marginal and dysfunctional individuals. One reviewer wrote:

> Charles Bukowski will probably survive as the closest thing to a truly damned poet that our, or any, culture has produced. For some twenty years now he has been a moral spokesman for the American lumpenproletariat, a chronicler of our urban degeneracy, whose dingy furnished rooms, drinking, and fornications are neither bohemianism nor self-indulgence, but a way of life. He writes almost exclusively of violence, dirt, sickness, hopelessness . . . (Anon., lv-lvi);

" '[E]verything' is a few bars, a roach-infested apartment, and a recurring sexual fantasy in which two people get a little drunk and make a kind of loud, indifferent love to one another" (Mitchell 465) wrote another. An early review, by Jack Conroy, was entitled "A Skidrow Poet" and characterized Bukowski as "the skidrow-mission stiff-greasy spoon-rented room bard" (5). However, a fair reading of the early poetry would, I think, find this emphasis on the marginality of its characters and events misplaced and while Bukowski writes of such phenomena and types, it is by no means the primary focus of the poems. (Reading such reviews, it would have come as a surprise to learn that the poet had been working for the U.S. Post Office for more than a decade and at the time of the later reviews was receiving a pension.) In any event, such a characterization does not reflect the content of his poetry of the last quarter century, during which he has written his finest poetry and the vast majority of his poems. In its undialectical way, such a criticism, though inaccurate, is symptomatic of the larger response to Bukowski's poetry. The attempt to marginalize the experience that is at the core of Bukowski's poetry, to rob it of its significance, is an attempt to deny the validity of that experience which is, in the main, not marginal but that of the American working-class.°

Bukowski's poetry is also, in fact, indebted to two of the major

40

movements in post-War American poetry, Beat and Confessional poetry, though remaining distinct from both. While formally indebted to the Beats, and an admirer of Ginsberg, there is a sense in which Bukowski is put off by the Beats' Ivy-League provenance and elitist/bohemian stance, their lack of an attachment to the labor market, as it were.° The example of the Confessionals also had an important effect on Bukowski's poetry and it is necessary to examine the relationship between his poetry and theirs to clarify his unique achievement. This is his treatment from a working-class perspective of what might at first seem confessional material. The resemblance exists because the poetry of both the Confessionals and Bukowski are a part of that "poetry of experience" characterized by Robert Langbaum as having at its core "the essential idea of romanticism . . . the doctrine of experience—the doctrine that the imaginative apprehension gained through immediate experience is primary and certain, whereas the analytic reflection that follows is secondary and philosophical" (35). In such poetry "[t]he emphasis on particularity (the autobiographical connection being one means of achieving it) is a guarantee that the poem is an authentic experience . . ." (48).

Confessional poetry paved the way for Bukowski by broadening the boundaries of what was considered acceptable poetic content, especially by heightening the emphasis on the personal, so that Bukowski's poetry was, in that respect, "within normal limits."° Since the extremely personal inevitably carried with it the mundane and petty events of everyday life, there was characteristic of the genre (as of the poetry of Williams and Brecht)— indeed, "vital to the advent of confessionalism"—

> [a]bove all . . . the willingness . . . to treat the unpoetic material present in abundance in modern urban life without the Wordsworthian compulsion to spiritualize the mundane or even to dignify it beyond its essential worth.°

Yet as subjective as Bukowski's poetry is, as much as he relates intimate details of his life, as much as "unpoetic" material provides the content of his poems, a fundamental difference between his poetry and that of the Confessionals remains, the difference of class. The working-class perspective from which Bukowski's poetry is written results in its content having a different kind of significance.

In his discussion of the confessional mode M. L. Rosenthal wrote that

> the private life of the poet himself, especially under stress of psychological crisis, becomes a major theme. Often it is felt at the same time as a symbolic embodiment of national and cultural crisis. Hence the idiom of our poetry can be at once private and public, lyrical and rhetorical. (15)

A "symbolic embodiment of national and cultural crisis" implies a privileging of the experiential content by virtue of a privileging of the poetic *persona* by some quality (status or unusual sensitivity). This is something absent from Bukowski's poetry. As is evident in some of his most effective poems (such as "out of the mainstream," "time is made to be wasted" and "overhead mirrors"), Bukowski's idiom is never public and rhetorical. Indeed, Bukowski explicitly rejects the idea of his experience as critical, or culturally symbolic.

The difference is apparent when we compare Bukowski to a poet like Robert Lowell. Lowell claimed an importance for his poetry by virtue of his own class position.° In "Skunk Hour," for example, perhaps Lowell's most famous poem, the narrator's linking of his existence to that of the "heiress," her bishop son and "our summer millionaire" makes a claim for the importance of the narrator's position. Bukowski, on the other hand, goes out of his way to avoid such a claim. The characters in "overhead mirrors" are socially insignificant—"a guy who operated a porno bookstore" and "a nudey dancer"— quite the opposite of "Skunk Hour's" rentier cast; the significance of "overhead mirrors" lies in the content being representative of a far broader class. A very different set of dynamics produces the events, as we shall see in a moment. It is not a question of the class origins of the poet, but of the class content of the poem (which includes its perspective). It is this proletarian content that his early critics rejected and that led to their consigning him to "skidrow" and the *"Lumpenproletariat,"* thus forcing on him a persona that it was the very point of his poetry to reject and that would only have been the other side of Lowell's Brahmin coin.

Special status had accrued to the content of confessional poetry because of the immanent claim of the poetic persona to either social (Lowell) or aesthetic (the Beats) superiority; the events themselves were deemed significant, representative of important changes in the (national) psyche just because of the significance of these personae. In Bukowski we now have the experience made significant by virtue of its proletarian quality, the opposite of its status under the Beats and the Confessionals. By removing the aura of privilege from this experience and revealing what Lowell (and the Beats) had in a way mystified or idealized, as ordinary proletarian pleasure(s), Bukowski registers a more significant social change than the earlier poets. Hence, the class perspective is crucial.

The proletarian perspective of these poems is important for another reason related to the question of (economic) value. We don't much care what happens to the narrator of "overhead mirrors" because he gives us no reason to see any worth in him. As will be seen in a moment, the narrator has rejected the whole idea of value. Such is not the case, however, in poems like "Skunk Hour' or "Waking in the Blue." Much of the effect of the latter comes from the reader's reflection of "what a waste!" as he sees the lives of America's elite decay at McLean's: the former "Harvard All-American fullback," for example, or " 'Bobby,' / Porcellian 29." What a horrible return on investment, he thinks. The experiences embodied in the poems of *Life Studies* are "symbolic," i.e., valuable because of the innate, i.e., class-derived, worth of those who have them. Because Bukowski does not—cannot—make such a claim, the "fusion" between public and private does not take place and the poems cannot function as representative.

One striking aspect of "overhead mirrors" resulting from this different conception of value, is the absence of any signs of guilt on the part of the narrator, something we might otherwise expect to find in someone destroying himself (as the narrator almost succeeds in doing). It is a quality that is pervasive in Lowell's poetry and, understandably, in confessional poetry, generally. Strictly speaking, what one confesses are sins, an issue for Lowell and again more or less nonexistent for Bukowski. This, again, relates to the question of value. The sin in Lowell is really the destruction of value, of the depreciation of all that dead labor invested in Lowell (and his fellow McLean's residents) by the previous generations of Lowells and Winslows.° Bukowski, on the other hand, as a worker, has little value other than his commodified labor-power: his proletarian experience is valueless, lacking in accumulation, worthless as symbol. This, the proletarian's brutal *realization* of his "worthlessness" in capital's terms, adds to the poem's power. There is no way *he* is going to achieve the kind of accumulation the *dramatis personae* of Lowell's poetry have done. *His* accumulation is more along the lines of "25, 26, 27 / cents"; the coke *he* buys is "low-grade crap." The narrator of "overhead mirrors" is destroying his labor-power with the low-grade coke, countering the devaluation inherent in that commodification, so that this "destruction" becomes at the same time a valuation process (in that he refuses the pre-ordained role of commodity). "Overhead mirrors" is, in fact, a massive assault on (the labor theory of) value (which holds that an individual's "worth" is directly related to his value as commodified labor power), depicting an attempt to sabotage value through the destruction of labor-power. A poem like "overhead mirrors" is thus quite different from "Skunk Hour" where the waste of a Lowell's mind is a horrible thing and the guilt thus proportionately large. There is no guilt in Bukowski because nothing of value is being destroyed, the cost of producing another worker is minimal compared to the costs of producing another Lowell; "overhead mirrors" is, in fact, positive in its refusal of commodification.

In Bukowski such "self-destructive" behavior has been regularized, mainstreamed, i.e., proletarianized. Taking drugs, drinking and womanizing are viewed as (culturally) significant in the Confessionals and (for slightly different reasons) in the Beats but have become ordinary proletarian pleasures for Bukowski, (tied to a refusal of work, of value). He has "decriminalized" them poetically by proletarianizing them, denying any value to the worker they destroy. There is no reason for guilt here.

We also see this theme of value reflected in the imagery of "overhead mirrors." Both Lowell and Bukowski rely heavily on a functional metonymy. Indeed, Lowell's shift in *Life Studies* from a figurative poetry to a more realistic mode was much remarked upon by his critics. Yet Bukowski's objects are quite different— far less valuable—from Lowell's. In "overhead mirrors," the narrator describes a night of terror, owing to a regimen of "buying coke, really / low-grade crap, sniffing that with / beer and scotch." One night is particularly harrowing:

> at times I
> got up
> and walked around
> turned the radio off and on, flushed the toilet
> now and then, ran all the faucets in the place,
> then shut them off, turned the lights off and
> on, got back on the bed, rested but not too long,
> got up, sipped water out of the tap,
> sat in a chair and took some coins
> out of my pocket and counted them: 25, 26, 27
> cents . . .
>
> (WT 237)

In the opening lines of the poem "Bukowski" has explicitly denied that his condition is unusual or especially valuable: "I wouldn't say it was a particularly low time, it was / a time" and this theme is underlined by the poem's place in the collection, in the context of which it is just one of tens of poems dealing with the narrator's various experiences. This is an important point. It is here that Bukowski's massive production becomes also a statement of content of which Lowell's slim volume's statement is the diametrical opposite. It is where the novelistic fullness of Bukowski's poetry has its effect: it is one poem out of more than a hundred; four pages out of 270. Thus, the relentless denial of a "critical" aspect to the experience—the refusal to see the experience as in any way exceptional, privileged, "valuable," all underlined by its place in the collection—is, paradoxically, part of what makes the poem powerful.

Bukowski, however, could not have written his poetry without the poetry of the Confessionals and the Beats, who paved the way for him. What they achieved for the solitary bourgeois/ bohemian, he appropriated for the working-class.° Emphasizing the confessional, the individualistic element obscures the class perspective of the poems and the effect of that perspective on poetic content. "Overhead mirrors" and other poems like it question the depiction of such experience as privileged; rather they reflect its transformation by and incorporation into the working class.

45

CHAPTER TWO:
THE INDIVIDUAL AND THE
SOCIAL IN BUKOWSKI'S
POETRY OF THE 80S

> Self-consciousness exists in itself and for itself in that, and by
> the fact that it exists for another self-consciousness; that is to
> say, it is only by being acknowledged or "recognized."

Hegel's classic exposition of self-consciousness in the *Phenomenology*, the struggle for recognition between *Herr* and *Knecht*,
took the form of a story just because the dialectical process proves
inextricably narrative. For their part, Bukowski's narratives, with
their lyrical subject inevitably revealed (often through a struggle) as part of a social world, have increasingly acknowledged
the dialectical nature of self-consciousness.

While the lyric clearly lends itself to expressing what is most
individual and Bukowski's "lyric realism" (the phrase is Tom
Clark's) executes that task admirably, his emphasis on the individual has caused readers to overlook the large social component in his poetry. The self in Bukowski's poetry is inevitably
defined through the other, producing lyrics that are more than
an abstract expression of individual consciousness. The social
world and the narrator are mutually defined through their interaction. Moreover, there is no attempt to transcend that social
world. Ultimately, Bukowski's threatened subject both refuses
and creates that social world—a world of manipulation, exploitation and domination. Bukowski's poetry of the 1980s showed an
increasing awareness of the dialectical nature of the relationship

between the self and the other, the individual and the social.

Bukowski's poems are often first-person narratives which include the narrator's subjective reaction to an ordinary incident, the core of which would be too slight even to qualify as incident were it not for the narrator's reaction. In their emphasis on this subjective reaction the poems have something of a romantic sensibility about them. Yet it is not so much romantic intensity of feeling which informs the poems as the subject's extensivity manifested most obviously in the length of the poems themselves. Ultimately, however, a dialectical relationship between subject and object is central to Bukowski's poetry, much as it was to "the romantic . . . poem of experience":

> whether the poetry of experience starts out to be lyrical or dramatic, whether it deals with a natural or human object, to the extent that it imitates the structure of experience, to the extent that its meaning is a movement of perception, it must be in final effect much the same—both lyrical and dramatic, subjective and objective: a poetry dealing with the object and the eye on the object. (Langbaum, 56)

In Bukowski's "sweater" the narrator has gone to the bank "to do some business." There is a problem with the computer and the narrator's teller asks another teller for help:

> then turning to the other girl
> she asked,
> "could you help me with this transaction?"
> the other girl didn't answer.
> my lady tried again: "Louise, would you
> please help me with this
> transaction?"
>
> "I'll be right back," Louise answered and
> closed her window.
> she then walked to one of the
> tables
> where an older woman was talking to a young man
> wearing glasses.
> Louise stopped about four feet from the
> young man
> folded her arms and began
> listening.
> then the young man spoke.

48

he had on a yellow sweater
only he didn't have it on,
he had it thrown about his shoulders
and the two empty arms hung down over his
chest.
they continued to converse as I
watched.
the young man did most of the talking
and as he did so he swayed
back and forth
ever so slightly
and the arms of his sweater swung
back and forth
back and forth
and he continued to talk and
sway
as I watched the empty arms
of his sweater swing
back and forth
back and forth

I don't like people who wear
loose sweaters over their backs
with arms dangling
and these types usually wear
sunglasses pushed back
into their hair
and I could sense
that what he was talking about
was utterly drab
useless
and probably
untrue
and
he had the bland unworried face
of somebody
to whom nothing had happened
yet
                    (WT 267–68, 17–72)

Louise continues listening to the young man and the narrator
decides to take a hand in the matter:

I began walking toward
them,
I had to make the first post
at the racetrack

and these three were
being rude, dumb, as if it was a
natural order of business.
I had no idea what I was going to
say
but it was going to be
good.
they stopped talking as I
approached.
then I heard the voice
behind me:
"Mr. Chinaski!"
I stopped,
turned.
"I got the computer to
function."

(88-107)

Though a first-person narrative, "sweater" presents an objective
description of the narrator's reaction to an everyday occurrence.
Certainly many readers of the poem have experienced a bank's
downed computer (at least before the advent of ATMs); at first
glance it hardly seems something worth writing a poem about,
let alone a poem of 133 lines. Yet Bukowski constructs his narrative so effortlessly, paces it so naturally that we do not feel
the length as disproportionate to the content; indeed, such length
is integral to the poem's effect—a part of the content—because
without this length we would not have the poem's gradually
mounting tension. Bukowski's effective melding of the objective
and the subjective is underlined by the poem's language: the first
fifty-five lines are factual description. Only at the end of this first
section does the poet intrude with the repetition of "back and
forth" which is both marked poetic language and indicative of
the narrator's increasing impatience. In the second section
(56–94), however, we are given the full force of the narrator's
reception of events through verbs of mental (and pre-mental)
process: "don't like," "sense," "thought."

The lengthy description gives the reader something of the feel
of the long wait (and eight minutes at a teller window—so near and
yet so far—can seem much longer than that) effecting an identification of the reader with the narrator. All the details (both of the
description and of the narrator's reaction), even the most trivial,
become relevant. This is important because, in spite of the

suspense generated, there is no satisfying resolution to the conflict. The expected release of a hostile interaction between Chinaski,
the man with the yellow sweater, and Louise never materializes
except in the oblique refraction of Chinaski's aborted intervention:

> but he no longer
> swayed
> and the arms of his
> yellow sweater
> no longer
> swung
> about.
>
> we'd spoiled each others'
> fucking
> day.
>
> (124–33)

It is a non-event. But it is testimony to Bukowski's faith in individual experience that he does not try to invent a response that
might ring false. Thus the poem, as absolutely true to his experience (granted we don't know what actually happened), is the
truer to ours than it would have been had he altered the given
to provide a dramatic climax (and perhaps an attempt at transcendence) to the events. He's frustrated, as is the reader. After
all, rarely does it happen that we say, or do, anything in such
situations, because for one thing, as Bukowski put it in "let nothing
ever happen," a poem where the narrator does do—and more
importantly—say something: "it's when you do things like that
too often that / they put you in the madhouse" (D 214). Indeed,
speech is often more dangerous than action.

The ending acknowledges the inescapable mutuality of the
world and at the same time suggests there is an irreconcilable
element of conflict in it. Within the poem this conflict is echoed
on a reduced level in the conflicts between the narrator's teller
and Louise, and Louise and the man with the sweater and the
woman he's conversing with. We have a chain of subjects with
conflicting desires. There is no human reconciliation, just the
resolution effected by the non-human mediation of the computer.

The a priori presence of human antagonism ("I don't like people who wear / loose sweaters over their backs / with arms dangling"), the fact that the narrator has no idea what he's going

to say indicate the pre-logical, emotional level of the event and thus hint at the oft stated idea in Bukowski that words are useless, though at times dangerous. What Chinaski was going to say in "sweater" would have been "good" only as it contributed to releasing his irritation and frustration at the man's rude behavior, not that it would have led to any resolution. Too frequent assertion of the self, he suggests, will lead to that self's being removed from the social world or, as in the closing lines of the poem, "out of the blue" (a poem about the impossibility of changing emotional attitudes by talking), even the world's being removed from the world:

> sometimes there was nothing to
> save
> except personal vindication of a
> personal viewpoint
> and that was what was going to cause
> that blinding white flash
> one of these days.
>
> (WT 266)

The focus of "sweater" is the narrator's experience. But because the narrator's world is presented with a good deal of realistic detail, and because the content of the narration is so overwhelmingly ordinary and mundane, banal in the one sense, the effect is of something beyond the subjective. As Langbaum put it: "The poet talks about himself by talking about an object; and he talks about an object by talking about himself" (53). The objectivity of the narration and setting are reinforced by the lack of figurative language or poetic diction. Indeed, a striking feature of the poem's language is the almost complete lack of what we so closely associate with poetry, metaphor and the kind of transcendence it implies.° There is not one metaphor or simile in the poem (excepting the half-dead "down"). This absence was increasingly a feature of Bukowski's poetry of the 1980s.

The ordinariness of the content and the avoidance of poetic language also result in the loss of any privileged quality attaching to the subject; the fact that no attempt is made at a hyper-naturalist representation of the mind allows, conversely, for a distinct personality to emerge. Bukowski provides enough detail to differentiate, but not so much that we lose sight of the individual. By always giving us the subject in relationship to a social world, rarely isolating it, he avoids the danger Lukács feared of "extreme individualization annul[ling] all individuality."

There is, however, another, refractive aspect of Bukowski's poetry. On the one hand, much of what we learn about the narrator in his poetry is through his actions: he goes here, he does this, he says that (as well as through others' characterization of him); but the narrator is also defined in defining others. To say of the bank employee

> he had the bland unworried face
> of somebody
> to whom nothing had happened yet

is to say something about both narrator and employee, the connection grammatically underlined by the "yet" which proleptically implies the relationship between the two. This is one of Bukowski's most effective techniques and meshes nicely with the detailed narrative form. This further refraction of the narrator constitutes a mutuality of characterization where neither subject nor object can be examined independently of one another. Such a characterization is integral to Bukowski's poetry and lends it greater objectivity than would any (specious) impersonality.

Had Chinaski missed the first post and decided to forego the track that day he might well have found himself

> eating my senior citizen's dinner at the Sizzler

> between 2 and 5 p.m. any day and any time on Sunday and
> Wednesday, it's 20% off for
> us old dogs approaching the sunset.
> it's strange to be old and not feel
> old
> but I glance in the mirror
> see some silver hair
> concede that I'd look misplaced at a
> rock concert.
>
> I eat alone.
> the other oldies are in groups,
> a man and a woman
> a woman and a woman
> three old women
> another man and a
> woman.

it's 4:30 p.m. on a
Tuesday
and just 5 or 6 blocks north is
the cemetery
on a long sloping green hill,
a very modern place with
the markers
flat on the ground,
it's much more pleasant for
passing traffic.

a young waitress
moves among us
filling our cups
again with lovely caffeine.
we thank her and
chew on,
some with our own
teeth.
we wouldn't lose much in a
nuclear explosion.

one good old boy talks
on and on
about what
he's not too
sure.

well, I finish my meal,
leave a tip.
I have the last table by
the exit door.
as I'm about to leave
I'm blocked by an old girl
in a walker
followed by another old girl
whose back is bent
like a bow.
their faces, their arms
their hands are like
parchment
as if they had already been
embalmed
but they leave quietly.

as I made ready to leave
again

I am blocked
this time by a huge
wheelchair
the back tilted low
it's almost like a bed,
a very expensive
mechanism,
an awesome and glorious
receptacle
the chrome glitters
and the thick tires are
air-inflated
and the lady in the chair and
the lady pushing it
look alike,
sisters no doubt,
one's lucky
gets to ride,
and they go by
again very *white*.

and then
I rise
make it to the door
into stunning sunlight
make it to the car
get in
roar the engine into
life
rip it into reverse
with a quick back turn of squealing
tires
I slam to a bouncing halt
rip the wheel right
feed the gas
go from first to second
spin into a gap of
traffic
am quickly into
3rd
4th
I am up to
50 mph in a flash
moving through
them.
who can turn the stream
of destiny?

I light a cigarette
punch on the radio
and a young girl
sings,
"put it where it hurts,
daddy, make me love
you . . .

(WT 277-80)

Another instance of Bukowski's 80s *Alltagslyrik,* "eating my senior
citizen's dinner at the Sizzler" (which I've quoted in full) centers
on something every bit as prosaic as the downed computer of
"sweater": having to wait for slow-moving old folk to exit a
restaurant. And once more, the length would seem disproportionate to the content yet is absolutely integral to the poem's
meaning.

Technically, the poem is quite assured: the alternating of long
compounded with very short clauses, the similes (quite unusual
for Bukowski at this time and hence all the more effective), the
effective juxtaposition of the suffering of aging signaled in the
passive participles of the fifth and sixth stanzas with the ruth-
less vitality emphasized by the vibrant present participles of the
last stanza are impressive. Capping the poem with the pop-song
quote gives it a surprising and effective closure with no hint of
transcendence but rather a graphic representation of the here
and now with which the narrator identifies in all its carnal materiality. The poem's humanity, though, derives from its unflinching confrontation of the mental and physical horrors of aging
with society's flat-markered denial; the narrator has granted the
aged their suffering refusing either to wish away, deny or paper
over real differences. The humor of "one's lucky / gets to ride"
is remarkable in that it doesn't belittle the couple or their suffering but reveals the narrator's empathy. With the narrator's understandably somewhat precipitous exit (as if fleeing Death
himself) from the parking lot the poem seems absolutely true
to both the situation and the narrator's reaction, and in this ex-
hibits one of Bukowski's strengths—acceptance and an absence
of moralizing. After the introductory stanza there is no subjective statement about the narrator's feelings. As in "sweater," the
narrator's emotions are not particularly complex but rather
typical. "Eating my senior citizens dinner at the Sizzler" is a

distinctly materialist, Southern California *Altersgedicht* with no transcendence and none intended. Threading his descriptions and observations along the theme of aging, allowing his consciousness free play over the minutiae of this ordinary moment, Bukowski yet manages to come up with a unified impression. Although there is no pointed moral, in fact no conventional "point" to the poem at all, at the same time it can not be taken as mere naturalistic description. It is one individual's vividly realized perception of one of life's poignant moments that attempts to do full justice to both the event and the subject's perception and reaction to it.

Apparently simple, even transparent, Bukowski's poems often have an "undecidable" quality when it comes to interpreting them: subjective expression or objective comment? In the best there is a mutuality which precludes easy dichotomizing. The frequency with which self-involvement yields (to) objective social commentary is surprising and this aspect of his poetry has been slighted. (Part of the significance of "sweater," for example, lies in those middle lines quoted above, another of Bukowski's "plebeian" reactions and as such significant in American poetry in the yuppified 1980s.) One function of Bukowski's "banal subjectivity" is to ground such apparently peripheral and unrelated socio-political comments: such asides contribute in important ways to the meaning of a poem. Indeed, the relationship to the social world is established through such comments and Bukowski's poetry would be very different without them. This can be seen by examining one such apparent "throwaway." It appears in the poem "There Are So Many Houses and Dark Streets Without Help." The ostensible theme of the poem is the narrator's "weakness" in getting lost when driving, and it focuses on one such experience in particular:

> one of the worst was leaving Santa Anita racetrack
> one evening
> I swung off into a side road to get away from
> traffic and the side road started curving and I got
> worried about that and cut off into another side road
> and I don't know how it happened but all the main
> boulevards vanished and I was just driving along
> these small roads and then the roads started going
> *upwards* as the evening darkened into night and
> I kept driving, feeling completely idiotic and

vanquished
I tried to turn off the upward grades but
each turn led me to a road going higher. . . .

I got higher and higher into the hills and then I
was on top of whatever it was and there was this
village all lit up by neon signs and the language
of the signs was all Chinese and then I knew that
I was mad.
I had no idea what it meant, I just kept driving
and then looking down I saw the Pasadena Freeway.
I was a thousand feet above it, all I had to do
was to get down there.
and that was another nightmare of trying to
work my way down from all those streets of rich
dark houses.
the poor will never know how many rich hide out
quietly in the hills.
I got down on the freeway after another 45
minutes and, of course, I got on in the wrong
direction.

(HP 109, 59–71, 76–92)

Once again we have the emphasis on the isolated subject; in fact
the cause of the narrator's losing his way is his attempt to assert
himself, to recover a subjectivity threatened by the crowd
("traffic"). But it is at just this point that he begins to lose control, reflected grammatically by the road becoming the subject
of the clause. The grammatical subject then switches back and
forth between the narrator and the road, although the narrator
(even when the grammatical subject) is hardly in control of the
situation: he is "worried," "do[es]n't know," is "just driving along,"
"feeling completely idiotic and vanquished." Each attempt at re-
gaining control is defeated: "I tried to turn off the upward grades
but / each turn led me to a road going higher. . . ." Finally, this
journey, over which the narrator has lost all control and about
which he is as much in the dark as ever, ends as unforeseeably as
it began with the fortuitous discovery that "the poor will never
know how many rich hide out / quietly in the hills."

Here, as in "sweater," we have a conflict, this time intra-
psychic. The poem seems even more tendentiously subjective.
Unlike "sweater," there are no other individuals (and possible
antagonists) in the poem. As in "sweater," the social connection

(and here it is consciously political) is constructed by the narrator's casual and apparently off-hand observation, seemingly interpolated into a poem to which it initially appears unrelated, almost a non-sequitur. Yet the mass of details that have preceded it do generate the remark and in the end it seems logical and motivated, rather than extraneous and forced; we feel the narrator's statement to be legitimate. As something forced upon his consciousness by experience (as opposed to something tendentiously injected into the poem) it has a similarly convincing effect on the reader.

Such a remark, because true, constitutes part of the beauty of a Bukowski poem. Its content and its position just after the climactic moment of the poem preclude its being a throwaway and the generic form of its presentation leaves it too marked to be anything less than an important part of the poem's meaning. It is more than an afterthought yet at the same time we do not feel that the poem has been pointed in this direction and the slight clumsiness of its placement works against a suspicion of rhetoric. Indeed, it is as if the force of this truth has caught the narrator (as well as the reader) by surprise, a genuine result of concrete experience. In fact the social reference is all the more convincing for its unexpected presence in a poem that seems so relentlessly self-involved. Finally, in a writer who occasionally asserts his lack of interest in political matters, a reference to the economic inequalities in American society becomes all the more effective. Such observations appear in more than a few of Bukowski's poems.

It is this quality of learning through experience—from experience—that constitutes Bukowski's bond with romanticism, "the core that remains unchanged" in romanticism and modern poetry, as Langbaum described it, noting that in such writing "the poet discovers his idea through a dialectical interchange with the external world" in contrast to "the traditional lyric in which the poet sets forth his already formulated idea . . ." (53). Such an interchange was increasingly a feature of Bukowski's poetry of the 80s.

This recognition of the social is in sharp contrast to the undialectical subjectivity present in much of Bukowski's earlier poetry. That stance represented the reactionary aspect of romanticism. It often consisted of statements of "already formulated ideas" bearing little relationship to concrete experience. It may be useful to look at an example of this earlier mode to underscore the significant change in this aspect of Bukowski's poetry. These are the middle stanzas of the poem "horse & fist":

> for me
> obedience to another is the decay
> of self.
>
> for though every being is similar
> each being is different
>
> and to herd our differences
> under one law
> degrades each
> self.

(P 108)

Considered abstractly, such sentiments possess a superficial attractiveness but they break down on examination. The emptiness of the rhetoric is effectively demonstrated in the confusion between obedience to a person and to a law expressing the society's will. Bukowski's position is a not uncommon reaction to ever increasing structures of domination in society;° however the idealist platitudes of a poem like "horse and fist" have been less and less evident in Bukowski's poetry, replaced by the recognition of the subject's ultimate mediation through the social world.

The extent to which the self feels threatened in Bukowski's poetry is reflected in the frequency with which assertion takes the form of a blanket refusal. The narrator is rarely positive in the Whitmanian mode of "I celebrate myself"; we would never expect such a subject to assert that what he assumes we also should assume, more likely the opposite: the protagonist reacts to society's demands by refusal and negation. Hence, it is often a defensive, threatened subject(ivity) as in the poem "I didn't want to," a particularly successful joining of narration and discourse:

> I was always a bad typist and I never learned to spell
> because I didn't want to.
>
> I never learned properly how to drive an automobile
> and I bought
> my first one off a used car lot for $35, got in with

60

> my drunken lady and almost ripped off the side of a
> hospital making my first left turn.
>
> I didn't want to learn music because I disliked
> the teacher with her white wig and her powdered face.
>
> I got stuck in ROTC because I didn't want to be an
> athlete and they put me in a manual of arms competition
> and I didn't want to win and I won and they gave me a
> medal and I threw it down a sewer.
>
> I didn't learn music and now I listen to
> more classical music than the first hundred people you'll
> pass on the street.
>
> (D 35, 1-15)

The subject asserts itself by refusing society's demands. Typing, spelling, driving, music, sports: typical demands (involving quite specific rules and conventions) on an individual being socialized. Sometimes the reasons for refusing are not even given and when given are sometimes idiosyncratic and trivial. But there they are. Of course it is not always easy to refuse, and sometimes what is refused is replaced by something worse, here the army (ROTC), the most authoritarian (outside of prison) of society's institutions. What is at issue is not necessarily the substance of the demand, but rather the fact that it is being demanded. That this is the case becomes clear when we learn that sometimes what is refused ultimately appeals to the narrator: "I hated poets and I hated poetry and I began to write / poetry" (18–19). Here the second "and" is important. It is suggested that there is no process other than chronology. Any possible mediation between the hatred and the writing is side-stepped. (Stylistically, this mimics Bukowski's refusal to "communicate," the undialectical, "metaphysical" aspect of his thinking, which I shall discuss in a moment). Uniting the disparate refusals is the absence of choice. Behind this absence is the narrator's sense that he is being exploited and/or manipulated. He may or may not want to do something, but whatever his wants, he wants to choose to do it, on his own terms, for himself, not for his parents, his teacher, the army, society.

In the poem "education," the narrator's mother has been called to school to see his teacher, who is upset because " 'he's not learning / anything.' "

61

> "oh, Henry," my mother said,
> "your father is so disappointed in
> you, I don't know what we are
> going to do!"
>
> father, my mind said,
> father and father and
> father.
>
> words like that.
>
> I decided not to learn anything
> in that
> school.
>
> (Y 31, 59–69)

This refusal to be exploited results in a refusal of dialogue, ultimately of speech, which is seen as manipulative and a trap. First,
dialogue presupposes an other, a possible threat to the individual.
Hence, as a corollary, dialogue, and speech, become suspect.
Speech, in such a situation, is never free, undetermined, but always determined and inextricably implicated in the social context, in issues of authority and submission, of power. In fact,
sometimes writing can seem a part of such an authoritarian structure and the impulse exists to try, somehow, to subvert this:

> I don't even want to write and when I write
> oft times a strange word will slip in and I'll leave
> it in or I'll make a typing error, say I will mean to hit a
> "g" and I'll hit an "h" and if it happens at the beginning
> of a word then I'll use a word beginning with "h."
> it doesn't matter.
>
> (46–51)

About a third of the way through "I didn't want to," the poem
shifts, revealing the source of the narrator's refusal and his identification of the subject with this refusal:

> it is difficult for me to get interested or angry.
> when a cop stops me for some infraction I simply sink
> into some great sea of disgust.
> "do you want to know what you did, sir?" he asks me.
> "no," I say.
> I have the same trouble with women.
> "Look, you just sit and don't say anything."
> they say. "now something is wrong if you just sit there
> and don't say anything!"

I drain my drink and pour another.
"Look," they say, "let's talk! let's work things
out!"
"I don't want to work things out," I tell them.
(33–45)

Cops and women (the constellation appears in other poems) replace the father and mother as the symbols of authority, have succeeded the family as the middle term between the individual and society), the locus of the primitive accumulation of exploitation, the original sin. The "trouble" is speech, dialogue—communication. The affectless, speechless stance vis-à-vis the policeman and the girlfriend are the threatened subject's only defence against "rational" authority. It doesn't matter that in all likelihood both cop and girlfriend are justified in their actions: as the mediating force impinging on the narrator they have to be refused, and the "simplest" way to do it is by refusing speech, "rational" discourse. To speak is to acknowledge the other, and the social world, and though rational in the narrower context, is not seen as such in the longer view because it is going to suck the subject into an authoritarian world of exploitation. To speak is to acknowledge domination which begins with language and results in the interesting paradox that the loquacity of the narrator of these poems is generated by a fear and distrust of words and speech as inextricably social. Indeed, as we have seen, the consequences of speech are sometimes seen as more dangerous than the consequences of action.

The dilemma faced by the Bukowskian protagonist is the mutual necessity of self and other, subject and object. It is an aporia from which the protagonist can never escape, except via empty statements like those of "horse & fist," or silence. Further complicating this condition is the fact that the world is constituted in a hierarchy of power and, as Hegel recognized, the master needs the slave. The subject in Bukowski refuses authority what Hegel termed recognition (*Anerkennung*) without which it (or its role, all too often the same thing) collapses, while yet remaining—technically—within the social world. One can see why Bukowski so admires Jeffers.° Yet (for reasons discussed in the next essay) Jeffers' "solution"—isolation—could not be Bukowski's.

Ultimately, Bukowski is refusing exploitation. Relationships are treacherous because, owing to the power struggle on which they are based, they inevitably end up in one person exploiting and/or dominating the other; mutuality, rather than dominance, is rare. In childhood it is the parents against whom one struggles, refusing to serve as the object of their need. Later, women have an innate power over men. (The fact that it is men's desire that grants them this power only makes the situation more troubling.) The risk is that once involved with a woman a man will become subject to the authority flowing from this power and since people inevitably (ab)use power, men become victims. For himself, Bukowski's protagonist refuses such authority because he is aware of its burdens. In the poem "everybody talks too much," he notices that the policeman who gives him the ticket has

> some sweat
> on his
> brow
> and the
> hand
> that held
> the
> ticket
> seemed to
> be
> trembling
> (Y 213, 48–58)

However it is not always easy to avoid victimization at the hands of authority. The tack Bukowski's subject takes is to preempt the "threat" of objectification and exploitation by immediately objectifying himself (and hence the other), as, for example, in the manual-at-arms competition, or by immediately objectifying the other (and inevitably himself). Refusing to speak, denying one's own and another's humanity is the weapon of choice. Both this refusal to speak and the reifying of an individual into a quasi-inorganic collection of parts spring from this underlying dynamic. The end of "I didn't want to" describes the death of a lover many years before along with the "death" of that first automobile:

> I really did buy my first automobile for $35 and I asked the man, "does the motor start? does it have a key?"
> it didn't have any springs or a reverse gear and to make the headlights work I'd have to hit a hard bump in the road,

and I had to park it on a hill to get it started,
it ran for two years without my changing the oil and when
     the car
finally died I just left it and walked away. the
drunken lady who had been along for that first ride past the
hospital, she lived a little longer, with me and without me,
but mostly with me, she died and I buried her one warm,
afternoon north of Anaheim, and the best thing about
her was she never said, "let's talk this thing out."

she was a typist for a large downtown furniture store
and she had the most beautiful legs I have ever seen before
     or
since.

I should have loved her more than I did but I didn't want
to.°

(74–90)

It is a poignant ending because, to the very end, the self is split
and the conflict resulting from this split is present in an especially troubling implication and/or admission: because one implication of the last four lines is that the narrator feels he should
have loved her more than he did *because* she had the most beautiful legs he had ever seen. This is not the ultimate interpretation I would want to make of the last sentence which is more
general in its application. It has, after all, been given its own stanza. Yet this particular juxtaposition can not be ignored.

There is another point concerning this split in the self. Why
should the narrator have loved her more than he did? Clearly
there can be no "should" in such matters. Clearly, too, there is a
temptation to link this "should" to the social world that has been
trying to tell the narrator what to do in the many previous examples in the poem. One thought is that the narrator may be
trying to get us on his side by equating his refusal here with the
earlier ones (which seem justified). More fruitful, I think, is to
substitute "couldn't" for the last three words of the poem. If such
a substitution is made, here and in the rest of the poem, I think
we get closer to the psychological truth embodied in the poem
though further away from the philosophical point Bukowski
would like to make. But there is no real resolution here; perhaps
the best we can do is to fall back on Bukowski's statement: "It
was [a choice] and it wasn't."

In general, the subject in Bukowski's poetry fears involvement in a system of domination. The stoic, unflinching attitude of his protagonist, here and elsewhere, is cognate to this refusal. Such an attitude is an attempt to refuse meaning (by visibly refusing to react) to interpersonal relations, to events, to the social world and to history because in the social world, as in the world of personal relations, involvement leads only to disappointment. These refusals attempt to deny meaning to human events by denying their effect on individual subjects. This becomes the ultimate objectification because in denying meaning one is denying one's own humanity.° What needs to be emphasized is that Bukowski's poems do treat such issues seriously, that they are ongoing concerns of his and that he is skilled at injecting significant ideational content into his narratives.

The refusal to speak is nowhere more striking, nor more effectively presented, than in "we've got to communicate," one of Bukowski's finest poems and perhaps the most extreme example of Bukowski's technique of characterization by refraction. In the poem the narrator's lover takes him to task for his refusal to talk about problems in the relationship. The narrator never speaks. He is only characterized by his lover:

> "I see you watching women getting in and out of their
> cars, hoping their skirts will climb up so you can
> see their legs.
> you're like a schoolboy, a peep-freak!
> and *worse* than that, you just like to *think* about
> sex, you really don't want to *do* it, it's only
> *work* to you, you'd rather stare and imagine.
> you don't even like to suck my breasts!"
>
>   (D 92, 9–16)

Not only does she characterize him generally, but she also describes him at the specific moment of the poem:

> "but look at you now, not a sound out of you, you just
> sit in that chair over there and pour drink after
> drink!
>
>   (35–37)
>
> . . . .
> but look at you *now!* all you want is one more drink and
>   then
> one *more* drink and you won't talk to me, you just keep
> lighting cigarettes and looking around the room . . ."
>
>   (84–86)

Such a procedure represents a dialectical reversal; the subject has now become alienated from itself and is objectified in its own poem, *it*, a speechless object, is being represented by *others*. It has effected its own worst fear by making itself into a speechless, powerless thing. Starting out full of itself and its own speech it has metamorphosed into a speechless victim. The poem is one of Bukowski's masterpieces; it is also one of his funniest (which is saying something). But what may not be immediately evident is how the humor is achieved. It results from the distance the narrator (the man, not the woman) has gained from himself, i.e., again, through his (successful) objectification of himself. And it is worth noting (and I shall discuss the dynamic again in the essays on the novels) that this is often the means through which Bukowski achieves his humor. In an odd way, his self-objectification represents a kind of justification for his behavior.

Three times in the poem the narrator's lover sums up her complaints in similar form: "you're afraid to look at a woman's pussy," "tell me, what's wrong with a woman's pussy?" "tell me, why are you afraid of a woman's pussy?" Hers is a valid question. The poem concerns the narrator's inability to sustain a relationship and his fear of intimacy, embodied in the lover's assertion that he is afraid to look at a woman's vagina. (As we will see in Chapter 4, female genitalia are potent symbols in the poetry.) Getting sucked into the vagina means much the same thing as getting drawn into speech. (And both sex and speech—at least at their best—are mutual.) When dialogue begins, autonomy is lost, or so the narrator sees it. (At the same time, as we will see in "looking for a job," sex can, from the male point of view, free a woman from work, that ultimate objectification.) The fear of intimacy is the same as the fear of speech. It is a fear of vulnerability, something the vagina aptly symbolizes.

The refusal to recognize the other, the metaphysical view of the individual, become most problematic when viewed from the perspective of work, the subject of the next essay. Here refusal and subjectivity become entwined in the issue of intra- as well as inter-class relations. Here, too, we encounter one of the most interesting and important areas of Bukowski's writing. For the poetry, it becomes a question of distinguishing the subjective refusal of the isolated individual within capitalist class relations from an objective refusal representative of a progressive class position within late capitalism. It is another area in which Bukowski's views underwent a profound change, reflected in the poetry of the 1980s.

CHAPTER THREE:
POETRY AND
THE WORKING CLASS

What *I've* tried to do, if you'll pardon me, is bring in the factory-workers aspect of life . . . something seldom mentioned in the poetry of the centuries.

(To Sean Penn)

The working-class consciousness that pervades Bukowski's poetry is as strong as it is for a good reason. For roughly fifteen years, beginning in 1941, Bukowski held a series of casual working class jobs and subsequently, for almost as many years, worked for the United States Post Office, first as a carrier, then for eleven years as a clerk. Bukowski's formal education had taken him through two years at Los Angeles City College where he majored in art and journalism and left without a degree in 1941. He might well have continued his education through the bachelor's degree which, in the 1940s, would have assured him entry to the middle-class. This, however, he did not do and his decade and a half of casual, working-class jobs, mostly in the service sector, as well as his career at the Post Office, left him with profound understanding of what Hans Mayer has called the "plebeian tradition" (10). Though it is now almost a quarter century since Bukowski worked at such jobs, the previous three decades have left their mark on his poetry.

Bukowski has written more poems depicting work and the American working-class experience than any other major American poet, more, perhaps than *any* American poet. Moreover, the extent to which work has provided the content of his poetry seems to have increased in the last decade and the attitude towards the working class expressed in these poems differs from that expressed in the earlier poetry.° Here I will examine four poems published in the 1970s and 1980s ("$$$$$$," "Yankee Doodle," "Sparks," and "transformation and disfiguration") in order to trace this shift in attitude towards the working class and towards the role of work in American society.

Bukowski's "personal revolt," his desperate attempt to preserve an "undegraded self," has sometimes been at others' expense and has brought him into conflict with individuals with whom one would have thought him in solidarity, i.e., with those who play the same role in the relations of production as he. "In this personal revolt," Raymond Williams wrote, "the best the individual can hope for is to minimize society's pressures: by detachment, by apathy, by skepticism, by seeing that at least he, and his family are all right" (109). Williams' conclusions are relevant to (some of) Bukowski's poetry:

> The personal revolt asserts individuality, in this world of impersonal abstractions, but the assertion, commonly, is also a withdrawal from social thinking: I and my family and friends are real; the rest is the system. But this, when sufficiently extended, not only confirms the elite's valuation of other people as masses. It also, in its denial or limitation of real relationships, helps people to regard themselves, in their social relationships as masses.
>
> (111)

This "personal revolt" has sometimes led Bukowski's protagonist into behavior which degrades others.

The poem "$$$$$$" shows this quite well by presenting such behavior in a social context where it inevitably has repercussions. The poem describes the reactions of the narrator's fellow-workers when on one payday it turns out that "Bukowski" has been so oblivious of such things as getting paid ("I've always had trouble with / money") that he has forgotten to pick up his previous paycheck. The poem goes on to relate another incident, indicative of his casual attitude in such matters, when he finds some money in his coat pockets that he had forgotten about. (The poem is quoted in its entirety, in sequence.)

$$$$$$

I've always had trouble with
money.
this one place I worked
everybody ate hot dogs
and potato chips
in the company cafeteria for
3 days before each
payday.
I wanted steaks
I even went to see the manager
of the cafeteria and
demanded that he serve
steaks. He refused.

(L 245, 1–13)

The poem is not without a socially progressive aspect. Bukowski,
though he may not share many people's passion for accumula-
tion, is no ascetic. There are things he wants and not only for
himself (although what he wants most is time). He accepts defeat,
in one sense, although he is not willing to reduce his demands
without a protest and not without refusing to contribute to the
production of any more surplus value than he absolutely has to,
through the attempt, perhaps, to separate income from produc-
tivity. (I say "perhaps" because it is not clear whether his absences
are paid absences; but even if they are not, his absence in all
likelihood slows down the rate of accumulation.)

I'd forget payday.
I had a high rate of absenteeism and
payday would arrive and everybody would
start talking about
it.
"payday?" I'd say, "hell, is this
payday? I forgot to pick up my
last check . . ."

"stop the bullshit, man . . ."
"no, no, I mean it . . ."

I'd jump up and go down to payroll
and sure enough there'd be a
check and I'd come back and show it
to them. "Jesus Christ, I forgot all about
it . . ."

(14–28)

He doesn't seem to understand their response:

> for some reason they'd get
> angry, then the payroll clerk would come
> around. I'd have two
> checks. "Jesus," I'd say, "two checks."
> and they were
> angry.
> some of them were working
> two jobs.
>
> (29–36)

"For some reason they'd get / angry": here the problematic aspect of Bukowski's revolt is exposed. The narrator's need to differentiate himself from society and to negate its conventional values makes for the bad faith of "some," which implies the narrator doesn't understand his co-workers' anger. Indeed, throughout the poem the narrator portrays himself as an innocent: he realizes the other workers are angry but can't for the life of him understand why. Both here and again in 33–34 the lineation also suggests that he's surprised. However, there is a question as to his honesty because it seems he does have an inkling of why they're angry when he tells us "some of them were working / two jobs."

One thrust of the poem is that the workers' "money-grubbing" attitude has made them bitter, humorless individuals (unable, for example, to selflessly appreciate another's good luck). On the other hand, the narrator's cavalier disregard of money reveals him as a free spirit, separating him from the mass of his fellow workers (and from the "masses" as well) with their petty, mundane concerns (such as supporting families) revealed in their concern with money.

The narrator's hostility is real, though probably unconscious. But his actions reflect a generalized, anti-social hostility rather than a particularized interpersonal one. They reflect, as well, the subject's desperate attempt to avoid being sucked into the net of conventional exploitation which is based, in Herbert Marcuse's words, on "needs, satisfactions, and values which reproduce the servitude of the human existence" (*Essay*, 6).

The central section of the poem presents a similar incident in more telling detail:

> the worst day
> it was raining very hard,
> I didn't have a raincoat so
> I put on a very old coat I hadn't worn for
> months and
> I walked in a little late
> while they were working.
>
> (37–43)

Once more the distance between the narrator and his co-workers is emphasized. Strictly speaking, there is no reason for him to tell us that he doesn't own a raincoat other than to underline his lack of interest in clothing and conventional forms of status expression. Absenteeism was mentioned earlier; now the narrator arrives at work "late / while they were working." We know that for most of the workday he'll be working and, judging from what Bukowski has written elsewhere, probably just as hard, if not harder, than most. However, here the contrast between the narrator and the other workers is emphasized. From one perspective, there is a positive side to his behavior because both lateness and absenteeism are a refusal to create additional surplus value and here an attempt to separate income from work; on the other hand, such behavior creates an emotional distance between the narrator and his co-workers. Even after he arrives he doesn't immediately begin working:

> I looked in the coat for some
> cigarettes
> and found a five dollar bill
> in the side pocket:
> "hey, look," I said, "I just found a 5 dollar
> bill I didn't know I had, that's
> funny"
>
> (44–50),

a piece of good luck not taken in the proper spirit:

> "hey, man, knock off the
> shit!"

Clearly, at this point it would have been politic for the narrator to drop the subject. The other workers have not responded in the way he thought they would (if he had given the matter any thought at all). Why go on? Apparently he can't see beyond his own good fortune to the envy he causes in the others.

"no, no, I'm *serious*, really, I remember
wearing this coat when
I got drunk at the
bars. I've been rolled too often,
I've got this fear . . . I take money out of
my wallet and hide it all
over me."

"sit down and get to
work."

(53–61)

The irritation of the other workers is understandable. The narrator has probably clocked in by this time, yet he's smoking a
cigarette and continuing to talk about finding money, indeed continuing to find money and to loudly advertise his find:

I reached into an inside pocket:
"hey, look, here's a TWENTY! God, here's a
TWENTY I never knew I
had! I'm RICH!"

"you're not funny, son of
a bitch . . ."

"hey, my God, here's ANOTHER
twenty! too much, too too
much . . . I *knew* I didn't spend all that
money that night. I thought I'd been
rolled again . . ."

I kept searching the
coat. "hey! here's a ten and
here's a fiver! my God . . ."

"listen, I'm telling you to sit down
and shut up . . ."

"My God, I'm, RICH . . . I don't even *need*
this job . . ."

"man, sit *down* . . ."

(62–81)

The narrator's public discovery of the money takes an interesting trajectory: $5.00—$20.00—$20.00—$10.00—$5.00. (It should
be borne in mind that the incident takes place no later than the
1950s and perhaps in the 1940s. Thus the total amount found—

$60.00—probably approaches a week's pay.) From the perspec-
tive of the other workers it would be difficult to imagine a more
damaging sequence. The narrator doesn't give them a chance
to prepare themselves for what's coming: the first five dollars
primes the pump, as it were; to begin with the twenties would
be to waste their shock value and what followed would be anti-
climactic. Starting with five dollars, however, alerts the co-
workers to what may be coming, while a more gradual five-ten-
twenty build-up would allow them to mobilize their psychic
defenses—weak though they inevitably are in such a situation—
against the financial onslaught. The narrator's sequence seems
the most painful for his audience and thus the most hostile and
again subjective assertion leads to a specious claim of superiority: " 'I don't even need / this job.' " The poem ends:

> I found another ten after I had sat down
> but I didn't say
> anything.
> I could feel waves of hatred and
> I was confused,
> they believed I had
> plotted the whole thing
> just to make them
> feel bad. I didn't want
> to. People who live on hot dogs and
> potato chips for
> 3 days before payday
> feel bad
> enough.
>
> I sat down
> leaned forward and
> began to go to
> work.
>
> outside
> it continued to
> rain.

                              (82–102)

That the other workers might think the narrator had planned
what happened implies two things: first, that the narrator already
occupies something of an outsider's place in the establishment
and second, that it is inexplicable to them that he doesn't realize

how they feel at his finding the money. But it is not that he wants them to feel bad; rather it is a case of the subject asserting itself and it is not only the money (though this is clearly welcome as buying him time) but the position it places him in vis-à-vis the others that provides the self with its gratification. It is again a question of "recognition" in Hegelian terms; in order for there to be a winner there has to be a loser. Thus the winner needs the losers, needs his inferiors when everything around him is telling him that *he* is a loser.° Yet in these earlier poems, Chinaski/"Bukowski" refuses to recognize a dialectic; there is no mediation, no recognition that it is a process, no acceptance of the other. It is as if the bucks stop there, with his discovery of the money. Everything is viewed abstractly and this is why the narrator lacks empathy. In the 1980s Bukowski's poetry grew to encompass the entire process, with a concomitant acceptance of others.

I think we finally accept, grudgingly, the narrator's profession of innocence, that he "was confused" and did not "want to make them feel bad." The narrator feels exposed. "Bukowski" has not been successfully integrated into the system, that is, he has not yet been completely subdued by an oppressive and hostile system intent only on extracting the last ounce of surplus value and this inevitably places him in conflict with those who have. Because no reasons are given for the fact that the workers are starving themselves on potato chips or working two jobs, it is implied that those reasons are not important. "Bukowski" scorns their voluntary "servitude." To survive in such an environment the narrator is compelled to medicate himself into an anesthetized oblivion where he runs the risk of losing even the small sum granted him to reproduce his life (such medication being one cost of reproduction not covered by health insurance—assuming there was any) and to make periodic attempts to leverage himself into a position from which, for however short a time, to achieve some slight distinction, a transient and delusive sense of self-worth.

But the narrator, too, is caught in a bind, the reverse of the others'. He notes that it is not just the time he finds the money, but also the times he neglects to pick up his paychecks that irritate his co-workers. When he does manage to get his check, he sometimes loses the money before he can even spend it at the bar, by having it stolen from him. For the narrator, there is a basic refusal to accept the connection between work and pay. It is this that all his behavior in the poem points to his trying to destroy, while it is this that the other workers have accepted, in some cases in spades. His "trouble" with money is with the place it occupies in the relations of production and in life. The demand for steaks in the company cafeteria is consonant with this. It is clear that the workers have to pay for their meals but the food is probably subsidized (else why the refusal to serve steaks?) and the demand for steaks is a further demand for loosing the wage from productivity. Ultimately, the poem is a critique of dollars, the cash nexus, the money economy—exchange-value—around which their lives are all—be it in acceptance or refusal—wound. However, although "$$$$$$" is an interesting poem, and not without its positive side, in the end the reader is left irritated and annoyed: the poem seems unresolved. The suggestion of bad faith in the narrator, in which unconscious hostility is combined with disingenuousness, results in the reader's not being certain how to take the poem.

In "Yankee Doodle," a poem published two years later we have another division, this time between the narrator and one coworker. Stylistically this poem approaches the poems of the 1980s but the content is once again an unresolved conflict at work. As in "$$$$$$" the emphasis is on the individual; the collective is almost completely excluded from the poem.

> I was young
> no stomach
> arms of wire
> but strong
>
> I arrived drunk at the factory
> every morning
> and out-worked the whole pack of them
> without strain
>
> (P 78, 1–8)

Also working there is

> the old guy
> his name was Sully
> good old Irish Sully

he fumbled with screws

and whistled the same song all day
long:

Yankee Doodle came to town
Ridin' on a pony
He stuck a feather in his hat
And called it macaroni . . .

(9–18)

Sully had been whistling this song (which apparently irritates the narrator) long before the narrator arrived on the scene:

they say he had been whistling that song
for years

I began whistling right along
with him

we whistled together for hours
him counting screws
me packing 8 foot long light fixtures into
coffin boxes

as the days went on
he began to pale and tremble
he'd miss a note now and then

I whistled on

(19–30)

Sully begins "to miss days . . . next I knew . . . Sully was in a hospital for an / operation." Finally Sully retires

and I realized that he had
never hated me, that I
had only hated
him

(48–51)

In this poem Bukowski approaches the form that he will use so effectively in "Sparks": lack of conjunctions and phrases rather than clauses. Although the sentiment, the *ressentiment* expressed make it even less successful than "$$$$$$," the narrator has begun to realize the mutuality of his relationship to the other workers.

For the most part, the narrator's emotional reaction to Sully and his whistling remains unexamined. We don't have a clue as

to why the narrator dislikes Sully, which is understandable because the narrator himself doesn't realize he dislikes him.
Although he nowhere says so, we assume that it is Sully's
whistling the song that so disturbs him: it is supposed such an
obvious irritant that the mere mention of it will make the narrator's feelings comprehensible. Indeed, the mention of this lack
of awareness strikes the one honest note in the poem and gives
it a redeeming moment. The narrator's realization that Sully did
not hate him, though he himself thought this (though this, too,
is never stated), but that he hated Sully makes clear that the narrator is projecting his own feelings onto Sully. But it is *not* made
clear. We can only assume that it is Sully's whistling of "Yankee
Doodle" and what it signifies: a mindlessly cheerful acceptance
of an exploited and alienated condition, that provokes (and
perhaps frightens) the narrator (the choice of a tune associated
with patriotism is an especially nice touch, identifying "patriotism"
with a mindless acceptance of exploitation); for an explicit ac-
knowledgment of this we have to wait for "Sparks."

"Yankee Doodle" is again a poem in which we cannot decide
whether the signs are "intended" or "symptomatic." Why does
the narrator persecute "good old" Sully? *Because* he is old,
and incompetent and the narrator is irritated that (after forty
years!) Sully has been given a lighter job while he (though "young
. . . strong" and recently hired) has a harder job? The poem
ends:

> then they let me go
> too
> I've never minded getting
> fired but that was one time
> I felt it.
>
> (54–58)

Again, it is not clear why the narrator "felt it." Sully, after all,
had already retired. Just as the hostility the narrator felt for Sully
was unexamined, so is the sympathy. Finally, the incident itself
seems more than a little unbelievable (there is a question as to
how much of it we are even *meant* to believe), i.e., the implication that Sully began to miss work, became sick and retired because the narrator began whistling along with him is a bit
far-fetched. In all likelihood forty years was quite enough for
Sully.

Thus we come to the problem of determining what the poem is "about." Charles Altieri notes that "[a]n expression of the self can be one that is intended, the self's act, or one that is symptomatic, the act of a self not in control of what it manifests" (24). In "Yankee Doodle," and to a lesser extent in "$$$$$$," the interesting aspects of the poems are not the "intended expressions of the self." The lack of explicitness is not suggestive in any positive sense because we feel that were things to be spelled out, this would weaken, not strengthen, the narrator's case by revealing the unacknowledged irrationality at the root of it.° At the end of the poem the narrator implies that he had some sympathy and fellow feeling for Sully. The "too" in the lines last quoted implies a similarity in the fates of both workers. Yet the cases are quite different: Sully retired, while the narrator was either "let go" (laid off), or "fired." The origin of such psychological dynamics is important because of their effect on the poems. In "$$$$$$" and "Yankee Doodle" the narrator does not feel himself as in any way allied with the other workers. The dynamic of "personal revolt," the false consciousness expressed in "horse and fist" has as its corollary the unconscious hostility and confusion of "$$$$$$" and "Yankee Doodle" which result in the lack of mediation and irresolution which flaw these poems.

In "Sparks," one of Bukowski's finest poems, we see the narrator in solidarity with his co-workers, indeed, hardly differentiated from them. The only division in the poem is between management and labor. There is no ambiguity and no doubt about where the narrator stands because he accepts his condition, an acceptance expressed in the paradoxical opening lines: "the factory off Santa Fe Ave. was / best." Paradoxical, because we don't usually associate anything good, let alone "best" with working in a factory (unless we own it). What is "best" reveals itself in comparison with "$$$$$$" and "Yankee Doodle."

One difference between "$$$$$$" and "Sparks" is the relatively detailed description of the job in "Sparks" ("Yankee Doodle" made a start in this direction): the work itself, the physical characteristics of the workplace, the conditions of hire, the description of the workers. In "$$$$$$," by contrast, we don't even learn what the work is. Because in "$$$$$$" an important feature is the narrator's refusal to identify with his co-workers, a more detailed description of their common tasks would not be to his purpose since it would suggest reasons for solidarity, rather than division. ("We" or "our" is not used once in the poem.) In "Sparks," however, the subject becomes collective and there is a corollary lack of emphasis on the individual or on conflict among the workers (though conflict is not avoided but, largely, absorbed). Collectivity becomes both a theme of the poem and its truth content (as false consciousness was in the earlier poems). It accounts for its integrity, purposefulness and lack of "unintended signs," all of which affect the language and content of the poem.

A notable linguistic feature is the poem's relative lack of conjunctions of which "Sparks" has noticeably fewer than "$$$$$$," especially lacking the use of "and" to join clauses. While polysyndeton remains a feature of Bukowski's style, it was more in evidence in his earlier writing. Conjunctions suggest flow, process, continuity. "Sparks," with its many gerunds and lack of conjunctions suggests a process without progress, a *perpetuum mobile* of exploitation. The omission of conjunctions between phrases is especially striking:

> most of us in
> white t-shirts and jeans
> cigarettes dangling
> sneaking beers
> management looking
> the other way
>
> not many whites
> the whites didn't last:
> lousy workers
> mostly Mexicans and
> blacks
> cool and mean
> (WT 27, 18–29)

Such terseness and lack of syntactic connection were rare in Bukowski's early poetry and were still marked in the poems published during the 1970s. "Sparks" is an imagist representation of working-class experience, though it evokes not so much a visual as an emotional atmosphere. The lack of conjunctions with their suggestion of progress, and the parallel adjective phrases and nominative absolutes with their verbs immobilized into participles emphasizing surface rather than depth produce an image frozen in time, lending an eternal quality to the experience and the social relations depicted. This lack of subordination registers Bukowski's preference for refusing explanation; here content obviates the need for a formally discursive spelling-out of the nature of things. Nor is there the need for a plot on which to hang significance as in "transformation and disfiguration." It suggests that description will suffice (though it is anything but mere facticity: the fact is, there is a context), the connections too obvious to need stating.

However, style alone does not make "Sparks" a powerful poem. It achieves its power because the narrator identifies with the other workers, with a collective, although collectivity in and of itself would not suffice, either. The fact that their situation is a class situation, objective and determined rather than contingent, ultimately produces the poem's power. That the subject of the poem is a group and not an individual is underlined by the fact that the narrator isn't introduced into the poem until line 46 and then only as one of a sub-group (whites) among the workers, and is only mentioned twice. Bukowski effects the identification of the narrator with his co-workers linguistically, as he establishes the fact that it is their identical roles in the relations of production that create solidarity. In roughly the first half of the poem, "we" or "our" appears in only 5% of the lines whereas in the second half roughly 40% of the lines have such a pronoun or possessive adjective and this suggests that working on the job together has created solidarity.

In "Sparks" the emphasis has been shifted from a subjective to an objective condition. The first two stanzas of the poem are almost pure job description. When it becomes necessary to shift from the third person, and the first person plural is inappropriate, Bukowski uses the second person plural, retaining the collective. What is a problem in their situation is equally a problem for all and gives force and depth to the description. Were it only the effect on one individual the problem of the objective condition as universal would be lost because any one individual can conceivably escape (as we will see in "transformation and disfiguration"). But such an escape remains just that, an individual('s) solution, and thus of only anecdotal interest. (In contrast to "$$$$$$," "Yankee Doodle" and "transformation and disfiguration" there is no anecdote in "Sparks.") The situation, and any possible solution, is very different for a class. But identification with a class, alone, is not enough, either. What is still necessary is the recognition of the true nature of the class position, i.e., of the exploitation involved and of the nature of class relationships:

> knowing we were
> suckers
> making the rich
> richer.
> (67–70)

In "Sparks" everything, to the extent that this is ever possible, is "an intended expression of the self," which here has assumed a collective character. The material is completely under the control of the poet.

But if this is true, then the recognition just mentioned raises certain questions. What was "best" about the factory? In what way did the workers "[give] them / better than they asked?" What could be good (let alone better or best) in such an alienated and exploited condition? "Best," of course, has nothing to do with the relations of production that obtain in the factory but rather with the human relations existing among the workers. Because the alienation is so great it allows (or forces) them to effect a complete separation between their work and the rest of their life, thus, paradoxically, allowing them to feel "fresh" after ten hours / of heavy labor"; "best" because their exploited condition is absolutely clear to them and so the work becomes secondary, even peripheral, the least important aspect of the job, to be dispatched in a clause of four syllables that is almost an aside, "the work got done," and immediately forgotten in the flux of human relationships. The solidarity of the workers was what was best.

In what sense, then, are we meant to take "better"? The word we would expect is "more" and the difference is important. It is a nice question as to which of the final two statements is the more puzzling: "We gave them / better than they asked," or "we gave them / nothing." Assuredly it is not here a case of Stakhanovites overfulfilling their quotas, because they do not give them more, but "better"; "better" in that "they" had not the right to expect that out of the "pack" of "Yankee Doodle" something as cohesive and unified as the "gang" in "Sparks" could develop, given that the process is deadly. It wasn't that "the work got done," because that, after all, is what management demands; it was that in and of itself more was produced than just product and surplus value. What was better was the "magnificence." It is an ironic usage: not "better" for management but for the workers.

In "Sparks," everything is intended, an expression of a trans-individual self. That everything is under the poet's control is, again, supported by the lapidary parataxis; the omission of rhetoric becomes the rhetoric by successfully disguising its rhetorical nature. The closing lines, among the most effective endings in Bukowski's poetry—

> we were some gang
> in that death ballet
>
> we were magnificent
>
> we gave them
> better than they asked
>
> yet
> we gave them
> nothing.
> (89–96)

—formally close the poem while opening it up philosophically by making the poem more than simple expression. The last clause is intriguing and important. To what extent, or in what way, is it a valid statement? Or is it just wishful thinking and a rewriting of history? Coming at the end of the poem, it seems to me quite effective, summing up, building on and expressing the tenor of what has happened, but its claim has to be elucidated.

Clearly the workers in the poem have given "the rich" their labor power. The work has "gotten done" and presumably surplus value has been created. It is not a question of gold-bricking or absenteeism as it is elsewhere in Bukowski. (Interestingly enough, it is never a case of sabotage. Perhaps this is too active— even committed—a form of refusal for the passive Bukowski protagonist.) And the workers know they are exploited. In just what sense have the workers given them nothing? In the sense, I think, in which Sully does give them something with his forty years and his retirement party. Implicitly, early on, he gave them the promise of reliability. And this is quite a bit. Nothing is so threatening to management/ownership as uncertainty. The workers in "Sparks" give "management" nothing in that and because they are not "touched" by the job (as Sully is). They know they are "suckers" and this knowledge is valuable. If the narrator is a "good" worker, it is for aesthetic reasons ("just for the rhythm of it"). Giving them nothing spiritually, as it were, is yet another refusal. ("Sparks" is a poem with a touch of idealism.) Of course in one sense the assertion is not, strictly speaking, correct; the narrator has not gotten away unscathed. As Bukowski put it in "guava tree," reflecting (as he has done all through the 80s), again, on those earlier years, when "it was always the other man's idea / the other man who was making all the money using me," "they got something, of course" (D 232). Therefore, although it is incorrect to say that they got nothing, what they did get was superficial compared to what they didn't get.

Moreover, it is in its character *qua* assertion that the statement, and ultimately the poem, gain additional force and significance. The workers have refused to make the deal Sully made, the retirement party for reliability. They know they're "suckers." (Sully, too, was a "sucker," but either didn't know it or wouldn't admit it.) But that knowledge is already the beginning of something. The integrity of the last lines lies in the workers' refusal to give up an important part of themselves (sometimes it is all that remains). It is their refusal to whistle while they work (though they have no illusions about their immediate situation). Because of that immediate situation, this assertion is not a light thing; it implies the workers' acceptance of a split in their humanity, "the split," as Lukàcs wrote in *History and Class Consciousness*, "between the worker's labor-power and his personality, its metamorphosis into a thing . . ." (99). Such an acknowledgement is never easy but it is a necessary step if the conditions which have produced such a split are ever to be changed in that "because of the split between subjectivity and objectivity induced in man by the compulsion to objectify himself as a commodity, the situation becomes one that can be made conscious" (168), and because the refusal is here generalized (in sharp contrast to the subjective refusals in "$$$$$$" and "Yankee Doodle"), it becomes potentially more powerful. "They" got nothing in that they did not get the workers to acknowledge any identity of interests with "them." They failed to co-opt them as they had Sully. The possibility of resistance is still present in the workers in "Sparks" and thus the possibility of change. Ultimately, capital will be able at almost any given moment, through the threat or, if necessary, the use of force, to extort surplus value from the working class. But its position is rarely as secure as it would like. The workers in "Sparks," by their refusal to give anything beyond that immediate bit of accumulation, preserve a necessary reserve of integrity and resistance.

All this is reflected in the language of the poem. One of its salient aspects, something that marks it in Bukowski's poetic oeuvre, is its almost complete avoidance of the first person singular pronoun. Had the last lines of the poem, quoted above, read: "I was some dancer / in that death ballet etc," they would not be without effect, just as the opening of "Yankee Doodle" is not without effect; but it would be narrow and limited compared to the present ending. The restriction of the grammatical subject of the poem to the first person singular would limit its applicability and possibly its appeal. The force of the poem derives from the identification of the individual with the group and the group's recognition of the alienated, exploited and collective nature of their condition. In the end, it is the absolute and unqualified recognition of solidarity among the exploited that gives "Sparks" its power.

While "Sparks" tells of a time when "Bukowski" and his fellow workers "gave them nothing" and of a job that "didn't touch us," such is not the case in "transformation and disfiguration." As the title indicates, here it is distinctly a case of the job having an effect—often traumatic—on the workers. Bukowski's title (a play on the Strauss tone poem, *Death and Transfiguration*) nicely denies any spiritual benefit coming from death—there are deaths in the poem but the narrator refuses to see them as in any way transfiguring. Ever the materialist, he chooses to emphasize their *disfiguring* power. The tone of the poem is resigned; the many conjunctions suggest an inexorable progression (in this case, of suffering) because here there is no thought of resistance, only the occasional individual escape. They have been captured, and unlike the narrator in "guava tree," who feels "like / the wolf who got out of the trap but without gnawing a / leg away," here the workers have been maimed, in some cases even destroyed, either directly as a result of the rigors of the job: Louie, exhausted from having to work two jobs, "fell asleep in bed / smoking a cigarette / the mattress caught fire / he burned to death. . . ." or indirectly as in the case of Ralph whose wife is unfaithful, at least in part because Ralph is working "eleven-and-one-half hours a night," and who is accidentally shot by his wife's lover. "Little tragedies" Bukowski terms them, with mild pathos.

> it was death and transformation
> and disfiguration:
> people found
> they couldn't walk anymore
> or they suddenly
> came up with speech defects
> or they were shaken by tremors or
> their eyes blinked or
> they came to work drugged or
> drunk or both
>
> it was terror and dismemberment
> and the survivors
> hunched on their stools wondering
> who would be next
> (WT 163, 49–62)

Not a pleasant picture of the U.S. Post Office, nor one that jibes with its public image (at least until recently). Ordinarily, we don't think of the Postal Service as the dangerous, quasi-industrial job that Bukowski depicts in this poem. For the general public a career with the Post Office has been considered a step out of the industrial working class. But the intensely routinized nature of the clerk's work and the equally extreme hierarchy of the postal bureaucracy make the job itself alienating and repressive in the extreme. As the sociologist Stanley Aronowitz wrote: "Post office work is commonly viewed as white-collar labor, but is characteristically perceived by the workers themselves as a variant of factory work" (311). It is one of Bukowski's achievements to have made us aware of this side of the job.

"Transformation and disfiguration" is similar to "Sparks" in that we largely view the situation from the group's perspective. This is established in the first stanza where, as in "Sparks," we have an introductory clause in the third person establishing the objectivity of the events being narrated:

> there were always little tragedies
> we heard about them on the job
> sitting on those stools
> eleven-and-one-half hours a night
> every bit of outside news
> was greeted by us
> much like the inmates of a prison camp
>
> every now and then
> a courier would come by and say
> "it's 3 to 2, end of the 3rd . . ."
>
> he never said 3 to 2 *who*
> because
> we were able to decipher all that
>
> (1–13)

The second and third stanzas about the baseball scores are important for showing the narrator as having come to terms with the apparently trivial aspects of job relations (something not true in "Yankee Doodle"). This is made clear when, at the end of the poem, in order to reduce the tension over the knifing-incident discussion, he himself asks, "I wonder who's winning / the old ball game?" That the "courier" doesn't have to name the team indicates that, at least in this respect—if not united—there is a common denominator, that the group's team is known, that the tone of the "courier's" voice is in itself enough to let them know whether the home team's ahead or behind. An interest in the sport is crucial. It's not so much a question of where one's particular sympathies lie (rooting for another team would be graciously tolerated, as evidence of democratic "freedom of thought") as of a litmus test for ingroup-outgroup status via interest in the sport itself. In the absence of any kind of unifying material (class) interest (and the postal workers are very different in their class consciousness from the factory workers in "Sparks") the workers need something on which they can unite as a group, however trivial.° Hence the progress of the local baseball team has to serve as the common bond, a topic promoting casual, day-to-day cohesiveness. As the team represents the city most of them live in, support of—or just interest in it—is felt to be asking very little (although it is not completely devoid of ideological significance: cp. "the national pastime.") and thus lack of interest, or outright aversion, becomes a sure sign of marginality.

But if the narrator is a part of the group, he is also, at times, apart; he talks to the other workers but only to learn about what has already become general knowledge. And the news is not good. The group here is a group that suffers and diminishes in the course of the poem as its members die or leave, the most important departure being the narrator's. This is a significant difference from "Sparks" where the integrity of the group is maintained, even vaunted, throughout the poem (with the minor exception of the few whites who "didn't last"). Here his departure emphatically separates the narrator from the other workers and determines the different effects of the two endings.

The ending of "transformation and disfiguration" is problematic and I shall discuss it in a moment, but first I want to discuss one effect of Bukowski's having chosen the third person: its more distanced perspective facilitates an objective analysis of the structural aspects of hierarchical work relations and the corollary recognition that the problem is systemic rather than individual:

> the supervisors brutalized us
> and the supervisors
> were in turn brutalized
> by their supervisors who
> were in turn brutalized
> by the Postmaster General
> who always demanded
> more for less
> and the public brutalized
> the Postmaster General
> and it was finally
> the little old lady
> pruning her garden roses
> who was the first cause
> of misery for everybody:
> Democracy at work
>
> (63–78)

89

Bukowski recognizes that it is the system—"democracy"—that is faulty. Apparently rational (clear chain of command and responsibility), it somehow irrationally perverts the demands of the innocuous individual into brutalizing work relations; something has gone haywire. At no level does it make sense, least of all at the level of the first-line supervisor who, as Bukowski put it in "guava tree," was "hired to cause me trouble / we were pitted against each other and that just wasn't / sensible because he was almost as poor as I." Yet it is at this, exploitation's most concrete level, that conflicts become most intense, in part because the larger class conflict goes unacknowledged:

> one night I asked,
> "where's Hodges?"
>
> (I don't know why but
> I was always
> the last to know anything
> perhaps because I was white
> and most of them were black)
>
> there was no reply
> about Hodges
> who was the meanest soup
> and *white*
> to top it all
>
> and I asked again
> and somebody said
> "he won't be around
> for a while . . ."
>
> and then
> in pieces and bits
> it was revealed to me:
> Hodges had been knifed
> in the parking lot
> on the way to his car
>
> and then
> it was inferred
> that everybody knew
> who did it

"would it be anybody
I know?"
I smiled

it got very quiet
Big George put his mail down
stared at me
he stared at me a long time

then he turned
started sticking his letters again

and I said
"I wonder who's winning
the old ball game?"

"4 to 2,"
somebody said
"end of the 4th . . ."
(79–119)

Thus the ultimate effect of these work relations is intra-class violence, foremen being "almost as poor" as and coming from the
same class as the postal workers themselves. Though there's an
indication of racial conflict, I don't think we are meant to see
the knifing as a racial incident, and indeed it is nowhere stated
that Big George is black. The fact that Hodges is white is only
the (vanilla) icing ("to top it all") on the situational cake, an added
irritant. His job, "to cause . . . trouble," is a function of the hierarchical structure of the work relations ("who always demanded /
more for less"). The note of resignation—defeat is perhaps not
too strong a word—in "transformation and disfiguration," as opposed to the triumphant tone of "Sparks," is a result of the different situation this poem describes: the exploitation involved in
working for the Post Office is not of the same order as that
present in the lighting-fixture factory; but the situation of the
workers in "transformation and disfiguration" is more disheart-
ening, in part, because the Post Office, as Aronowitz noted, is
seen as white-collar work, as a career.

While the poem is impressive in its detail, in its wedding of
narrative with discursiveness, the ending remains problematic:
"Hodges never came back / and soon / I got out of there too"

(120–122). Two careers with the U.S. Post Office have ended. One reading might view the narrator's leaving as evidence that he feared a racially motivated attack. It is clear why Hodges never came back, but it is not clear why the narrator leaves. After all, Hodges was management and the most concrete instrument of exploitation and brutalization. The ending begs the question by suggesting that the narrator left for the same reason that Hodges did. It heightens the effect of the poem but only by injecting a false sense of drama into it. It seems to have "ignored the full play of forces that go into making the resolution" (Altieri, 25). I think the poem would have been more effective (and had more integrity) had it ended six or three lines earlier. (Early in his career, closure had been a problem for Bukowski, though in the poems of the 1980s he seems to have resolved the issue.) As it is, though, the ending is unambiguous, a pseudo-resolution.° The narrator's leaving has a trace of the "I-don't-even-*need*-this-job" attitude expressed in "$$$$$$." This reduces the effect of all that has preceded it in the poem because the narrator has now separated himself from the group. (One might argue that Bukowski really did leave the Post Office, but of course he left the lighting-fixture factory, too.) The difference in treatment of racial difference between "transformation and disfiguration" and "Sparks" is interesting: though the group of workers in "Sparks" was racially mixed, this was not a cause of conflict.

The individual perspective is evident in the narrator's distance from the group and injects a hint of falseness into it. This seems to me the case with "old" in " 'I wonder who's winning / the old ball game?' " which is too ironic for the actual context. The question is meant to reduce the tension by unambivalently referring back to common, if trivial, interests. "Old" works against this goal. It suggests a tone more in line with the feelings of rueful reminiscence, of retrospective distance present in Bukowski at the time he wrote the poem rather than what "Bukowski" was likely feeling at the time of the incident. Such distance is, however, along with the last three lines, historically determined, revealing escape as possible only for the individual subject. ("Old" comes from the subject escaped.) The problem and the individual solution are aptly resumed in "guava tree":

```
before there was always much for me to do
but it was always the other man's idea
the other man who was making all the money using me
and also the foreman he hired to cause me trouble
we were pitted against each other and that just wasn't
sensible because he was almost as poor as I, it was
tiring and deathly like something sucking at
your blood.
well, I wasn't a revolutionary, I only wanted to save
my own ass, I figured that would be easier than saving
humanity's ass . . .
```
(D 232, 6–16)

Both "transformation and disfiguration" and "Sparks" are in their way remarkable attempts to come to terms with the exploitation and alienation of a class society, as manifested over a quarter of a century of U.S. history. While they are not primarily documentary poems, their value as documents should not be overlooked. It is one of Bukowski's strengths as a poet that he has managed to capture history and social dynamics in his poems without vitiating their aesthetic power.

CHAPTER FOUR:
METONYMY

> But the greatest thing by far is to have a command of metaphor. This alone cannot be imparted by another; it is the mark of genius, for to make good metaphors implies an eye for resemblances. (1459a)
>
> Aristotle

As the quotation from the *Poetics* suggests, the dominance of metaphor as the poetic figure par excellence has a long history. "The language of poets is necessarily metaphorical," M. H. Abrams writes, "because these figures of speech disclose the unity behind the apparent diversity of phenomena . . ." (357). Yet, poets periodically rebelled against the overuse of the figure and to the extent that such movements propounded a simpler, more "natural" diction there was a tendency towards metonymy. David Lodge wrote of one such reaction among the romantics who

> thought of themselves as replacing one, inauthentic, kind of metaphorical writing . . . with another, more powerful kind . . . which didn't necessarily express itself through a profusion of metaphorical figures. Wordsworth's effort to purify the language of English poetry entailed forcing it back towards the metonymic pole. . . . (118)

Yet metaphor always seemed to reassert itself. In 1948, Cleanth Brooks wrote: "One can sum up modern poetic technique by calling it the rediscovery of metaphor and the full commitment to metaphor" (799).

Perhaps the most influential modern theorist of metonymy and the scholar who prompted others to think more seriously about its uses was the linguist Roman Jakobson who saw in the two modes profoundly different ways of expressing reality. In his essay "Two Aspects of Language and Two Types of Aphasic Disturbances," he divided language as a whole into metonymic and metaphoric poles, viewing the first as characteristic of prose, the second of poetry. Metonymy involved contiguity, metaphor similarity. In an earlier essay he wrote: "The basic impulse of narrative prose is association by contiguity, and the narrative moves from one object to an adjacent one on paths of space and time or of causality; to move from the whole to the part and vice versa is only a particular instance of this process."° Jakobson broadened the traditional literary definitions of the terms and it is in his general sense, as refined by Charles Altieri, who speaks of a "functional metonymy," that I will be using them. Analyzing Flaubert, Altieri wrote:

> We need a literary term to distinguish Flaubert's typically ironic symbols from symbols that promise a potential communal intensification of shared meanings. . . . I want . . . to apply to the distinction between ironic and traditional or romantic symbol the terms metonymy and metaphor as developed by Claude Lévi-Strauss out of Roman Jakobson's work. . . . I find them suggestive because they relate specific rhetorical forms to more general operations of functions of the mind., We might then speak of metaphoric and metonymic functions.°

The "redeeming feature" metonymy offered the writer was that, "so long as he does not impose his own single interpretive structure on the images, the poet himself remains concealed in the absence they evoke" (104).

Bukowski's early poetry had shown the influence of Surrealism; Neruda, specifically, has been suggested as an influence, as have the Imagists and William Carlos Williams.° Both movements granted metaphor and simile important places in poetry and both figures appear not infrequently in Bukowski's earlier poetry. But by the 1980s, they had been almost completely jettisoned either in favor of metonymy, or as part of a complete avoidance of traditional figurative language. This persistent rejection of metaphor, the figure most completely identified with poetry, has, I think, had a beneficial effect on his poetry.

☆

The poem "retired," from Bukowski's 1986 collection, *You Get So Alone at Times That It Just Makes Sense* is a striking example of this trend in Bukowski's poetry. (The complete poem is quoted.)

retired

pork chops, said my father, I love
pork chops!

and I watched him slide the grease
into his mouth.

pancakes, he said, pancakes with
syrup, butter and bacon!

I watched his heavy lips wetted with
all that.

coffee, he said, I like coffee so hot
it burns my throat!

sometimes it was too hot and he spit it
out across the table.

mashed potatoes and gravy, he said, I
love mashed potatoes and gravy!

he jowled that in, his cheeks puffed as
if he had the mumps.

chili and beans, he said, I love chili and
beans!

and he gulped it down and farted for hours
loudly, grinning after each fart.

strawberry shortcake, he said, with vanilla
ice cream, that's the way to end a meal!

he always talked about retirement, about
what he was going to do when he
retired.
when he wasn't talking about food he talked
on and on about
retirement.

he never made it to retirement, he died one day while
standing at the sink
filling a glass of water.
he straightened like he'd been
shot.
the glass fell from his hand
and he dropped backwards
landing flat
his necktie slipping to the
left.

afterwards
people said they couldn't believe
it.
he looked
great.
distinguished white
sideburns, pack of smokes in his
shirt pocket, always cracking
jokes, maybe a little
loud and maybe with a bit of bad
temper
but all in all
a seemingly sound
individual

never missing a day
of work

(Y 17–18)

Here we see Bukowski writing in the vein brought into prominence by the later Robert Lowell, whose poetry took a decided
turn for the metonymic with *Life Studies*. (Indeed "retired" seems
a working-class version of "Terminal Days At Beverly Farms.")
But Bukowski is even more reticent than Lowell. Absent from
Bukowski's poem is any overt comment on his father and his
father's life. Comment there is, and not always particularly subtle,
but it is all in the choice—not of words—but of facts and details,
of actions described: the food his father ate, and in a nice touch
he notes that the immediate cause of his death was his failed
attempt to consume the—in context—healthiest substance mentioned, water (possibly an amused reference to "Bukowski's" fa-
bled alcoholism, something which had yet to kill *him*), how he
consumed it, the fact that he was wearing a tie when he died,
that he smoked, that he "never made it to retirement," that he

"never miss[ed] a day / of work." All these things, in fact almost everything in the poem, damn the father; and by inference we get a good idea of how "Bukowski" felt about him. But we get it almost solely from the metonymic details. Bukowski's poetic strength is his refusal of overt comment. This is closely allied to his reliance on one form of narrative, the chronicle, a narrative, in Walter Benjamin's phrase, "free from explanation," the "chaste compactness" of which "precludes psychological analysis." "[I]t is half the art of storytelling," Benjamin wrote in his essay, "The Storyteller," to keep a story free from explanation as one reproduces it. . . . the psychological connection of the events is not forced on the reader. It is left up to him to interpret things . . ." (89).

Narrative lends itself to incorporating such details because it is based on the apparent contiguity of sequential time. Apparent, because just as the choice of metonymic details is left open to the poet, so is the choice of what to include in the narrative sequence. In Bukowski, the refusal to psychologize is closely connected to the preference for metonymy, for things, rather than explanation. Such explanation is the overt interjection of a subject which, less and less often in Bukowski, provides explicit meaning. Bukowski avoids explanation not only by refusing overt comment but by refusing the implicit comment of moralizing adjectives. Their absence further objectifies the depiction. The metonymic details that ultimately "condemn" the father are themselves often presented indirectly: the narrator doesn't say that his father wore a tie, but rather that "his necktie slipp[ed] to the / left," nor that he smoked, but that he had a "pack of smokes in his / shirt pocket."

Here the contrast with Lowell is revealing, evident when we look at the second stanza of "Terminal Days at Beverly Farms":

> Father and Mother moved to Beverly Farms
> to be a two minute walk from the station,
> half an hour by train from the Boston doctors.
> They had no sea-view,
> but the sky-blue tracks of the commuters' railroad shone
> like a double-barrelled shotgun
> through the scarlet late August sumac,
> multiplying like cancer
> at their garden's border.

Although "Terminal Days" clearly employs a functional metonymy, it is more closely allied than "retired" to that aspect of the modernist tradition that, in Donald Hall's words, "asked for a poetry of symmetry, intellect, irony and wit" (25), a request which Lowell, with the poem's plethora of pregnant adjectives, moderately poetic diction, personification, portentous similes and quoting of examples of his father's idiolect, amply fulfills. By contrast, Bukowski uses no metaphors or similes, his diction is resolutely unpoetic and the poem is almost completely without adjectives. (Perhaps "jowled" can be seen as metaphorical but it involves so little in the way of substitution that it only underlines how rigorous is Bukowski's antipathy towards the figure.) Bukowski rejects traditional poetic resources far more emphatically than did Lowell.

The poem metonymically characterizes the father, giving us, obliquely, a picture of his life. Indeed, the title— "retired" rather than "retirement"—is metonymic in the term's narrow meaning giving us a partial aspect of the individual for the whole. It is also more vivid and specific than "retirement" because its grammatical passivity suggests something suffered by a particular individual. Yet, on reconsideration, the title also suggests that the poem will be about his father's life in retirement, suggested by having the opening words of the poem spoken by the father. Of course, the poem cannot be about retirement because his father "never made it to retirement." Rather the poem is about his father's life.

The crucial final stanza of the poem, emphasizing the father's submission to capitalist work discipline, suggests at least a part of the latent content. The deeper relationship, again suggested metonymically, is that of the father to conventional values in general and, most importantly, to the work ethic in particular. Pork chops, pancakes, butter, syrup, bacon, coffee, mashed potatoes and gravy, chili and beans, strawberry shortcake and vanilla ice-cream: it would be hard to find a more conventional American diet of its era; indeed its conventionality (really stereotypicality) is heightened by some of the collocations: strawberry shortcake *and* vanilla ice cream, pancakes *with* syrup, butter and bacon, chili *and* beans. In the case of pancakes it would seem superfluous to note the butter and syrup and even more so, in the case of chili, to add the beans. The father becomes reified through the plethora of food items. There is also the suggestion, with the 1980s heightened awareness of nutrition and health in the background, that his father is killing himself. Though, taken individually, some of the items are undeniably healthy, in almost all cases, and certainly when the list is considered as a whole, this is a diet for death. Not only the diet, high in starches, fat, caffeine and nicotine (the cigarettes always on his person emphasizing addiction), but the manner in which it is consumed: "jowl[ing]" and "gulp[ing]" the food and coffee in and down suggest a compulsive aspect to the processes—indeed, quasi-masochistic in the case of the coffee—as if the process has gotten beyond the control of the individual, as if he has become a machine automatically reproducing itself.

As food kept the father going in the most basic sense, so, it would appear, did the prospect (because it never materialized into more than "talking about") of retirement fuel him spiritually (as it would seem to do many others). Retirement becomes a kind of afterlife in which all the horrors of the routine job are compensated for and it is this reverse Faustian pact that Bukowski has constantly reacted against in his writing. Both the reified, compulsive quality of his father's reproduction of his life and the "deal" he has made reflect the larger whole of submission to convention, metonymically realized in the phrase, "his necktie slipping to the / left." For Bukowski, the tie has always been one of those signs he has seized on when negatively characterizing a male for conventional behavior, as for example in the poem "we've got to communicate," where the narrator is being upbraided by his lover: "but no, / you don't *like* Lance, do you? / he wears a necktie, and he's into real estate" (D 93).

"Retired" is a prime example of metonymic *écriture*. As Jakobson wrote: "Show us your environment and I will tell you who you are. We learn what he lives on, this lyric hero outlined by metonymies, split up by synecdoches into individual attributes, reactions and situations" (313). Altieri noted the advantage the technique holds for the poet because "by objectifying his materials, he need not identify himself with any single object or single perspective" (104). In "Terminal Days," Lowell does not really do this: true, he chooses objects, but with his pregnant, almost symbolic adjectives and metaphors, he is far from concealed. Perloff saw Lowell as "fus[ing] the romantic 'poetry of experience' with the metonymic mode perfected by the great realist novelists of the late nineteenth century. The style born of this fusion marks a turning point in the history of twentieth-century poetry" (99). While Perloff is right to note the significance of the increasing use of metonymy in the poems of *Life Studies*, it is Bukowski who has most fully exploited this poetic mode. In "retired" Bukowski condemns his father (or rather his father is made to convict himself) almost completely in terms of his actions, all of which then culminate in the most damning fact of all: his never missing a day of work. Yet the implied author barely inserts himself into the poem. The facts are unqualified and indeed the only judgments allowed into the poem, in the penultimate stanza, appear there indirectly, as the judgments of others.

Just as important as his metonymic bent is Bukowski's resolute refusal of metaphor. Jakobson wrote that "[i]n normal verbal behavior both processes are continually operative, but . . . under the influence of a cultural pattern, personality, and verbal style, preference is given to one of the two processes over the other" (110). But Bukowski doesn't just prefer metonymy; he virtually excludes metaphor from his poetry of the 1980s. Some readers are threatened by such a presentation of the world, as if the lack of figurative language automatically deprives a poem of meaning, or at least of poetry. After the stripping of rime and a regular rhythm begun by Whitman and furthered by numerous twentieth-century (especially American) poets, the removal of metaphor from poetry, may seem one more nail in its coffin. Altieri feared that "[m]etonymy poses . . . the possible appropriation by behaviorist perspectives or by a more general analytic view that reduces phenomena to facts" (110).° But this hardly seems possible; the subject is inevitably interested. Metonymy serves to conceal the subject, not abolish it.

Unlike "retired," Bukowski's poem "overhead mirrors" is a poem more strictly concerned with the narrator's own experience. What links all the details of the poem is narrative contiguity, what Jakobson called "the context." They are not metaphoric substitutes for anything else, for "entities conjoined in the code but not in the given message." Any larger meaning

102

arises out of their role as details composing the narrative; they are "relationships [that] derive not from structured patterns but from connections or associations perceived in time or space" (Altieri, 104). Such relationships are more convincing than patently artificial formal patterns which reveal the hand of the poet. They can be more convincing than metaphor because so apparently "unpoetic." The details, however, are not randomly chosen; as Perloff wrote: "metonymic structure is far from artless" (88). The passage beginning "it was one of those nights you remember" from "overhead mirrors" (see p. 45, above) is an example of how the "the creation of an empty background [i.e., no universal] forces one to attend to the energy present in particular objects experiences and thoughts" (Altieri, 109). There is little in the way of a broader context, let alone patterned structure backgrounding these actions. The actions themselves are the most trivial imaginable and are—trivial though they are—themselves canceled by being immediately undone (turning the radio, faucets and lights off and on), and their inconsequentiality then heightened yet again by (continual) repetition: "I kept turning . . ." Indeed, the repetition of these meaningless actions provides the only formal structure within the poem and thus its only formal assertion of meaning: the piling up of clauses suggests that pure inertial movement is as close as we get to meaning. Even the proffered aid of the narrator's friend, "the porno guy," who, knowing the narrator is sick and may need him, gives him the phone number of the motel where he and his girlfriend will be, is pointless:

> "got a pencil?"
>
> "yeh . . ."
>
> "it's . . ."
>
> he gave me the number.
> I didn't have a pencil, I couldn't
> move.
>
> "thanks," I said.
>
> (W 236, 51–57)

Here the lack of constructed meaning, of a formal patterned structure, is represented both by the actions and by their linguistic representation in the poem; and again a key feature of the latter is the almost total absence of adjectives that might reveal the narrator and a meaning along with (in lines 58–78, as well) a tremendous number of verbs—action without qualification.

An inability, or unwillingness, even to assign a cause to his condition is made clear in the characterization of the porno store operator, who is depicted as capable of both exploitative and thoughtful behavior: " 'we'll fix you up,' said the porno bookstore / guy (who was also selling me / the watered-down coke)." Yet the narrator's continuing to buy the "low grade coke," noted without comment, causes the reader to wonder just what is going on. Thus the metonymy is clearly "not artless." To label it behaviorist does not do justice to the dialectic of surface and depth, openness and subtle determinacy that metonymy allows, indeed fosters in a poem, qualities which go a long way toward forcing the reader to think and think twice about what the poem may mean in spite of the fact that "Bukowski" explicitly downplays significance in any larger context:

> "I wouldn't say it was a particularly low time, it was
> a time and I tried to adjust spiritually
> to most matters.
> which meant: not expecting much and not getting much.
>
> (1–4)

He makes clear that this is no epiphany that he is about to describe and that—materialist that he is—its only significance lies as a phenomenon within a naturalist framework, a biological extreme case, "but sickness is another matter."

The title of the poem, another metonymic detail, refers to "the only friends I had . . . a nudey dancer and / a guy who operated a porno bookstore" who, aware of the narrator's condition, call him one evening:

> "listen, Babs and I aren't working tonight,
> we're going to a motel with over-
> head mirrors and X-rated tv, we're going to
> relax and fuck . . ."
>
> (40–44)

But, title or not, it remains just a detail which (as often in Bukowski) when used as the title throws the reader off, rather than involving him in any kind of metaphoric or symbolic meaning, i.e., in its particularity it denies any broader meaning (though it does ultimately participate in the meaning of the poem). There is no patterned structure, no universal, although the drug experience is (minimally) contextualized in the narrative:

> I was living in a cheap court in Hollywood
> in between women
> and I was buying coke, really
> low-grade crap, sniffing that with
> beer and scotch.
> I got mentally very depressed and physically
> sick.
> I couldn't eat.
> it got so I just ingested
> coke, scotch and beer.
>
> (6–15)

"Overhead mirrors" refuses a patterned structure, a larger meaning, in part by virtue of its refusal of metaphor. Indeed, the one overt attempt at pointing a moral: "if you don't fight death it will / just move in," is really a pseudo-universal of the type favored by Bukowski in his existentialist moods. Irrelevant, it comes out of nowhere and quickly returns there, unsupported by anything in the poem. Indeed, its irrelevance underscores the materialism of the depiction. Its superficial presence only suggests all the more that the nexus of the poem lies elsewhere because, for one, death is *not* fought in the poem. There is no fight in the poem, against death or anything else. The only resistance is inertial. Indeed, to "fight death" by turning radio, lights and faucets on and off and flushing the toilet, i.e., to reassure oneself of one's existence through activating the mechanical paraphernalia of modern society, would seem to suggest how defenseless we have become.

The force of the poem rests on two things. The first is its concreteness, its "attention to the energy present in particular objects, experiences and thoughts," in its "look[ing] very carefully." But more importantly its force lies "precisely in establishing differences, in breaking through easy abstractions or myths

of human community, to make one intensely aware of the oppo-
sitions and contradictory desires which constitute the human
condition" (Altieri, 134). It is this capacity to "establish differences,"
an inherent characteristic of metonymy, that makes it so useful
to Bukowski. The differences in Bukowski's poetry (not just in
"overhead mirrors" but in many of the poems discussed so far)
do "break through easy abstractions or myths of human community." Negation and the refusal of identity, here made clear
through metonymy, are central to Bukowski's achievement.

Yet at the same time negation is asserted, it is softened somewhat through a metonymic string at the end of the poem. This
dialectic is represented by a continuum whose two ends are
reflected in the details of the "porno guy" and his girlfriend having
sex in the motel room with the overhead mirrors, and the narrator, at the end of the poem (after he has completely recovered
from his night of horror), buying a newspaper:

> the next morning I didn't puke.
> I got up, took a good crap, took a
> lukewarm bath, dressed and walked to the
> corner of
> Hollywood and Western
> put a dime in the box
> got a *Herald-Examiner*,
> remembering decades back when there
> was a newspaper in L.A.
> called the *Herald-Express* and another
> called the *Examiner*
> and they merged rather than
> kill each other off.
> and carrying that paper back
> I felt that I had lived a long
> time
> though not a very wonderful one,
> I took the paper back to my place,
> sat on the couch
> and began to read it
> fascinated, finally, with what the
> other people
> were doing.
>
> (112–134)

One meaning of the poem, created through the juxtaposition of these details is an assertion of this balance between self-absorption and a recognition of the world outside the individual subject. It is not watching oneself in mirrors, although even people who do that are involved with more than themselves.

The various aspects of Bukowski's poetry that I have been discussing in these chapters are all present in the last poem I will discuss, "looking for a job." This is a poem of the working-class, strongly subjective in its refusal of work, and a self-contained narrative relying on metonymy, sometimes in the strict sense of the term; as in "there are so many houses and dark streets without help" the ostensibly controlling subject becomes objectified and the metonymic images of particularization suggested in "transformation and disfiguration" are here consciously asserted as ultimate fate.

looking for a job

> it was Philly and the bartender said
> what and I said, gimme a draft, Jim,
> got to get the nerves straight, I'm
> going to look for a job. you, he said
> a job?
> yeah, Jim, I saw something in the paper,
> no experience necessary.
> and he said, hell, you don't want a job,
> and I said, hell, no, but I need money,
> and I finished the beer
> and got on the bus and I watched the numbers
> and soon the numbers got closer
> and then I was right there
> and I pulled the cord and the bus stopped and
> I got off.
> it was a large building made of tin
> the sliding door was stuck in the dirt
> I pulled it back and went in
> and there wasn't any floor, just more ground,
> lumpy, wet, and it stank
> and there were sounds like things being sawed in half
> and things drilled and it was dark
> and men walked on girders overhead
> and men pushed trucks across the ground
> and men sat at machines doing things

and there were shots of lightning and thunder
and suddenly a bucket full of flames came swinging at
my head, it roared and boiled with flame
it hung from a loose chain and it came right at me
and somebody hollered, HEY, LOOK OUT!
and I just ducked under the bucket
feeling the heat go over me
and somebody asked,
WHAT DO YOU WANT?
and I said, WHERE IS YOUR NEAREST CRAPPER?
and I was told
and I went inside
then came out and saw silhouettes of men
moving through flame and sound and
I walked to the door, got outside, and
took the bus back to the bar and sat down
and ordered another draft, and Jim asked,
what happened? I said, they didn't want me, Jim.
then this whore came in and sat down and everybody
looked at her, she looked fine, and I remember it
was the first time in my life I almost wished I had a
vagina and clit instead of what I had, but in 2 or 3 days
I got over that and I was reading the
want ads again.

(B 172–73)

The poem (quoted in full) opens with the narrator quite active
in his environment and apparently in control. The metonymy
begins in earnest as soon as the narrator gets on the bus to go
to the job site, at which point objects begin taking over, indicating the incipient objectification of the narrator and his resulting
loss of control. With "watched," because of its passive aura (if
not grammatical passivity), the mood begins to shift and this shift
is completed in the following clause when "the numbers g[e]t
closer" to the narrator who is now the object. "Numbers" is a
powerful synecdoche here; the conversion of space into time is
effective because it puts both concepts in play at once, the effect, in this case of anxiety, or fear. (Take your pick.) It is a good
example of how effective Bukowski's resolute avoidance of
metaphor can be.

The synecdochic use of numbers and the metonymic trans-
position/transformation of subject for object together form a kind
of metonym to the second power. The full, unelided sequence

would go something like this: "The numbers on the buildings [or street signs, since there is no way to determine which is meant] became numerically closer to the number of the building [or street] housing the business that had placed the want ad in the paper." This double objectification results because "numbers" stands for street signs or the buildings on which the numbers appear and of course each group of numbers doesn't itself change but is rather succeeded by a different group of numbers; secondly, what is static, the "numbers," becomes dynamic and the subject, while what is dynamic, the narrator carried along on his bus, becomes static and the object.

To say "I watched the numbers" is an unmarked expression but then to say "the numbers got closer" is unusual and an indication of a deeper psychological dynamic. The narrator is so horrified at the thought of the possibly impending job that his fear prevents him from even contemplating the job in anything like its true dimensions. (Significantly, the type of work involved is not even mentioned in the poem; we get an idea of what it might be through the literally hellish synecdoche describing the job site.) It is as if he is being forcibly dragged towards some unnameable horror rather than going somewhere of his own free will. His ambivalence is so great that it results in a projection which reverses the true dynamic of the situation; the only way the narrator can conceive of himself meeting such a fate is if it is just that, fated, against his will, that is, to project himself as passive and objectified. Space, in a way, is transformed into time via the numbers and thus, become more easily quantifiable, allows a specious control over the oncoming event while at the same time prolonging the agony in that numbers alone more tellingly represent the abstract and inexorable quality of the narrator's fate.

Lines 16–39 constitute the description of the workplace and the metonymy is especially effective here. We have a depiction of the workplace in the form of its own mini-narrative within the larger narrative. The narrator provides a lot of descriptive detail, but it is the detail of process, not of static description: verbs (especially in the attributive position to nouns), surprisingly, not adjectives (again marked by their absence) in a passage which is so consciously and purposefully descriptive. Though the poem was written in the early seventies and thus exemplifies the extreme polysyndeton that Bukowski exhibited earlier in his career, this paucity of adjectives and, even more, the reliance on verbs and verbals foreshadow poems like "Sparks" and "transformation and disfiguration." A rough count, in which I also take as adjectives those verbals in attributive position, yielded 7% of the words in the lines under discussion being classified as adjectives.° Especially from line 21 on the emphasis on verbal descriptions effects another dynamism-in-stasis that is quite striking. In such lines as

> and there were sounds like things being sawed in half
> and things drilled and it was dark
> and men walked on girders overhead
> and men pushed trucks across the ground
> and men sat at machines doing things
> and there were shots of lightning and thunder

(21–26)

Bukowski synthesizes movement and stasis through both the unarticled nouns and verbs, especially copula, whose heavy use adds to the static quality. The anaphoric "and" (twice in the poem it begins lines seven times in a row) gives the effect of perpetual motion and at the same time suggests an endless present—yet another kind of stasis.

The reduced number of adjectives are all the more effective when they do appear. Detail—even pointed, realistic detail—can obtrude and clutter a passage. But an increased use of metonymy does not necessarily mean an overuse. In Bukowski, it is rather a preference for the one figure over the other. It should also be noted that the adjectives Bukowski does use are of the most basic and "objective" kind: "large," lumpy," "wet," "dark." (Lowell, for example, in "Sailing Home from Rapallo" uses "fiery," "crazy," "azure," "spumante-bubbling" in addition to less marked choices.) In fact, whenever possible, Bukowski seems to avoid even these basic uses, circumventing them with a construction like "made of tin" in line 16. There is the impression that here anything more than the stark depiction of things and states would be less.

Bukowski's achievement, however, results as much from his avoidance of metaphor as it does from his reliance on metonymy. There are few metaphors in the poem. "Getting the nerves straight" (a half-dead metaphor in any case) is the most apparent

110

while "shots of lightning and thunder" are not immediately apparent as such, so closely does Bukowski tie even his sparing use of metaphor to the phenomena being described. In fact, part of what makes this description powerful is that it does not stand for anything, in the substitutive sense, other than itself. Nothing is "absent"; there is only the "empty background." Here we are "forced to attend to the energy present in particular objects, experiences, thoughts." And what these constitute here are work and the conditions of work as they exist for the American working class. "Looking for a job" by emphasizing the objects and conditions of work forcefully depicts the differences inherent in different work roles, "breaking through easy abstractions of myths of human community."

Indeed, it is this that the poem effects so well. Any metaphoric language would only weaken Bukowski's depiction of reality; by relating it to some other, absent half it would detract from what is being depicted, and to the extent that it suggested a "shared community" it would be denying the reality confronting the narrator, and not just the narrator. On the other hand, there is rarely the danger of the poem falling into pure facticity because throughout the depiction is informed by the element of refusal: "hell, you don't want a job, / and I said, hell no, but I need money." No more than this is needed to redeem the metonymic details of the poem—there is no danger here of "phenomena being reduced to facts." In this sense there is no absence. Jacques Lacan saw metonymy as analogous to the psychic displacement that wishes to avoid censorship; in Bukowski's poems, metonymy reverses the process and functions to foil the censorship exercised by social constructions wishing to deny unpleasant aspects of reality.

One interesting linguistic detail is the omission of any article, definite or indefinite, before the nouns in lines 21–26. As a stylistic device it appears in a number of Bukowski's descriptions of work emphasizing the alienation of the process being described;° but here there is an additional, subtler effect attached to the word "men" because of the omission. Because it is not any one, specific integral "man," nor group of men (let alone mankind), the impression is of some men doing this, some men doing that: that they are each individually partial components of some larger

unity but that that larger unity is not here, is only represented
by a part of it. The abstraction is such that it suggests itself as
a metonymic part of some larger whole. This impression is reinforced later in the poem when the narrator sees "silhouettes of
men / moving through flame and sound." A silhouette is a less
than complete representation of a whole. Lacking the final dimension, it produces the image of a ghost-like presence, as though
the workers have now become shades, a part of their former
selves, work having ferried them across that Stygian DMZ between life and the shadow existence of the no longer fully alive
which is perhaps the truest representation of the condition of
alienated labor.

Closure was sometimes a problem for Bukowski, and the
ending of "looking for a job" does at first seem problematic.
The end is sometimes the point in a Bukowski poem where—
especially if Bukowski senses that the narrative has failed to make
the point—he will go ahead and make the point for it. Such a
procedure may result in sentimentality or sententiousness. Sometimes after reading a poem, especially one of his earlier poems,
readers may find themselves thinking the poem would have been
better off ending earlier. Formally, "looking for a job" might be
improved by ending after line 43. It has brought the narrator
back to the bar where the story began, thus providing a nice
symmetry and also ending on an effective psychological reversal perfectly consonant with the underlying subject/object split
that the poem began with, i.e., projecting the narrator's refusal
of work onto those who might have hired him. It would be effective not just for its accurate representation of the defense
mechanism of projection but also because it fittingly presents
the narrator as the object of others. The possibly gratuitous
tacking-on of the prostitute, a traditional symbol of objectified
humanity, can strike the reader as a bit too pat. But Bukowski,
pushing the image of the prostitute one step further by synech-
dochically representing her as only vagina and clitoris, and pushing this even further by using the truncated colloquialism, "clit,"
perhaps justifies his ending. We have an image of disembodied
female genitalia which, if a male could only somehow possess
them, would guarantee him a life free of work. (It is assumed that
sex cannot be work.) It is one of the most brutal partializations

112

imaginable. (Images of both men and women being mutilated, cut up into pieces either by others or by themselves do appear in other poems of Bukowski's. Furthermore, the image of work as performing this same function is suggested, for example, by the imagery and content of "transformation and disfiguration.") However, it forces us, in turn, to reflect back on the situation of the workers in the poem. If the narrator has the least desire to be, literally, a prostitute rather than to subject himself to conditions of work such as he has just witnessed, it should give the reader pause when considering such conditions. From the narrator's point of view, what such objectification does to people is clear. If, at first, they were, however vaguely and partially, "men," they soon lose even that vague substantiality and become shades.

"Looking for a job" is one of Bukowski's strongest statements against the attempt to find a unifying structure beyond the material conditions of particular, not universal, existence that would somehow negate the alienation embodied in commodified labor power. The unity implicit in the worldview elucidated by Abrams (see above, p. 21) is categorically denied by Bukowski. The predominance of the metonymic mode and the complete avoidance of metaphor result from his refusal to engage in a search for this non-existent unity. Any attempt to deal with the despondency or pessimism that the lack of a unifying structure causes some to feel has to begin here, with the objective conditions of the worker's existence.

Metonymy is such a strong presence in Bukowski's poetry just because it expresses his refusal to recognize any unit larger than the particular individual and his (work) experience; at the same time this preference for partialization objectifies the individual. Thus there is a dialectic at work in Bukowski's poetry: on the one hand the subject in Bukowski's poetry is straining to maintain its integrity through continual self-assertion, isolation and the refusal of a larger collectivity in which it fears being submerged and losing all individuality, and yet this refusal, in turn, produces the metonymy which, ultimately, effects that subject's own objectification.

I don't want to leave the poem, however, without making clear how comical a poem it is. The fate of the poor working stiff who recognizes the need for work but, confronted with a good deal more than he had bargained for, just isn't up to it, is funny. The fact that this is not a good bargain and the narrator's realization of just how bad a bargain it is play an important part in creating the humor of the poem, as humor can be a last-ditch effort to cope with an impossible situation. The narrator went looking for a *job* and what he found was *work,* and plenty of it. "The descent to hell is easy," Vergil noted and the narrator of "looking for a job" sees how easy is that slide and how horrible a hell it is (the impression is that that "bucket full of flame" is *aimed* at him). Yet while the humor should not be overlooked, neither should it be taken as trivializing the situation. We should not infer that because Bukowski uses humor then, somehow, what he is describing can't be so bad. On the contrary, the humor comes from a realization of just how bad the situation is.

EXCURSUS: BRECHT

To my knowledge Bukowski has never mentioned Brecht in his published work, an odd omission because their work has much in common. Neither the plebeian logic of Mother Courage nor the cunning of Schweyk is foreign to Henry Chinaski. The rejection of bourgeois values in Brecht's *Hauspostille* and the posthumously published love sonnets finds its analogue in Bukowski's early collections. Brecht's anti-sentimental "Remembering Marie A," to take an early example, is not dissimilar to Bukowski's love poetry in its frequently jaundiced treatment of sexual relations. There is a provinciality to both poets, reflected in their antipathy to New York, Brecht's Augsburg partisanship and Bukowski's fondness for the sub/urban L.A. and the provincial San Pedro. Both careers progressed from a lyrical anarcho-vitalism to a more rational analysis of social relations, reflected in Brecht's commitment to Marxism and in the social democracy of Bukowski's later poetry. The similarities can be grouped in three categories: 1) the working-class perspective (and its plebeian sub-set) that informs the best poetry of both poets, 2) the materialist worldview and 3) the "alienating" technique, reflected in Brecht's "critique of empathy" and Bukowski's renunciation of metaphor and preference for metonymy.

The working-class perspective: In both writers there is a progression from an anarchist, free-floating rebellion (represented by the Baal persona of the early Brecht): hard, subjective, coarse (even brutal), with a suspicion of the emotions, through an unmediated identification with the marginal and asocial to a more systematic and reasoned engagement on behalf of the

115

working class. This identification was not the same for both writers. Brecht's was that of a European marxist intellectual not of the working class himself (though his family's connection to the bourgeoisie through his father's position was quite recent; indeed, Brecht's emphasis on his "peasant" roots is thematised— somewhat ironically—in one of his most famous poems, "Of Poor B.B."). Bukowski's perspective is more that of the worker in Brecht's "Questions From A Worker Who Reads":

> In what houses
> Of gold-glittering Lima did the builders live?
> Where, the evening that the Wall of China was finished
> Did the masons go?°

Bukowski experienced exploitation on his own person, and poems such as "Sparks," "transformation and disfiguration" and "guava tree" attest to this in a way Brecht's poetry could not. This accounts for the power of those first-hand reports from the factories and the Post Office: Bukowski's "little tragedies" exemplify Brecht's view of "the 'little worlds' " as "front-line sections of the larger battles."° The plebeian world view forms a sub-set of the working-class perspective. It results in that privileging of vulgarity (in its narrow and broad senses) which is significant in both Bukowski and Brecht and in basic ways determined the style and content of both writers.

In both cases this plebeian trait directly influences the writer's style. There is a visible line from the "alienation" of the routine (cp. the influence of Jackie Gleason on Bukowski) back through vaudeville to the commedia dell'arte and other "folk elements," elements which Brecht saw as "epic": "the epic elements I brought with me 'into the business' from the KARL-VALENTIN-theater, the open-air circus and the *plärrer*" (AJ, 50). "The v-effect is an old artistic method, known from comedy, certain branches of popular theater . . ." (AJ, 137). Note, for example, the broad humor of Brecht's wedding scenes, one of the most vivid being that in the fifth act of the 1930 film *Kuhle Wampe* where the Valentin influence is most pronounced.

The popular, plebeian element is also reflected in both writers' interest in sport. "Bukowski"/Chinaski's nights at the Olympic Auditorium are matched by Brecht's interest in boxing and six-day bike riding. It may be recalled that Brecht contemplated writing

116

a biography of (and wrote some twenty-odd pages on) his friend, the German middleweight champion Samson-Körner. While it is true that Brecht saw the positive value of collective athletic participation (a strong element in *Kuhle Wampe*) and Bukowski emphasizes the Darwinian virtues of boxing and horse racing, both writers appreciate sports, and the epic style in which they celebrate such activities is similar. Compare, for example, Brecht's "Tablet to the memory of 12 World Champions":

> I start the series in the year 1891—
> The age of crude slugging
> When contests still lasted 56 or 70 rounds
> And were only ended by the knockout—
> With BOB FITZSIMMONS, the father of boxing technique
> Holder of the world middleweight title
> And of the heavyweight title (by his defeat of Jim Corbett on
>   17 March 1897).
> 34 years of his life in the ring, beaten only six times
> So greatly feared that he spent the whole of 1889
> Without an opponent.
>
> (152)

with Bukowski's apotheosis of Norm van Brocklin in "the gentleman and the bastard," who, when "each game seemed to go down to / the last second / always before crowds of / 100,000 in the good times of / the fifties" (WT 3–7) would come in late in the game with the Rams behind,

> fresh and
> mean
>
> points
> behind
> going for broke
> throwing
> for broke
>
> those high
> towering
> passes, perfectly
> leading his
> swift ends

```
                    time after
                    time
                    always fighting
                    the clock
                          (46–67)
```

Materialism: Part of the materialist aesthetic shared by Brecht and Bukowski manifests itself in the emphasis on bodily functions (including sex) as natural and the anti-asceticism reflected in the appreciation, for example, of that primary product of modernity, the automobile. Bukowski's fondness not only for his "good old Volks" but for the BMW that resulted from his late financial success expresses this. Brecht's fondness for cars found expression in an advertising poem, "Singende Steyrwägen":

```
          We hold the curve like tape
          Our motor is:
          Steel that thinks.
          . . . . . . . . . . .
          We drive you without so much as a jolt
          so that you think you're lying
          in water
          . . . . . . . . . . .
          So quietly do we drive you
          that you think you're driving
          the shadow of your car.°
```

Theirs is not an anti-technological world view, a romantic reaction against modern life. Bukowski's positive valuation of space probes is at one with Brecht's positive valuation of science (though the question clearly troubled Brecht in the late 1930s: witness his wrestling with the problem in the various versions of *Galileo*). And Bukowski, too, in his manic American manner appreciates the materiality of the car as

```
          [I] roar the engine into
          life
          rip it into reverse
          with a quick back turn of squealing
          tires
          I slam to a bouncing halt
          rip the wheel right
          feed the gas
```

go from first to second
spin into a gap of
traffic
am quickly into
3rd
4th
I am up to
50 mph in a flash
                    (WT 279, 87–102)

Clear expressions of this materialism (better: Epicureanism) are found in poems like Brecht's "Pleasures" (448) where so many of the pleasures are both ordinary and sensuous. Bukowski's poem "Yes" (D 138–40) enumerates similar pleasures.

Critique of Empathy, metonymy: The most striking convergence of the two poets is in the poetic form itself. While Brecht never relinquished closed forms entirely, the best of his poems, and by far the majority of them, are in free verse. He, too, made frequent use of the narrative, from the early ballads, through the parables, legends and chronicles of the late 1920s and 1930s, most notably in the *Svendborger Gedichte.* In the best of such poems, for example "Der Dienstzug," Brecht, too, renounces metaphor almost completely and relies on a functional metonymy to lend his verse an objectivity not at all dissimilar to Bukowski's. (See also, for example, the poem "Weigel's Props" [427], a veritable paean to metonymy. This metonymic bent accounts, I think, for the great success of translations of Brecht into English and Bukowski into German.) In a more general sense, Brecht's "Critique of Empathy," his attempt to "alienate," distance, his reader from the events being described finds its analogue in the lapidary descriptions and ironic tone of Bukowski's later poetry. In Brecht, as in Bukowski, the everyday as lyrical content was privileged as basic to the lyric's communicative function. Brecht's skill in making the ordinary, the "banal," meaningful is on a par with Bukowski's. The "sentimentality, lack of authenticity and of a relation to reality" that Brecht criticized in the bourgeois lyric were likewise objects of Bukowski's scorn as expressed, for example, in his essay, "A Rambling Essay on Poetics and the Bleeding Life written while Drinking a Six-Pack (Tall)" and the poem, "*Kenyon Review.* After the Sandstorm."°

The number of areas—specific and general—where there are striking similarities between the form and content of Brecht's and Bukowski's poetry suggests a cognate dynamic helpful in revealing (the later) Bukowski as a social lyricist.

THE FICTION

CHAPTER FIVE:
WORK, REFUSAL OF WORK
AND THE JOB IN *POST OFFICE*
AND *FACTOTUM*

The only human essence of labor which approximates to the
concreteness of capital is the refusal of work.°
                                                    Toni Negri

1

No contemporary American novelist has treated work as ex-
tensively or intensively as Bukowski. The salient characteristic
of Bukowski's first two novels is their focus on work. Indeed,
Bukowski's outstanding achievement is his depiction of work,
most notably in *Post Office* (1971) and *Factotum* (1975). Moreover,
the latter marks a turning-point in the treatment of work in the
American novel.

For ideological reasons work has not been a popular topic
in contemporary American fiction, when compared, for example, with its place in writing from the former socialist bloc or
in earlier periods of American literature; there, indeed, its treatment had often been connected with writing sympathetic to leftist
politics. The socialist writers of the turn of the century dealt with
work as their treatment of it formed part of an engagement on
behalf of the working class. Novels such as Upton Sinclair's *The
Jungle* (1907), Jack London's *The Iron Heel* (1908) and *Martin
Eden* (1909) and his autobiography, *John Barleycorn* (1913), and

Theodore Dreiser's *Sister Carrie* (1900) and *An American Tragedy* (1925) provide vivid images of work, but the focus is never work per se. Later, Jack Conroy's *The Disinherited* (1933) is moving in its depiction of exploited workers and the unemployed during the early stages of the Depression. But it is a *Tendez-roman*: the reader feels the novel progressing towards an overtly political resolution and the hero's joining the Communist Party as an organizer, the "conversion ending," seems somewhat pat. Robert Cantwell's *The Land of Plenty* (1934) is an impressive novel but focuses on a strike, a moment of no work, as does John Steinbeck's better known *In Dubious Battle* (1936). Perhaps Edward Dahlberg's *Bottom Dogs* (1930) comes closest in mood to *Factotum*, but work is not the primary focus. Harvey Swados' novelistic collection of stories, *On the Line* (1957), though marked in the Eisenhower 50s for its interest in work—specifically alienated assembly-line work—and remarkable for that alone, also evades important issues and ends in a mild apotheosis of the union. This brief summary does not, of course, do justice to the many American novels written in this century that do treat work in some fashion.

Bukowski, however, while not consciously a proletarian or engaged novelist, has yet managed to do more towards fulfilling leftist theory as concerns the role of the novelist in bourgeois society than have more committed novelists, "dispel[ling]," in the words of Engels' well-known letter to Minna Kautsky about such fiction, "the dominant conventional illusions concerning [real] relations." He has done this by changing the focus of the discussion. Because the novels from the turn of the century through the 1950s treating such subject matter were often *Tendenz* novels, the content was openly linked to a political tendency, ranging from Conroy's Marxist-Leninist Communism to Swados' left-liberalism. Yet Bukowski, uncommitted and "apolitical" as he was, depicted alienated labor and sketched a mode of working-class resistance in ways having much in common with contemporaneous New Left analyses.

Post Office and *Factotum* represent an important change in novels treating work and working-class experience. They reflect the changes that American society had undergone since the Second World War—they have as their content an American

124

working-class life from 1940 to 1970—and also reflect the events of the 1960s and early 1970s. Both of these facts are important: without the events of the 1960s the material might well have ended up—if it had ended up being written (and published) at all—as something like *On the Line.* On the other hand, without the content—the jobs—of those three decades and without the three decades of jobs, the result might have been something like the writing of, for example, Raymond Carver.

What is different about these novels is their relentlessly negative depiction of all aspects of work and a fundamental questioning of its usefulness. While previous writers did not glorify work, it was seen as necessary. What was wrong was that the worker was being exploited: either he was being worked too hard, or he wasn't being paid enough, or both, but the necessity of (the) work itself was never questioned. This was true of the early socialist novels as well as of the proletarian novelists of the 1930s. In Swados' novel there is the beginning of an attitude that is most clearly presented in Bukowski: that there is no way such work is anything but degrading and an assembly-line worker is never going to to be "middle-class." In other respects, however, *On the Line* was a last vestige of the 1930s rather than a sign of things to come, whereas Bukowski's novels represent an important change. Nor were they merely an isolated individual response, but rather reflections of historic socio-economic developments taking place in the United States in the 1960s and 1970s (the culmination of that had begun earlier in American history) as well as of more recent twentieth-century technological developments. Bukowski's response to such developments was something quite different from that of any previous writer. His refusal of work (for such it is) is an implicit call for its abolition. Radical as such a demand seems, he was by no means alone in making it.

2

Bukowski's representation of work can easily be viewed as merely the subjective, indeed, idiosyncratic, response of a dissatisfied and disgruntled individuals. This, however, is not the case. But in order to show how historically determined his attitude

125

to and representation of work are, it will be necessary to prepare with some thoroughness the socio-historical foundation for my discussion of the novels. Some of this analysis may strike the reader as alien, indeed alienating. Yet if Bukowski's real and substantial achievement is to be fully appreciated, such spadework has to be done.

As far back as the middle of the 19th century there had been a movement in the United States to reduce the working day in response to the increased intensity of work in industrializing capitalism, to take at least some of the benefit of increased American technological efficiency in the form of shorter hours, as well as in higher wages (as opposed to taking it solely in the form of the latter). The movement fluctuated for a century but continued making progress into the 1930s and through the early days of Roosevelt's New Deal. But with Roosevelt's opting for full employment, or at least increased employment, what had been a real movement towards reduced work was defeated.°

The sharp fall in hours worked per week that took place in the first quarter of the 20th century was due to a factor unique to American capitalism: its intensive mechanization. The historian Gabriel Kolko has written:

> there is no question that American capitalism developed within the context of a quite distinctive technology unlike that of Western Europe, and this in turn both created and built upon a no less diverse and unique working class. Capital- and technology-intensive to an unprecedented degree, American industry created a rhythm of life and an extraordinarily disciplined and numbing division of labor which made possible a higher standard of living even as it demanded more exhausting and alienating labor. . . . Until 1919 capital investment was geared, unprecedentedly, to utilizing technological innovations to replace labor, and the manhours worked as a ratio of manufacturing output fell by almost one-half between 1900 and 1929.

> (72)

This "unique working class" produced a unique worker. One of the first to describe this "Fordized" worker was Antonio Gramsci. Commenting on Frederick Taylor's methods of scientific management, he wrote:

126

> Taylor is in fact expressing with brutal cynicism the purpose
> of American society—developing in the worker to the highest
> degree automatic and mechanical attitudes, breaking up the
> old psycho-physical nexus of qualified professional work, which
> demands a certain active participation of intelligence, fantasy
> and initiative on the part of the worker, and reducing produc-
> tive operations exclusively to the mechanical, physical aspect.
> (302)°

In order to produce and maintain such a worker his life as a
whole had to be controlled, by "preserving outside of work, a
certain psycho-physiological equilibrium which prevents the phys-
iological collapse of the worker, exhausted by the new method
of production" (303).

This meant that drinking and womanizing had to be controlled. In fact, Gramsci saw Prohibition resulting from the need
for the new man, and not as an aspect of the Puritan strain in
America civilization. About womanizing he wrote at some length:

> "Womanizing" demands too much leisure. The new type of
> worker will be a repetition, in a different form, of peasants
> in the villages. The relative stability of sexual unions among
> the peasants is closely linked to the system of work of the coun-
> try. The peasant who returns home in the evening after a long
> and hard day's work wants the *"venerem facilem parabilem-
> que"* of Horace. . . . It seems clear that the new industrialism
> wants monogamy: it wants the man as worker not to squander
> his nervous energies in the disorderly and stimulating pursuit
> of occasional sexual satisfaction. The employee who goes to
> work after a night of "excess" is no good for his work.°
> (304–05)

I hope to make clear in my discussion that Bukowski's depiction
of the American worker corroborates Gramsci's explanation of
the function of Fordist labor-relations practices, which in turn
allows us to see Bukowski's depiction as possessing a certain
universality. What has been seen as the idiosyncratic response
of an "alcoholic" malcontent is an objective class response. It
should be made clear that Gramsci's caveat about " 'womanizing'
demand[ing] too much leisure" has to be seen in a broad sense.
Womanizing is never just sexual; otherwise prostitution would
serve the same function. It is a convenient term for the whole
social apparatus accompanying it. It is the pursuit, and the time

127

it takes, that monogamy (in Gramsci's view) is aimed at defeating.

The crisis of the 1930s, closely following the amazing increase in technological efficiency of the first quarter-century, had prompted a call for shorter hours as one means of providing work for a greater number of people. As noted, Roosevelt rejected this option, and eventually World War II pulled the American economy out of the Depression. The release of pent-up demand after the War led to the (for the most part) flush times of the 1950s. Hence it wasn't until the 1960s that, for both economic and cultural reasons, the issue of work and alienated labor again began to be widely discussed. Several factors contributed to this: the crisis of legitimacy created by the Vietnam War resulted in an increased willingness to question a number of issues previously deemed moot; the ever-increasing technological efficiency of the American economic system, due now to the perfection of the computer microchip, had put mankind at that point envisioned by Marx in the *Grundrisse* of 1857–58 (discussed below) where human labor-power was no longer a significant factor in the production of wealth; finally, mental labor was being collapsed into physical labor at an astonishing rate, as increasingly jobs previously differentiated from those of the industrial proletariat came to resemble that archetype of alienated labor, the factory; and those who worked them were aware of it. ° "The most characteristic feature of modern labor," Aronowitz wrote "is the convergence of mental and manual labor" in that

> Government employees, those engaged in retail and wholesale trades, and workers in corporate bureaucracies performing manual operations on accounting machines or typewriters can hardly be considered radically different from industrial workers in general. The transformation of the office into a large-scale organization had been accompanied by the imposition of efficiency engineering or scientific management upon work relations. . . .
>
> (312)

All these factors combined to create a mood (whether in Swados' auto assembly-line worker or Bukowski's postal clerk—and there were wildcat strikes in both industries at the end of the 1960s and the beginning of the 1970s) where a reexamination of traditional American values with respect to work could be undertaken. Work and the "work ethic," that had been positively valorized

128

in Franklin, Alger and others, were now undergoing an agonizing reappraisal.°

A fundamental shift in the Left's attitude to work also took place. The increasing influence of Marx's *Grundrisse* (containing his economic manuscripts of 1857–58 and notebook extracts from 1850–51, but first published in 1939 and not published in English until 1973) was an important factor in this New Left analysis of the role of work in late capitalism. Marx had written:

> But to the degree that large industry develops, the creation of real wealth comes to depend less on labor time and on the amount of labor employed than on the power of the agencies set in motion during labor-time. . . . Labor no longer appears so much to be included within the production process. . . . As soon as labor in the direct form has ceased to be the great wellspring of wealth, labor time ceases and must cease to be its measure, and hence exchange-value . . . of use value. (704–705)

One of the most influential New Left reanalyses of the role of work—and influenced by the publication of the *Grundrisse*—was Herbert Marcuse's, undertaken in such books as *Eros and Civilization* (1955), *One-Dimensional Man* (1964) and *An Essay On Liberation* (1969). In *Eros and Civilization* Marcuse elaborated a reading of Freud influenced by the Frankfurt School's Marxist cultural critique. In post-revolutionary capitalism, domination was maintained through the

> specific reality principle that has governed the origins and the growth of this civilization. We designate it as performance principle in order to emphasize that under its rule society is stratified according to the competitive economic performances of its members.
>
> (40–41)

Marcuse is not merely criticizing class society; he is pointing out what he views as the irrationality of a situation that while once necessary, is no longer so. The freeing up of man's libidinal energy, its liberation from the temporal constraints of the workday, which should have followed upon the lessening need for his alienated labor, has not occurred; the domination originally necessary—based on an economy of scarcity—has remained as that condition of scarcity is (potentially) no more. The principle which had made sense in an economy of scarcity (roughly speaking: "the harder you work, the more you get") no longer makes sense, and domination through this principle has been irrationally "exercised by a particular group or individual in order to sustain and enhance itself in a privileged position" (33–34). The core of Marcuse's analysis is his critique of the persistence of the performance principle in a society where it is no longer necessary, a society in which, in contrast to that of Franklin's *Autobiography*, the Alger novels or even Taylor's steel mills, human labor has been effectively divorced from the production of wealth. Marcuse emphasized that the increased productivity of industrial society had not only not been used to diminish alienated labor, but had been retained in order to sustain class societies, which by their very nature would never abolish such labor:

> For the world of human freedom cannot be built by the established societies, no matter how much they may streamline and rationalize their dominion. Their class structure, and the perfected controls required to sustain it, generate needs, satisfactions, and values which reproduce the servitude of the human existence. This "voluntary" servitude (voluntary inasmuch as it is introjected into the individuals), which justifies the benevolent masters, can be broken only through a political commitment in the infrastructure of man, a political practice of methodical disengagement from and refusal of the Establishment, aiming at a radical transvaluation of values.°

However idealist Marcuse's solution may be, my point here is that the issues he was the first to raise for a large audience in his books of the 50s and 60s sprang from a socio-economic matrix in which Bukowski's novels were also embedded; Bukowski's novelistic response was the literary cognate to social criticism like Marcuse's.

Although it is clear that a reevaluation of the function of work was taking place from a variety of political perspectives, very little of this reevaluation appeared in the fiction of the period. Bukowski's decision to undertake a thorough treatment of this area is in and of itself a significant contribution. His success is all the more remarkable because there was so little for him to build on in the immediate past and because (in part a result of this lack) the way in which he did it constituted a sharp break with earlier treatments.

3

Post Office is a short novel and one of its strengths is its focus on work, on the job, and on its effects on the individual. My analysis of it will be somewhat skewed because I have left out the personal relationships (in the novel Henry Chinaski marries, divorces and fathers a child) and will probably make the novel seem more a *Tendenzroman* than it may appear to be. Yet, as its title suggests, Bukowski has in mind an institutional critique, and that institution is not only the U.S. Post Office in the 1950s and 1960s but the institution of bureaucratized work in the United States. That work was Bukowski's central concern became clear with the publication of *Factotum*, four years later.

Post Office is Bukowski's critique of (neo-)Taylorism and Fordism. Though the events of the novel take place a good three-quarters of a century after Taylor's initial studies in scientific management, and forty years after the publication of *Scientific Management*, Bukowski's critique centers on the worker who has been de-skilled and reduced to mindless repetition ("All you moved was your right arm") and little autonomy. That such a critique is no anachronism (nor limited to traditional industrial jobs) was also acknowledged by the authors of *Work in America* (a government-sponsored study undertaken to investigate the worrisome dissatisfaction of American workers with their jobs), when they noted that "the anachronism of Taylorism" was a significant factor in job dissatisfaction:

> It should be noted that Taylorism and a misplaced conception of efficiency is not restricted to assembly lines or . . . the manufacturing sector of the economy. The service sector is not exempt. . . . [where Tayloristic practice] rigidifies tasks, reduces the range of skills utilized by most of the occupations, increases routinization, and opens the door to job dissatisfaction for a new generation of highly educated workers.
>
> (19)

Bukowski's novel makes it clear that that door was wide open at the Post Office.

The reader of *Post Office* soon realizes the unpleasant nature of postal work. The novel's second sentence ("It was Christmas season and I learned from the drunk up the hill, who did the trick every Christmas, that they would hire damned near anybody . . ." [9/13])° both suggests that such work can be compared with the most alienated labor and that one has to anesthetize oneself in order to be able do it. As a substitute carrier, Henry Chinaski works only when a regular worker fails to show up and "the regulars usually called in sick when it rained or during a heatwave or the day after a holiday when the mail load was doubled" (10/14). The work itself is inhumanly demanding and made worse by the presence of a sadistic supervisor:

> There were 40 or 50 different routes, maybe more, each case was different, you were never able to learn any of them, you had to get your mail up and ready before 8 a.m. for the truck dispatches, and Jonstone would take no excuses. The subs routed their magazines on corners, went without lunch, and died in the streets. Jonstone would have us start casing the routes 30 minutes late—spinning in his chair in his red shirt—"Chinaski take route 539!" We'd start a halfhour short but were still expected to get the mail up and out and be back on time. And once or twice a week, already beaten, fagged and fucked we had to make the night pickups, and the schedule on the board was impossible—the truck wouldn't go that fast. You had to skip four or five boxes on the first run and the next time around they were stacked with mail and you stank, you ran with sweat jamming it into the sacks.
>
> (10/15)

This is clearly an unreasonable situation, and Chinaski, as a reasonable man, attempts to rectify it. He realizes that such behavior on the part of a supervisor rests on the acquiescence of those he is dominating. Since workers have rights, he tries to do something about the situation:

> The subs themselves made Jonstone possible by obeying his impossible orders. I couldn't see how a man of such obvious cruelty could be allowed to have his position. The regulars didn't care, the union man was worthless, so I filled out a thirty page report on one of my days off, mailed one copy to Jonstone and took the other down to the Federal Building.

After being made to wait an hour and a half, he is

taken in to see a little grey-haired man with eyes like cigarette ash. He didn't ask me to sit down. He began screaming at me as I entered the door.

"You're a wise son of a bitch, aren't you?"

"I'd rather you didn't curse me, sir!"

"Wise son of a bitch, you're one of those sons of bitches with a vocabulary and you like to lay it around!"

He waved my papers at me. And screamed: "MR. JON-STONE IS A FINE MAN!"

"Don't be silly. He's an obvious sadist," I said.

"How long have you been in the Post Office?"

"3 weeks."

"MR. JONSTONE HAS BEEN WITH THE POST OFFICE FOR 30 YEARS!"

"What does *that* have to do with it?"

(10–11/15–16)

The humor in the passage comes in part from Chinaski's low-key attitude. Throughout the novels, it is something that remains constant in Chinaski's behavior vis-à-vis management and often results in a situation being comic that in real life most likely was not. The humor, I think, also results from Chinaski's implacable and unalterable position: I don't need this job. Yet of course he *does* need the job(s); if he didn't need them Bukowski wouldn't have written an entire novel about finding them, losing them and having to find them again. Chinaski's stance is utopian and so diametrically opposed both to the stances of his immediate antagonists (the bosses) and to that of his real condition in life (he has to work at least some of the time) that a humor of incongruity results. The humor also comes from the way in which his depiction of the "little grey-haired man" cuts across the pretentious jargon with which organizations present their "rationality." This is no "appropriate," "professional" handling of the "interview."

Unsatisfied, Chinaski returns to work at the station, where he is harassed by Jonstone who repeatedly writes him up for various infractions, ranging from lateness to leaving his cap on top of his locker after a memo was circulated stating that this was contrary to Post Office procedure. Chinaski accepts this state of affairs, knowing "from my trip downtown that any protest was useless" (13/21). The Post Office affects others, too, for instance, one G.G., who

133

had been a carrier since his early twenties and now he was in his late sixties. His voice was gone. He didn't speak. He croaked. And when he croaked he didn't say much. He was neither liked nor disliked. He was just there. His face had wrinkled into strange runs and mounds of unattractive flesh. No light shone from his face. He was just a hard old crony who had done his job: G.G. The eyes looked like dull bits of clay dropped into the eye sockets. It was best if you didn't think about him or look at him.

(27/42–43)

G.G. is unfairly accused of child molestation and this begins to affect his performance:

Although G.G. knew his case upsidedown, his hands were slowing. He had simply stuck too many letters in his life—even his sense-deadened body was finally revolting. Several times during the morning I saw him falter. He'd stop and sway, go into a trance, than snap out of it and stick some more letters. I wasn't particularly fond of the man. His life hadn't been a brave one, and he had turned out to be a hunk of shit more or less. But each time he faltered, something tugged at me. It was like a faithful horse who just couldn't go any more. Or an old car, just giving it up one morning.

(28/44–45)

Unable to box up his mail in time, owing to a last-minute addition of a "bundle of circulars," G.G. "put his head down in his arms and began to cry softly" (28) and then runs up to the locker room. The complete lack of solidarity among the workers is emphasized as nobody helps G.G. (though Chinaski tries) nor shows even the least interest in him. And, as happens with alarming frequency in Bukowski's writings about work, the affected worker never shows up again:

I never saw G.G. again. Nobody knew what happened to him. Nor did anybody ever mention him again. The "good guy." The dedicated man. Knifed across the throat over a handful of circs from a local market—with its special: a free box of a brand name laundry soap, with a coupon, and any purchase over $3.

(29/47)

Towards the end of the novel the effect of the job is again discussed. Chinaski has quit the Post Office only to return a short time later, this time as a clerk rather than a carrier. The change in jobs is important because it allows Bukowski to generalize his critique of work since the work of the postal clerk is more purely "mind" work than that of the carrier. It may not be mental work of a very high order, but the task is no longer primarily physical. It is an example of what Marcuse, in *An Essay on Liberation*, called the "dematerialization of labor" (41) and the work, though no longer physical, remains "debilitating" (13). This is apparent on the very first evening of work (Chinaski works evenings):

> After nine or ten hours people began getting sleepy and falling into their cases, catching themselves just in time. We were working the zoned mail. If a letter read zone 28 you stuck it to hole no. 28. It was simple. One big black guy leaped up and began swinging his arms to keep awake. He staggered about the floor. "God damn! I can't *stand* it!" he said. And he was a big powerful brute.
>
> (41–42/67)

As with the carrier job, there are oppressive supervisors and irrational work rules:

> No talking allowed. Two 10 minute breaks in 8 hours. They wrote down the time when you left and the time when you came back. If you stayed 12 or 13 minutes, you heard about it.
>
> But the pay was better than at the art store. And, I thought, I might get used to it.
>
> I never got used to it.
>
> (42/68)

Like the carrier's job, the work is debilitating over the long term, too:

> 11 years shot through the head. I had seen the job eat men up. They seemed to melt. There was Jimmy Potts of Dorsey Station. When I first came in, Jimmy had been a well-built guy in a white T-shirt. Now he was gone. He put his seat as close to the floor as possible and braced himself from falling over with his feet. He was too tired to get a haircut and had worn the same pair of pants for 3 years. He changed shirts twice a week and walked very slow. They had murdered him. He was 55. He had 7 years to go until retirement.
>
> "I'll never make it," he told me.
>
> They either melted or they got fat, huge, especially around the ass and the belly. It was the stool and the same motion and the same talk. And there I was, dizzy spells and pains in the arms, neck, chest, everywhere. I slept all day resting up

for the job. On weekends I had to drink to forget it. I had come
in weighing 185 pounds. Now I weighed 223 pounds. All you
moved was your right arm.

(104/179)

In addition to these burdens there are other aspects of the job
that are at least as bad, such as the inflexible "rationality" of the
system. At one point, towards the end of his career as a postal
clerk, Chinaski is called in for "counselling." It has taken him
longer to sort a tray of mail than the standard requires:

> "Look, you took 28 minutes on a 23 minute tray. That's
> all there is to it."
> "You know better. Each tray is two feet long. Some trays
> have 3, even 4 times as many letters than others. The clerks
> grab what they call the "fat" trays. I don't bother. Somebody
> has to stick with the tough mail. Yet all you guys know is that
> each tray is two feet long and that it must be stuck in 23
> minutes. But we're not sticking trays in those cases, we're stick-
> ing letters."
> "No, no, this thing has been time-tested."
> "Maybe it has. I doubt it. But if you're going to time a man,
> don't judge him on *one* tray. Even Babe Ruth struck out now
> and then. Judge a man on ten trays, or a night's work. You
> guys just use this thing to hang anybody who gets in your
> craw."
> "All right, you've had your say, Chinaski. Now, I'm telling
> YOU: you stuck a 28 minute tray. *We* go by that. Now, if you
> are caught on another slow tray you will be due for AD-
> VANCED COUNSELLING!"

(105/180)

Bukowski is making two points here: first, the ultimate irrationality of a system that is presumably rationalized ("this thing has
been time-tested."). The problem with much performance evaluation is that anything that can be quantified (number of letters
sorted, articles published, claimants interviewed) is then used
as the basis of decisions that also imply a judgment on quality
(correctness of the clerk Chinaski's sorting of mail). Here, of
course, even the quantifying of the task is handled clumsily.
Chinaski's criticism is correct; and his second point, concerning
the arbitrary nature of its use, and of what is often its real function, is also valid. The two are related. If the system were truly
rational, i.e., constructed with a view to the costs and benefits

136

for those working in it and not only for those it serves, it would not function in as irrational and arbitrary a manner as it does here. The arbitrariness is heightened by the "counsellor's" last words on the matter which, at the same time, give the lie to the whole interview. Chinaski is allowed his "say," i.e., in a purely formal bow to work-place "democracy" he's allowed to speak. But the counsellor "tells" Chinaski, and that's that. This also contributes to the humor in the terms "counselling" and "ADVANCED COUNSELLING." They are purely formal terms, just as Chinaski's "say" has been a purely formal one. The humor comes—once again in Bukowski—from the gap between appearance and reality.

Bukowski's critique of work is not limited to its effects on the job. He also wants to show that its tentacles reach out into the life of the worker outside of work, that work serves broad functions of social control, that, in effect, "Fordism," as well as Taylorism, is not dead. Gramsci had seen such behavior on the part of management as the expression of its need to control the workforce, "to elaborate a new type of man suited to the new type of work and productive process" (286).

> The attempts made by Ford, with the aid of a body of inspectors, to intervene in the private lives of his employees and to control how they spent their wages and how they lived is an indication of these tendencies. . . . Someone who works for a wage, with fixed hours, does not have time to dedicate himself to the pursuit of drink or to sport or to evade the law.

At one point in the novel Chinaski calls in sick to spend some time with an old girlfriend.

> At that time, when you called in sick the post office sent out a nurse to spot check, to make sure you weren't nightclubbing or sitting in a poker parlor. My place was close to the central office, so it was convenient for them to check up on me. Betty and I had been there about two hours when there was a knock on the door.
> "What's that?"
> "All right," I whispered, "shut up! Take off those high heels, go into the kitchen and don't make a sound."
> "JUST A MOMENT!" I answered the knocker.
> I lit a cigarette to kill my breath, then went to the door

and opened it a notch. It was the nurse. The same one. She
knew me.

(55–56/94)

This bit of Fordist labor relations is then matched by a similar
story that Betty tells about a former boyfriend who worked for
the county, after which Chinaski remarks "Damn, they won't let
a man live at all, will they? They always want him at the wheel"°
(57/96).

Bukowski also depicts work as a means of exercising ideological control, demonstrating its usefulness in indoctrinating the
citizenry and he shows that the function of such indoctrination
is increased production, rather than a response to any real threat.
Since the Post Office was a government agency, it was all the
more easily (and thus all the more crudely) managed.° In this
instance it occurs, appropriately enough, during a training session (the passage reflects the era of the novel's composition and
underlines the political content of Bukowski's writing: it is hard
to imagine such a passage being published in the 1950s or even
the early 1960s). A training instructor is lecturing before a large
map ("[I]t covered half the stage"):

> Then he said, "Look here. That's *Alaska!* And there *they*
> are! Looks almost as if they could jump across, doesn't it?"
> "Yeah," said some brainwash job in the front row.
> The Italiano flipped the map. It leaped crisply up into it-
> self, crackling in war fury.
> Then he walked to the front of the stage, pointed his
> rubber-titted pointer at us.
> "I want you to understand that we've got to hold down
> the budget! I want you to understand that EACH LETTER YOU
> STICK—EACH SECOND, EACH MINUTE, EACH HOUR, EACH
> DAY, EACH WEEK—EACH EXTRA LETTER YOU STICK BE-
> YOND DUTY HELPS DEFEAT THE RUSSIANS! Now, that's all
> for today."

(46/76)

Although *Post Office* is a first-person narrative, and the idiosyncratic protagonist underlines the novel's subjective tone, objectivity is achieved by showing the effects of the job not just
on Chinaski, but on his fellow-workers as well, by revealing either
their physical decay or concrete symptoms of psychological
decline, as, for example, their dress.

138

Beyond this, Bukowski shows almost no one prospering under the system. The few examples of those who advance or are satisfied, are special cases, exceptions proving the rule. Both Tom Moto, a carrier from Chinaski's early days with the Post Office, who reappears briefly as a supervisor, and the woman who hands him his resignation forms, "a young black girl . . . well-dressed and pleased with her surroundings. . . . I would have gone mad with the same job" (110), are minority-group members with lower expectations regarding work. Bukowski is no racist and what he suggests by such examples is that only those who suffer discrimination, and are thus thankful for any opportunity, find such work acceptable.

4

In his first novel, Bukowski's critique focused on the alienating and exploitative nature of the job. In effect, *Post Office* is a critique of the persistence of Taylorist and Fordist management techniques into the 1950s and 1960s and a depiction of the de-skilling and the transformation of "mind-work" into factory type labor. Bukowski's standpoint, in his critique, is akin to that of the labor sociologist Harry Braverman in its avoidance of the issue of (radical) consciousness. This is one reason why the political aspect of his work has been overlooked. In *Labor and Monopoly Capital*, Braverman wrote: "No attempt will be made to deal with the modern working class on the level of its consciousness, organization, or activities. This is a book about the working class as a class *in itself*, not as a class *for itself*."° This does not mean that an individual's subjective consciousness is without value, but rather that its value is limited for an objective analysis.°

What is important throughout *Post Office* is that Chinaski refuses to accept the alienated situation as normal. For all his cynicism and personal alienation, Chinaski is representative of a new class of worker, educated and unwilling to accept the rigidified bureaucratic relations that obtained in mid-century America. His is the attitude of the worker of the 1960s and later, although the events he is writing about occur in the 1950s and early 1960s. (It is difficult to tell to what extent such attitudes were present in the 1950s but remained unexpressed in the atmosphere of the Cold War.) It is the worker that was so troubling to the authors of *Work in America*, who spoke of the "challenge" presented by the "alienation and disenchantment of blue-collar workers" (xv) and who found "convincing evidence that some blue collar workers are carrying their work frustrations home and displacing them in extremist social and political movements or in hostility towards the government" (30). Bukowski's critique of the persistence of scientific management techniques is also significant. Scientific management had supposedly been superseded by the "Human Relations" school in the 1920s (of which the "counselling" episode is an example) but *Post Office* shows that this was not the case.

While Bukowski's critique in *Post Office* focused on a large bureaucratic institution, in *Factotum*, he criticized the institution of work per se. In the course of the decade the novel spans, Henry Chinaski holds twenty-odd jobs in New Orleans, Los Angeles, New York, Philadelphia, St. Louis, Miami Beach and San Francisco.° Work is always his reason for being anywhere. Hence the emphasis on work emerges more clearly and the effect is more powerful than in the earlier book. Still, if *Post Office* was still mainly about work, *Factotum* is a novel that is even more centrally about work, and more important, about the refusal of work.

Factotum, in fact, is the clearest statement of what might be called the refusal-to-work ethic, as well as its justification. It is because of this justification (discussed in the next section) that it marks a turning-point in the treatment of work in novels about the American working-class. The hermetic world of *Factotum* makes Bukowski's critique all the more effective: work is the world and the world is work. The representation of many horrible jobs, as opposed to just one, reinforces the powerful dead-end impression that is one of the novel's great achievements. It is not that one happens to have a horrible job: jobs are horrible.

Factotum focuses on the experiences of Henry Chinaski as he travels around the United States, working. Although Chinaski crosses the country from coast to coast four times in the course of the novel, most of the novel takes place in Los Angeles. Chinaski also has relationships with several women, the main one with Jan Meadows, with whom he lives on and off for almost a decade.

140

This aspect of the novel ends about two-thirds of the way through the book and from that point on Chinaski undergoes a gradual, though seemingly inexorable, decline, climaxed (if that's the word) when, at the very end of the novel—sans woman, sans home, sans job—he goes to a burlesque show in downtown Los Angeles where, watching a stripper perform, he "couldn't get it up."

Factotum begins with the protagonist out of work, and throughout the book work figures as an intrusion into one's otherwise pleasant (or at least tolerable) existence, as in Chinaski's first brush with it in the novel:

> I went out on the street, as usual, one day and strolled along. I felt happy and relaxed. The sun was just right. Mellow. There was peace in the air. As I approached the center of the block there was a man standing outside the doorway of a shop. I walked past.
> "Hey, BUDDY!"
> I stopped and turned.
> "You want a job?"
>
> (13)

It is not just the work itself that is so horrible but the felt presence of the job throughout life. Even when not at work the job is still there, deforming people and human relationships in a variety of ways (so closely is individual self-esteem tied to work):

> I remember how my father used to come home each night and talk about his job to my mother. The job talk began when he entered the door, continued over the dinner table, and ended in the bedroom where my father would scream *"Lights out!"* at 8 p.m., so he could get his rest and his full strength for the job the next day. There was no other subject except the job.°
>
> (13)

Looking for a job is also an unpleasant process: "Even during World War II when there was supposed to be a manpower shortage there were four or five applicants for each job. (At least for the menial jobs)" (55).

Before people have jobs they are contorting life histories (not to mention themselves: "trying to look ambitious" [15]) to appear acceptable:

> I had elaborated on my work experience in a creative way.
> Pros do that: you leave out the previous low-grade jobs and

describe the better ones fully. . . . Of course, since all my previous jobs were low-grade I left out the lower low-grade.

(127)

And, "I lengthened my tenure at the jobs I had previously had,
turning days into months and months into years" (159), or lying
outright about their present situation: " 'You're married?' 'Yes.
With one child. A boy. Tommy, age 3' " (170), or ingratiating themselves hypocritically: "I had to demean myself to get that one—I
told them that I liked to think of my job as a second home. That
pleased them" (102). The anxiety doesn't end with getting a job:
"The work was easy and dull but the clerks were in a constant
state of turmoil. They were worried about their jobs" (16). Nor
is such anxiety limited to the lower levels: "I sat across from the
editor, a man in shirt sleeves with deep hollows under his eyes.
He looked as if he hadn't slept for a week" (18). Not only is work
routine, boring and poorly paid, but there is far too much of it:

> The problem, as it was in those days during the War, was
> overtime. Those in control always preferred to overwork a
> few men continually, instead of hiring more people so every-
> one might work less. You gave the boss eight hours, and he
> always asked for more. He never sent you home after six hours,
> for example. You might have time to think.
>
> (57)

(This had been a significant part of Bukowski's critique in *Post
Office*, too: "It was twelve hours a night . . ." [60/101].)

These are, of course, more or less obvious instances of
Bukowski's critique, though no less telling for that. But perhaps
even more effective, because so subtly expressed, are the ways
in which he smuggles his critique into the linguistic structures
of the novel. Nowhere is this more apparent than in the descriptions of work seen through Chinaski's eyes (especially when the
possibility arises of Chinaski doing any of that work). In his
descriptions of people at work he creates an aura and a distance
that manage to be both humorous and menacing. Such passages
strongly contrast with the concreteness of so much of Bukowski's
writing. Following the opening assault quoted above, chapter 3
continues:

> I walked back to where he stood. Over his shoulder I could
> see a large dark room. There was a long table with men and
> women standing on both sides of it. They had hammers with
> which they pounded objects in front of them. In the gloom
> the objects appeared to be clams. They smelled like clams. I
> turned and continued walking down the street.
>
> (13)

This description is striking in the distance it effects between the
reader and the activity, work: Chinaski, looking over a shoul-
der, in the gloom, to a large dark room. The vagueness produced
by the omission of the definite article in the fourth sentence and
the uncertainty produced by "appeared" and "like" combine to
create the impression of a situation so routinized, dehumaniz-
ing and just plain depressing that we feel it would be too unpleasant to the narrator to have to describe it in more detail.
Chinaski's dead-in-his-tracks stance further contributes to the impression of immobility and impotence to which the spectator has
been reduced. A similar description occurs a few pages later,
on the occasion of a job interview at a newspaper:

> I sat across from the editor, a man in shirt sleeves with deep
> hollows under his eyes. He looked as if he hadn't slept for a
> week. It was cold and dark in there. It was the composing room
> of one of the town's two newspapers, the small one. Men sat
> at desks under reading lamps working at copy.
>
> (18)

Once again, the omission of the articles in the last sentence de-
humanizes the work process. As in the first description, these
are de-individualized individuals, people robbed of any identity,
unqualified by even an article and in this they are one with the
inorganic objects which constitute their work and environment:
"desks," "reading lamps," "copy." By omitting the articles, giving
us quasi-telegraphic sentences, Bukowski abstracts the process
and universalizes it. We see people objectified, almost non-human,
zombies: objects working on objects. Because of these stylistic
characteristics, the processes described are also, and are meant
to be, representative of work in general, rather than of any
specific job. The regular rhythm of the final sentence lends it
a narrative, epic broadness which underlines the universality of
the events being described. (With one more foot it would be a

perfect dactylic hexameter, the line of the classical epic.) This, in turn, imparts a stateliness to the description of the work and the contrast between the stately form and the mundane content produces a mock-heroic effect.

One final point about the language in this paragraph shows how subtle (and political) Bukowski's seemingly uncomplicated prose is. In the penultimate sentence Bukowski writes "small" rather than "smaller," the word we would expect in a comparison of two things. Why? Because, by making the adjective absolute rather than comparative, the inferior position is emphasized. If the comparative aspect were emphasized, then the possibility of change would be felt to be greater because it would be shown to be small only in relation, and for something "small" to grow relatively, either with respect to itself or to something else, that is to become "larger," is conceivable in a way that the categorical change from "small" to "large" is not. Bukowski has cast the issue in these terms because he wants to suggest a connection between the editor's looking "as if he hadn't slept in a week" and his newspaper's secondary position: it is behind in the competition and has to overtake, or at least catch up with, its rival and the effort to do this is affecting the editor. One of the themes of the novel, as well as of Bukowski's work generally, is that to be successful (in society's terms) one has to make unwarranted sacrifices, even, sometimes, of one's own body.

Even when it isn't a question of Chinaski himself working, Bukowski depicts work negatively. At one point there is a fire in Chinaski's apartment building:

> I went to the door and opened it. There was thick smoke in the hall. Firemen in large metal helmets with numbers on them. Firemen dragging long thick hoses. Firemen dressed in asbestos. Firemen with axes. The noise and the confusion was incredible. I closed the door.
>
> (101)

The anaphoric "Firemen" and the pseudo-sentences, the omission of articles and the lack of any kind of subordination which might clarify the relationship between men and objects so closely identify the workers with the work as to suggest the inevitability of work completely objectifying the worker. Work objectifies people; people then objectify each other; the world becomes a

144

world of objects. Such is Bukowski's syllogism and the extent to which individuals are objectified in *Factotum* is striking.

5

In *Factotum* Bukowski offers a radical, generalized critique of work and its function in U.S. society and, for the first time, a strategy of resistance.° In *Factotum* the refusal to work has become systematic and programmatic. At the newspaper in New Orleans, sent to borrow type from the competing paper: "I found a place in a back alley where I could get a glass of beer for a nickel. . . . [T]he nickel beer place became my hangout. The fat man began to miss me" (19); at the bicycle warehouse he is fired for lateness (verging on absenteeism): "You've been showing up for work at 10:30 for 5 or 6 days now. How do you think the other workers feel about this? They work an eight hour day" (94); at the *Los Angeles Times,* assigned to shine a brass railing that runs around the building (a task which "appeared to be the dullest and most stupid" of all the jobs he had ever had), "I polished about twenty-five feet of the railing, turned the corner, and saw a bar across the street. I took my rags and jar across the street and went into the bar" (147–148). Refusal is by no means always tied to drinking, but the relation of the two deserves comment. Although Bukowski has written much of drinking alone, in *Factotum* this is by no means always the case, as the two examples just cited show. The bar represents not just alcohol but a humane alternative to the lack of human relationships that usually characterize the workplace. There is an interesting depiction of this on the second page of the novel, after Chinaski has gotten a room:

> I was in a room on the second floor across from a bar. The bar was called The Gangplank Cafe. From my room I could see through the open bar doors and into the bar. There were some rough faces in that bar, some interesting faces. I stayed in my room at night and drank wine and looked at the faces in the bar. . . .
>
> (12)

This is a revealing passage: Chinaski, on the outside looking in is drawn to the bar, but hesitant and ambivalent about joining that society (after all, there were "rough" as well as "interesting" elements in it). It is not so much the drinking, per se, as the bar community that is attractive to the shy outsider, a community where the performance of alienating work is not the measure of success. In fact, in chapter 22, the most extended treatment of this community, in which Chinaski cleans the venetian blinds for drinks, the camaraderie of the group is exemplary, the two notable exceptions being the manipulative and exploiting manager who tries to cheat Chinaski out of his "pay" and the faithless prostitute. That incident is notable in another way, Chinaski's implicit refusal of the wage, the connection between work and income. As soon as he is paid, he buys everyone drinks with the money and in the end winds up *owing* the manager.

At the job at the *Times*, Chinaski, given another chance, is assigned inside janitorial work:

> I finished both the ladies' and the men's restrooms, emptied the wastebaskets and dusted a few desks. Then I went back to the ladies' crapper. They had sofas and chairs in there and an alarm clock. I set the alarm for thirty minutes before quitting time. I stretched out on one of the couches and went to sleep.
>
> (153)

Unobserved, he repeats the procedure the next night, though this time he is caught sleeping and fired.

At the Hotel Sans, his last job in the novel,

> I was assigned to the loading dock. That loading dock had *style*: for each truck that came in there were ten guys to unload it when it took only two at the most. I wore my best clothes. I never touched anything.
>
> (191)

This last example of refusal is interesting, and funny. I think the humor results from Bukowski's vivid and concrete illustrations—indeed, proofs—of Chinaski's not working: the fact that he could wear his "best" clothes (also an interesting indication that his wardrobe allows of such categorizing) and as the ultimate proof the fact that work, as it were, didn't lay a hand on him. Yet, as so often in Bukowski, there is something else going on here. The key word in the passage (and Bukowski makes sure we recognize it as such) is "style." It is an odd choice because one doesn't ordinarily think of a loading dock as having a style. We usually attribute that quality to humans or things that in some way reflect a person, i.e., the *person*ality: clothes, physical gestures, prose. By using the word here Bukowski is humanizing the loading dock and what humanizes it is its *lack of work*. This is clear because that is the only quality of the loading dock revealed in the passage. Once again, in Bukowski, humanity is a function of the lack of exploitation (and at a 500-percent-plus oversupply of labor, the coefficient of exploitation here is very low indeed; in Chinaski's case, it is nil).

But the clearest statement of the refusal-to-work ethic and also its justification—and it is this justification that marks a turning-point in the treatment of work in novels of the American working class—come midway through *Factotum*.

> At the auto parts warehouse I did less and less. Mr. Mantz the owner would walk by and I would be crouched in a dark corner or in one of the aisles, very lazily putting incoming parts on the shelves.
> "Chinaski, are you all right?"
> "Yes."
> "You're not sick?"
> "No."
> Then Mantz would walk off. The scene was repeated again and again with minor variations. Once he caught me making a sketch of the alley on the back of an invoice. My pockets were full of bookie money. The hangovers were not as bad, seeing as they were caused by the best whisky money could buy.
> I went on for two more weeks collecting paychecks. Then on a Wednesday morning Mantz stood in the center aisle near his office. He beckoned me forward with a motion of his hand. When I walked into his office, Mantz was back behind his desk. "Sit down, Chinaski." On the center of the desk was a check, face down. I slid the check face down along the glass top of the desk and without looking at it I slipped it in my wallet.
> "You knew we were going to let you go?"
> "Bosses are never hard to fathom."
> "Chinaski, you haven't been pulling your weight for a month and you know it."
> "A guy busts his damned ass and you don't appreciate it."
> "You haven't been busting your ass, Chinaski."
> I stared down at my shoes for some time. I didn't know what to say. Then I looked at him. "I've given you my *time*.

It's all I've got to give—it's all any man has. And for a pitiful buck and a quarter an hour."

"Remember you begged for this job. You said your job was your second home."

". . . my time so that you can live in your big house on the hill and have all the things that go with it. If anybody has lost anything on this deal, on this arrangement . . . I' ve been the loser. Do you understand?"

"All right, Chinaski."

"All right?"

"Yes. Just go."

I stood up. Mantz was dressed in a conservative brown suit, white shirt, dark red necktie. I tried to finish it up with a flair. "Mantz, I want my unemployment insurance. I don't want any trouble about that. You guys are always trying to cheat a working man out of his rights. So don't give me any trouble or I'll be back to see you."

"You'll get your insurance. Now get the hell out of here!"

I got the hell out of there.

(112–113, emphasis in original)

Here Bukowski has shifted the grounds of the relationship between worker and employer. It is in this one instance, above all others, that he most differs from his contemporaries and his predecessors who have written about work. (One proof of the significance that he attributes to this incident is that the passage just quoted constitutes all of chapter 49 of *Factotum* and is placed almost exactly in the middle of the novel.) With his refusal to claim sickness Bukowski makes it quite clear that this is no fluke but a principled refusal. The mention of the sketching is important because, while it may be seen as hinting at a kind of aesthetic moralism, that is not its main function. Working lazily is still working, the concept of a wage tied to production is still—however tenuously—present. This connection disappears when work ceases.

When Henry Chinaski says, "I've given you my *time*. It's all I've got to give—it's all any man has," and ignores the fact — indeed, admits it—that he hasn't been working, let alone "busting his ass," he is breaking new ground in the relation between the working class and capital (at least in fiction) by divorcing the wage not just from productivity increases (a more moderate working-class demand and the basis of the consensus between

148

labor and management from roughly the 1940s through the early 1970s) but from production *tout court*. The fact that he hasn't been working—the paramount issue from Mantz's point of view—is asserted to be meaningless from Chinaski's. The logical next step is that he should be paid for *not* working and this follows with the *demand* for unemployment insurance.

This is the point where Bukowski's novel is cognate with the New Left analyses of labor-capital relations discussed earlier, in that both are a reaction to a fundamentally different technological-economic social structure. Because labor was now divorced from productivity, a revolutionary working class no longer had to be a class that worked:

> [T]he key to capitalist accumulation is the constant creation and reproduction of the division between the waged and the unwaged parts of the class. . . . the cutting of the link between income and work is the decisive point at which the class recompose[s] itself.
>
> (*Midnight Oil*, 110, 113)

and it was in "this cycle [i.e., the capitalist crisis of the late 1960s and early 1970s] that the struggle for income *through* work change[d] to a struggle for income *independent* of work. The working-class strategy for *full employment* . . . became . . . a general strategy of the *refusal of work*" (110).° "In the Tendency [the divorce of labor from production] capital is pushed *beyond value*. Once labor ceases to be the well-spring of wealth, value ceases to be the mediation of use-values."°

This is the significance of Chinaski's demand for unemployment insurance. While unemployment insurance is still tied to work, because one has to have worked in order to be eligible, the connection is much looser, and the idea that it is a "right," something expected by the worker—like paid holidays and annual leave—is marked, and certainly not a demand encountered in earlier proletarian fiction. The idea that the worker would prefer *not* to work goes against the grain of traditional socialist ideology, where work, and the worker, were glorified.° (A clarification of the U.S. unemployment benefits policy is perhaps helpful here. Practically speaking, the employer has a good deal to say in determining whether or not an employee receives benefits after he is terminated. Although the reason for Chinaski's being

149

fired here—laziness—might be a little hard for the employer to prove, Mantz, if he wanted to, might well have gotten Chinaski denied benefits for other reasons—whether they were true or not—such as lateness or absenteeism.)

In the past there had been a connection between work and wealth. With the increased efficiency of technology, and hence the increasingly small part played by human labor in the production of wealth, that connection (the "law of value") has ceased, and because the causal relationship between human labor and wealth has in fact ceased to exist, distributing that wealth on the basis of one's work no longer makes sense. Value has here been dispensed with. Chinaski, too, realizes that "labor no longer appears as an integral element of the productive process" and that with the irrelevance of labor-time in relation to wealth, "exchange-value" [ceases to be] "the measure of use-value."

This state of affairs underlies the forms that Chinaski's refusal takes, forms that may at first seem somewhat problematic because of their individualistic nature. There is no instance of any kind of collective refusal in either *Post Office* or *Factotum*. The traditional American vehicle for such action had been aptly assessed by Henry Chinaski on the second page of *Post Office* when he noted that "the union man was worthless" (9/15). Here, too, Bukowski echoes New Left analyses, sharing, e.g., the analysis of American labor unions made by Kolko: "the fact remains that American unions have found it infinitely simpler to adjust to capitalism, or even to help manage it within their own industry, than to replace it" (158). The absenteeism, the lateness, the malingering, the pilferage, all the minor forms of resistance, must be seen in the context of changes that were taking place in the relationship between labor and capital in the 1960s and 1970s, as part of a broader movement reflecting objective social change, rather than mere subjective maladaptation. This is underscored by the fact that

> The movement for shorter hours during the Vietnam War largely took place in small campaigns against overtime (sometimes under union auspices, more often informally) and in the decisions of countless, especially young workers to absent themselves from work, sometimes on a regular basis. The latter phenomenon . . . helped to spawn a huge literature

150

concerning absenteeism, turnover and the "revolt against work."°

(Kolko, 272)

Aronowitz noted that "[t]he wildcat strike of postal workers in 1970 took place over the heads of the union leadership and became a national strike without central coordination or direction" (250).

Although the incident at the auto parts warehouse takes place sometime in the late 1940s or early 1950s, it was written in the early 1970s. It reflects the attitudes of tens of millions of American workers influenced by the events of the 1960s and it reflects historic technological changes. It is a measure of Bukowski's authenticity as an artist that he so perfectly captured a broad historical current of feeling in so unique and idiosyncratic a work of art. Underlying all the humor, the serious intent of *Factotum* must be recognized. It is no accident that Bukowski took four years to write it while he completed *Post Office* in three weeks.° It is strikingly unified in content, style and tone. That it reflects a growth and change in worldview—indeed, an increasing politicization—on Bukowski's part is clear not only when one compares it with *Post Office* and the earlier stories, but when one sees reflected in later works, poems as well as fiction, the worldview first expressed in this novel.

EXCURSUS:
MILLER

Because of the explicit sexual passages and the chauvinist attitude towards women displayed in his writing, Henry Miller is
the writer readers are most often reminded of when reading
Bukowski; and the similarities between the two writers extend
beyond their treatment of women and sex. They both came from
quasi-immigrant German-American families, the first language
of both was German (which both forgot) and both dodged the
draft; both wrote strongly autobiographical fiction, began publishing late (if one ignores Bukowski's false start in the 1940s) and
both painted. Perhaps their primary area of congruence,
however, is that of work or more correctly, refusal of work. "Why
must everybody *work*?" (109) asked the fictional Henry Miller
of "The Tailor Shop" (though he performs very little work in that
story), a question neither Miller nor Chinaski ever stopped asking or ever answered to their own satisfaction. The fundamental experience of Miller's work life, his nearly five years as a
personnel manager at Western Union from 1919 to 1924, was
so crucial to his writing that he—as if under some compulsion—
tried to capture it on four different occasions between the years
1922 and 1942: in *Clipped Wings, Moloch, Tropic of Capricorn* and
Sexus. It equaled in extensivity, if not intensity, his obsession with
June Mansfield Smith (the Mara/Mona of his fiction). As he later
wrote: "I held the job for almost five years and still consider it
the richest period of my life."° Both Miller and Bukowski have
negative attitudes towards the American Dream. Miller's first serious attempt to write a novel was an explicitly *anti*-rags-to-riches
story or, as he put it in *Tropic of Capricorn*: "I was determined to

wipe Horatio Alger out of the North American consciousness" (34). Yet notwithstanding these important similarities, Bukowski and Miller are profoundly different writers with strikingly different worldviews. These differences may best be explored using the concepts of narcissism and the petty-bourgeois consciousness. **Narcissism:** Norman Mailer, a sensitive critic of Miller's work, wrote of Miller's narcissism: "It is too simple to think of the narcissist as someone in love with himself. One can detest oneself intimately and still be a narcissist. What characterizes narcissism is the fundamental relation. It is with oneself" (138). Miller, Mailer wrote, "has . . . eschewed the incomparably finicky and invaluable literary task of trying to place people in society, he never really writes about society except through metaphor" (139). This is the fundamental difference between Miller and Bukowski and it is a very important difference, reflected in what they write about and how they write. Miller's dialogue is with the self, Bukowski's with the world. Friends remarked on Miller's fetish of cleanliness, his feel for fine clothing, so contradictory to his otherwise bohemian lifestyle; "Bukowski"/Chinaski's relationship to clothes is quite the opposite, as is his rejection of Bohemia. Yet the paradox is only apparent. Miller's concern is with the self and clothes are intimate expressions of that self and so is personal appearance, something about which Miller is always quite fastidious. Chinaski's slovenliness is the symbol of his troubled relationship with the world. (Miller has no interest in his own relationship with the world.) By dressing down, and continually letting us know about it, Chinaski is also continually *discussing* that relationship and this—the self's relationship with the world—is one of the main concerns of his writing. Miller's interest stops at his body and what's contiguous with it; Bukowski's interest *begins* there. Bukowski is endlessly fascinated by *other peoples'* bodies; Miller rarely describes them. Mailer noted that it was the "vibrancy of the role" that the narcissist feels and the Miller of the fiction is always accused by his friends of playing a role, of not really caring. Chinaski has just the one "role" and part of its charm is the consistency with which he plays it. Miller's intense narcissism is the reason that so much of his writing takes as its subject-matter *writing*; and this becomes doubly self-reflexive when his writing is about writing about himself. With the partial exception of *Women* very little of Bukowski's fiction concerns itself with writing. Even in *Women* the writing most often manifests itself through poetry readings, i.e., as *work*, that is as a *relation to the world* and indeed as conflict. For Miller writing is claustral, cloistered (typing in the front room of his parents' Bushwick home or even hiding in the closet) or—most hermetic of all—in his head, those million words composed on the way to the tailor shop: "Each morning I write a new book, walking from the Delancey Street station north toward the Waldorf" (111); "the narcissist," as Mailer put it, "suffers from too much inner dialogue." The ultimate evidence of Miller's profoundly self-ish attitude to the world is the remarkable fact that, as Mailer notes, after three novels and 1600 pages, we know so little of Mara/Mona, the great love and obsession of Miller's life, really not much more than we do after she is first introduced into the fiction. Partially it is that Mona played so many roles herself but more to the point is the fact that Miller's real interest is in himself and not others. After all, he only wants to know so much about Mona in order to know himself better. In one sense, the difference between the two writers is reflected in their different obsessions with women. Miller's great fear is that Mona is a lesbian. His third novel, *Crazy Cock,* is devoted to discovering whether this is true and, if so, what it means. Chinaski's great concern is that his women are whores. Clearly the great threat of the lesbian relationship to the male psyche is that it holds the potential of obliterating it entirely. This the "whore" does not achieve. Chinaski can only be upset at women if he has "invested" (emotionally, let it be stressed) something in them. Miller, on the other hand, is someone for whom the prostitute is almost the ideal woman. Indeed, although Miller's biographers have never clearly established whether June was unfaithful to Miller with other men (or with women), it seems that part of Mona's attraction for "Miller" was the strong possibility that she would be unfaithful. The prostitute is so attractive just because nothing of the man's own emotions will be invested in her (and thus alienated from the self). On the other hand, for Chinaski, the possible infidelity of the woman is so troubling just because he *has* invested something of himself, his feelings, in her.°

The "petty-bourgeois ideological sub-ensemble": The last—
and most important—difference relates to class. Miller's origins
were those of the "true" petty-bourgeois. After working as a journeyman tailor for a while, his father managed (through his wife's
inheritance) to buy a half-interest in a tailor shop. ° After a few
years of keeping his head above water, he failed and suffered
a slow but continual financial, emotional and physical decline.
Miller himself never wanted any part of the business, recognizing what it had done to his father, and only "worked" there reluc-
tantly. (In the fifty-odd pages of "The Tailor Shop," he is shown
working for all of a half page.) Yet in a perverse and parodic
manner, Miller himself sometimes imitated this petty-bourgeois
idea of individual advancement through some scheme, the most
farcical of which was his and June Smith's "shuffling from table
to table in smart Manhattan cafes and restaurants trying to sell
sweets from a suitcase" during their time together in Brooklyn
and New York in the 1920s. ° Miller ultimately played something
like the role of pimp, as June would go inside and use her beauty and seductive charm to sell the candy while Miller waited outside. Whether it is as a personnel manager for the Cosmodemonic
Telegraph Co., or trying to cash in (too late, of course) on the
Florida land boom of the 1920s when he winds up a "newsie"
on a street corner in Jacksonville: "I shall never forget the first
time I yelled 'Paper—whatta you read?' I felt like the center of
the universe. My voice stuck in my throat and I blushed to the
roots of my hair," in Miller, the petty-bourgeois individualist,
never leaves. ° In Bukowski, Chinaski never works at a job where
his position is that much different from the others, or where
individual initiative makes a difference. Moreover, he rarely has
a job involving public contact whereas Miller's jobs were not
infrequently sales jobs where personality was a factor. Chinaski's
rise into the supervisory ranks at the end of *Factotum* lasts scarcely a few Sundays. In fact, Chinaski has contempt for advancement. With some exceptions, the businesses he works for are
relatively large, often with some fairly bureaucratic tendency
present. His is the world of bureaucratized and/or "rationalized"
routine work. One difference between the two authors is a result
of this worldview, and that is their markedly different prose styles
and fictional techniques. Miller's long sentences, chapterless

156

novels and endless "philosophizing" (charming though this can be) reflect an underlying attempt at finding a meaning, whether of an individual or a cosmic nature. These, of course, are anathema to Bukowski whose techniques are all constructed to limit meaning: short sentences, short paragraphs, short chapters and (relative to Miller) short novels. Miller, though, no less than Bukowski saw the destructive aspect of the American dream. Indeed, perhaps the most poignant passage in "The Tailor Shop" comes toward the end when a customer needs his tuxedo "sent up right away." Miller's father, the "boss tailor," says he'll send the boy right up with it. The cutter having left,

> The boy that he's sending up with the tuxedo right away is himself and it doesn't matter much because he will duck round by the trade entrance and nobody will be the wiser. Nobody looks more like a millionaire than a boss tailor delivering a tuxedo to Mr. So-and-So. Spry and spruce, shoes shined, hat cleaned, gloves washed, mustache waxed. They start to look worried only when they sit down for the evening meal. No appetite. No orders today. No checks. They get so despondent that they fall asleep at ten o'clock and when it's time to go to bed they can't sleep any more.
>
> (125)

Miller's response to all this was a refusal more global than Chinaski's (and in the end it is a kind of affirmation), to ultimately expatriate himself and choose the life of a bohemian in Paris. He suffered intermittent episodes of poverty similar to George Orwell's but for a longer period of time (*Tropic of Cancer* was published in 1934, one year after *Down and Out in Paris and London*), poverty the extremity of which Chinaski never endured. Yet even as he refused work and chose to scrounge and indeed in a very methodical way *scrounging* became his job and he treated it as such, as something having very little to do with *him*, even as he did all this, in his ears the phone was ringing for "waybills" at the Cosmodemonic Telegraph Company as he tried to capture that experience in his writing of the 30s. It is interesting to note that "Bukowski"/Chinaski never "scrounges"; to my knowledge in Bukowski's entire oeuvre, his protagonist never borrows money. For Miller, borrowing becomes as routine as the wage: "I spent the morning borrowing right and left";

". . . even as I was saying thank you to my friend McGregor for the ten-spot which I had wrung from him after the most humiliating wheeling and cajoling"; "'Listen,' I said, 'lend me a dollar, will you? I've got to eat, I'm famished.'" Miller's apparent rejection of value ultimately becomes the establishment of value of a different sort, in line with his petty-bourgeois leanings. Miller could easily have been that "charmer" at the end of *Factotum* who asks "do you need somebody who is a good conversationalist. Somebody who can meet and talk to people? I have a certain amount of charm" and who, failing to immediately perform, is cruelly rejected by Chinaski: "Can't use you, you're a stiff." Chinaski has clearly rejected the bohemian "theory of value," too. For Bukowski, the bohemian mode of existence has always been anathema. ("The word here is *rent*," Chinaski notes to a girlfriend.) Indeed, his frequent derogation of artists and intellectuals can also be seen as privileging the working-class perspective. Work informed almost all the best of Miller's writing but he reacted differently than did Bukowski. The relation of the individual with the world that informs Bukowski's work, mediated through alienated labor, is the most significant difference between the two writers.

CHAPTER SIX:
POLITICS, CLASS AND
THE PLEBIAN TRADITION

1

Bukowski's attitude to politics can be characterized as a hard-won lack of interest. In 1981 he told a *Los Angeles Times* interviewer: "There is no political motivation in me"(6). His response to William Packard was more measured. Asked "Are you interested in national, international affairs, do you consciously restrict yourself as to what you will and will not write about?" he replied:

> I photograph and record what I see and what happens to me. . . . I am not a man who looks for solutions in God or politics. If somebody else wants to do the dirty work and create a better world for us and he *can* do it, I will accept it. In Europe where my work is having much luck, various groups have put a claim on me, revolutionaries, anarchists, so forth, because I have written of the common man of the streets, but in interviews over there I have had to disclaim a conscious working relationship with them because there isn't any.
>
> (320)

Yet this is a modest and not unambiguous denial. Politics—broadly defined—has played an important, if at times surreptitious, role in Bukowski's writings. Bukowski's own reference to the content of his work suggests as much.

There are several reasons why we may be tempted to regard Bukowski as an apolitical novelist. In reading his novels it is particularly easy to identify the protagonist with the author and thus the views of the one with those of the other; hence we may all too easily take Henry Chinaski's disparaging comments on politics, politicians, voting and the like as representing the author's views in this area. But as the above quote indicates, Bukowski's own views are substantially more nuanced and moderate than Chinaski's. Secondly, even Chinaski's views are neither as unnuanced nor as unvarying as readers might think, given some of his specific statements. Finally, the representation of politics in Bukowski's novels must be seen as involving more than just the protagonist's views, no matter how central he is to them.

It is indeed hard to recall any positive comment in the novels on any aspect of formal politics. Yet such criticism as Bukowski's (and Chinaski's comments) at least implies a more positive standard from which to judge and thus reflects an implicit demand while such a decidedly negative stance suggests that the issue is charged. Political events are, with one exception, marginalized in the novels and it is the consistency of such treatment that hints at the latent power they hold for the author, as does the fact that there was a moment when politics was extremely important for Henry Chinaski. While my discussion will center on *Ham On Rye* in which, atypically, politics are treated explicitly and in some detail, I will begin with a brief discussion of the earlier novels where political events enter only peripherally.

In the 1960s and 1970s the civil rights and anti-Vietnam War movements dominated politics in the United States and we might reasonably expect novels of that era to reflect this. In fact, in *Post Office*, a short chapter is devoted to the 1965 riots in the Watts section of Los Angeles. The disturbance is presented objectively and the only comment that can be read from it is a subtly humorous identification of Chinaski with the blacks. Shortly before that chapter, the conflict between Chinaski and the blacks at the station (and thus black-white relations in American society) is shown through a humorous scene of verbal sparring, but it is clear that Bukowski has no intention of treating such issues in depth. The other important political issue of the 1960s was the Vietnam War which is ignored to an even greater extent. It is mentioned only in passing when Chinaski is describing the beginning of a relationship with Fay, a woman with whom he later has a child: "Fay had grey hair and always dressed in black. She said she was protesting the war. But if Fay wanted to protest the war, that was all right with me" (84/143).

Even more remarkable is the omission of history and thus politics from Bukowski's second novel, *Factotum,* much of which takes place during World War II. The mention of the end of the War almost as an afterthought is striking: "At some point during one of our hellish nights World War II ended. The War had always been at best a vague reality to me . . ." (100). The marked syntax and choice of words here emphatically reveal the extent to which history has become peripheral, even trivial; especially the use of "hellish"—too striking to be accidental—to describe Henry and Jan's life together, in light of the millions of hellish nights endured by the millions of people directly affected by the War is a provocative indication of what Bukowski feels is important, of the absolute reduction of everything to the level of the individual. Moreover, the end of the War is seen solely as something adversely affecting Chinaski: "The war . . . was over. And the jobs that had always been difficult to get became more so" (100).

The theme of *Women* is personal relationships and hence politics is rarely mentioned. The novel was not only written after the Vietnam War had ended but also treated that period when the United States was winding down its involvement in the War which had become, after the invasion of Cambodia, and Kent State in 1970, less divisive. More striking is the complete ignoring of the domestic political events associated with the Watergate crisis and their repercussions. This is striking because this was a moment in contemporary American history when the very legitimacy of the government was being questioned. The historian Howard Zinn wrote:

> In the early seventies, the system seemed out of control—it could not hold the loyalty of the public. As early as 1970, according to the University of Michigan's Survey Research Center, "trust in government" was low in every section of the population.
>
> (529)

Yet nothing of this gets into the novel, a remarkable omission. This having been said, however, directly and indirectly the

161

political makes its presence felt in the novels, most explicitly in *Ham on Rye*. I propose now to treat this aspect of the novels under three headings: politics per se (i.e., politics in the narrow sense of formal democracy), class, and class consciousness. As the most narrowly circumscribed, and also the weakest presence, I shall treat politics first.

2

For several reasons *Ham on Rye* is the most satisfying of Bukowski's novels. First of all, it is that here he treats in a serious and extended fashion a number of issues that remained unexamined in the earlier novels: relations with and between his parents, relations to the social world of his peers, and the most important for our present purposes, politics. With respect to this last point, Bukowski suggests that these first two sets of relationships are significant for understanding the character of Henry Chinaski's early involvement in right-wing politics.

Chapter 52, which describes this involvement, is the only extended treatment of politics in Bukowski's novels. While it would be incorrect to say that the novel has been leading up to this episode, it is fair to suggest that Bukowski wants us to see Henry Chinaski's early years as explaining his later behavior (and implies a like causal dynamic for similar behavior in others) and that Bukowski's explanation is primarily psychological.

In his classes at L.A. City College, shortly before the United States' entry into World War II, Chinaski begins to speak out against the U.S. becoming involved in the War, preaching an anti-democratic, fascist line:

> Sometimes as the instructors talked on and on about the evils of nazism (we were always told to spell "nazi" with a small "n" even at the beginning of a sentence) I would leap to my feet and make something up:
> "The survival of the human race depends upon selective accountability!"
> Which meant, watch out who you go to bed with, but only I knew that. It really pissed everybody off.
> I don't know where I got my stuff.
> "One of the failures of Democracy is that the common vote

guarantees a common leader who then leads us to a common apathetic predictability!"

I avoided any direct reference to Jews and Blacks, who had never given me any trouble. All my troubles had come from white gentiles. Thus, I wasn't a nazi by temperament or choice; the teachers more or less forced it on me by being so much alike and thinking so much alike and with their anti-German prejudice. I had also read somewhere that if a man didn't truly believe or understand what he was espousing, somehow he could do a more convincing job, which gave me a considerable advantage over the teachers. °

"Breed a plow horse to a race horse and you get an off-spring that is neither swift nor strong. A new Master Race will evolve from purposeful breeding! . . ."

I loved it. I could make up anything I liked.

(236–37)

Chinaski continues taking this line at the college and attracts fol-lowers. At one point a group of them attend a meeting of the Americans for America Party in Glendale:

It was a large handsome house. We were met at the door by a fat smiling boy who looked like he had spent a lifetime eat-ing chestnuts by the fire. His parents didn't seem to be about. His name was Larry Kearny. We followed him through the big house and down a long dark stairway. All I could see was Kearney's shoulders and head. He was certainly a well-fed fel-low and looked to be far saner than Baldy, Igor or myself. Maybe there would be something to learn here.

(239–240)

The meeting begins with the pledge of allegiance, irking Chinaski: "My God, I thought, I am in the wrong place!" Then, from be-hind a desk on a raised platform, Larry Kearney makes a speech.

He explained that since this was the first meeting, he would preside. After two or three meetings, after we got to know one another, a president could be elected if we wished. But meanwhile . . .

"We face here, in America, two threats to our liberty. We face the communist scourge and the black takeover. Most often they work hand in hand. We true Americans will gather here in an attempt to counter this scourge, this menace. It has got-ten so that no decent white girl can walk the streets anymore without being accosted by a black male!"

Igor leaped up. "We'll kill them!"

"The communists want to divide the wealth for which we

163

have worked so long, which our fathers labored for, and *their* fathers before them worked for. The communists want to give our money to every black man, homo, bum, murderer and child molester who walks our streets!"

(240)

Eventually the meeting breaks up and after some drinking and a half-hearted attempt (instigated by Igor) at Russian roulette, Igor, Baldy and Chinaski rent a boat at Westlake Park, row out and shoot holes in it with Igor's old pistol and have to swim in. A final reference to Chinaski's Naziism is made in chapter 54. Chinaski is still attending L.A. City College, where he has an exchange with the Anthropology teacher, "a known Communist . . . a large man, casual and likeable. . . .":

> "Chinaski, you don't believe all that Nazi hokum you're spreading around, do you?"
> "I'm not saying. Do you believe your crap?"
> "Of course I do."
> "Good luck."

(249)

Henry Chinaski is clearly an example of an anti-authoritarian personality, and for someone who reacts against authority, a movement that has as one of its basic tenets unquestioning submission to a leader would hold little attraction. Hence, when he says, "I wasn't a nazi by temperament or choice," we can believe him. (Indeed, as one German critic has pointed out, Chinaski would, "because of his name and his physiognomy have been listed as belonging to the 'slavic *Untermenschen*' by Hitler's race specialists. . . .")°

Chinaski's Naziism is presented as a reaction against the mindless anti-German expressions of the time: "I didn't like to see the whole German nation, the people depicted everywhere as monsters and idiots. . . . Out of sheer alienation and a natural contrariness I decided to align myself against their point of view" (236), i.e., against a war hysteria, and against the majority acceptance of liberal ideas. I think this is one valid explanation of Chinaski's motive in joining such a group. Further, because he receives a positive response to his outbursts and attracts other students, he achieves recognition on the campus as well. All this gives him a transient feeling of belonging, something like what he had earlier experienced with the group of petty criminals he drank under the table in an incident closely preceding chapter 52. Chinaski is a loner, but not by choice. (As a boy he is portrayed as wanting friendships but being prevented by circumstances from forming any; he is also shown as tyrannized by a brutally sadistic father and left to his fate by a mother who is powerless to intervene.) He describes himself as having no political interests in common with these people; indeed, his standard line is that he believes in nothing. He is neither a racist nor a patriot. His speechifying in class is presented as absurdist: "I would leap to my feet and make something up. . . . I don't know where I got my stuff. . . . I could make up anything I liked" (237). (It is also true, however, that in the penultimate sentence he is avoiding responsibility; and in blaming *others*—"the teachers more or less forced it on me"—there is a patent bad faith.)

On the other hand, it is hard to escape the feeling that in the end something has been avoided. In the late 1930s, such behavior clearly had consequences. Although the tone of the presentation modifies in important ways Chinaski's fascist politics, the reader still has to make a judgement on such behavior. It is perhaps the only moment in the novel where the reader feels an element of bad faith on the part of the author. For example, what does Chinaski mean when he says that he "avoided any *direct* reference to Jews and Blacks?" At the very least, there are unanswered questions here. Perhaps, also, a reader's uneasiness results from the slightly comic aura that envelops the episode as a whole, as well as from the not entirely convincing asides (asides which the reader hears but not the audience at L.A. City College in the late 1930s), for example, the sentence, "I don't know where I got my stuff," which, to me, seems evasive and suggests an unwillingness on the part of Bukowski to probe a little deeper or to reveal a little more.

But more crucial than Henry Chinaski's motivation for a fair evaluation of the episode as a whole (and any interpretation we might make as to the novel's politics) is how Bukowski depicts the other individuals drawn to such a movement, most of whom he portrays as misfits: for example, Baldy, a friend Chinaski has known since junior high, where he was also depicted as a misfit (and whom, in an earlier incident at the College, Chinaski humiliated):

> Coming out of Current Affairs I ran into Baldy standing there with a guy five feet tall and three feet wide. The guy's head was sunk down into his shoulders, he had a very round head, small ears, cropped hair, pea eyes, tiny wet round mouth.
> A nut, I thought, a killer.
> "HEY, HANK!" Baldy hollered.
> I walked over. "I thought we were finished, LaCrosse."
> "Oh no! There are *great* things still to do!"
> Shit! Baldy was one too!
> Why did the Master Race movement draw nothing but mental and physical cripples?
>
> (238)

Later, in the passage quoted earlier, Larry Kearny, the one person not shown as an obvious misfit, is depicted as clearly fascist, a racist and, if not paranoid, opportunistically manipulating the paranoid fears of his confused listeners.

That Henry Chinaski has no real commitment to fascism is emphasized by Bukowski's placing the incident right after his marathon drinking session with a group of petty criminals, friends of his friend Becker. Both incidents are portrayed as stages in Chinaski's attempt to find some meaning in life, or at the very least something in which he can participate. The only constant is drinking and when, after the speeches of the evening, Chinaski, Igor and Baldy end the evening drinking, it is suggested that this and the socializing are the real attractions. Moreover, the only politically involved individual who is depicted positively in the entire incident is the Communist instructor of anthropology. He is the only person who holds political views out of belief in a cause, something Chinaski finds a mistake but Bukowski implicitly characterizes positively through the positive depiction of the instructor. The most devastating portrayal of an individual, and thus of a political position (and indirectly of conventional electoral politics) is that of the student body president, Boyd Taylor:

> He was very popular with the students, the only man in the history of the college to be elected president twice.
> "Hey, Chinaski, I want to talk to you."
> I'd never cared too much for Boyd, he was the typical good-looking American youth with a guaranteed future, always properly dressed, casual, smooth, every hair of his black mustache trimmed. What his appeal was to the student body, I had no idea. He walked along beside me.

"Don't you think it looks bad for you, Boyd, to be seen walking with me?"

"I'll worry about that."

"All right. What is it?"

"Chinaski, this is just between you and me, got it?"

"Sure."

"Listen, I don't believe in what guys like you stand for or what you're trying to do."

"So?"

"But I want you to know that if you win here and in Europe I'm willing to join your side"

(237–238).

Thus the political spectrum ranges from misfits and disturbed individuals on the right, through rank opportunists in the center to sincere committed idealists on the left. Ultimately, Chinaski himself would seem to have been a New-Deal liberal, at least in economics:

> I liked Franky [Franklin D. Roosevelt] because of his programs for the poor during the Depression. He had style too. I didn't think he gave a damn about the poor but he was a great actor, great voice, and he had a great speech writer. But he wanted us in the war. It would put him into the history books. War presidents got more power and, later, more pages.
>
> (266)

Politics repels him because one inevitably loses one's individuality in the crowd. His favorable reaction to Roosevelt is in part elitist, a result of Roosevelt's style, an individuality that sets him apart from the average man. At the same time, he is not taken in by Roosevelt's professed motives. Underlying Chinaski's rejection of electoral politics is a demand for more extreme action in response to the crises of the late 1930s and this—combined with his unhappy personal situation—it is suggested, led to his brief flirtation with fascism.

3

For a contemporary American writer, Bukowski is uncommonly aware of social class. Nowhere in his novels, however, does it play as prominent a role as in *Ham on Rye*, where history, too, is an important part of the novel. *Ham on Rye* is a

Bildungsroman, of sorts, and this form with its emphasis on growth and change would seem to require historical particulars. Bukowski endows his protagonist with a fair amount of biographical detail, primarily in what he tells us of Henry Chinaski's father, and thus finds it difficult to avoid history completely. Though presented in a foreshortened perspective, it is the minor saga (or New-World parody thereof) of a German-American *Buddenbrooks,* complete with the decline into alcoholism and Art. In the figure of Henry Chinaski, Sr., we have an individual who, in another writer's hands might have developed into the protagonist of his own novel or at least assumed the stature of, say, the father in Butler's *The Way of All Flesh.*

Henry Chinaski, Sr. has suffered that most horrible of all American fates, downward social mobility. His father had been an officer in the German army and thus solidly middle-class and, after emigration to the United States, the head of a construction firm. However he no longer has any money, having "drunk it up and given it away." Of his three sons, one, Ben, is a drinker and womanizer, dying of tuberculosis, another, John, is a ne'er-do-well, wanted by the police for counterfeiting dimes and for raping a young woman to whom he had given a ride on his motorcycle. The third is Henry, Sr., Chinaski's father, who is possessed of a *ressentiment,* truly Nietzschean in its intensity, resulting from the decline in social status the family has suffered (along with the knowledge that he will inherit no money) and motivated also by a desire to recoup the family's fortunes through his son's rising above the father's station in life.

Bukowski's depiction of the father is an extremely effective rendering of an individual shaped—warped, really—by social class. Though a member of the working class by virtue of his jobs: milkman and museum guard (and unemployed during part of the Depression), his is clearly the class consciousness of a petty bourgeois, indeed that of a "new" petty bourgeois, as the phenomenon has been described by the political scientist Nicos Poulantzas, which:

> experiences its exploitation chiefly in the wage form. . . . Although they are hostile to the "rich," the petty-bourgeois agents are often still attached to wage differentials. . . . What we are faced with here is the permanent fear of proletarianization

. . . as a result of the insecurity experienced at the level of earnings, and in the form of a monetary fetishism.°

This is the class into which Chinaski, *père* has fallen. *His* social status is below his father's. (Although to what class his father belonged after coming to the United States is not made clear, it is obvious that a former officer in the German army and the head of a construction firm in the United States—though nothing is said about the firm's size—possesses a higher status than does his milkman son.) While Chinaski, Sr.'s two brothers have accepted, though somewhat dysfunctionally, their déclassé position, he has not. Though he has *become* proletarianized, having fallen into the reserve army of the unemployed (a far cry, this, from the *Offizierkorps* of his father), he refuses to accept this accomplished fact and appears terrified of becoming what, in point of fact, he already is, a member of the working class. Though possessed of that hostility towards the rich noted by Poulantzas, he is quite incapable of doing anything about it.

Early in the novel there is a powerful depiction of an incident that reveals his impotence within the established order. One Sunday the family takes an empty picnic basket and goes for a drive among the orange groves outside of Los Angeles. They stop at a grove:°

> Then we were between two rows of orange trees, shaded from the sun by the branches and the leaves. My father stopped and reaching up began yanking oranges from the lower branches of the nearest tree. He seemed angry, yanking the oranges from the tree, and the branches seemed angry, leaping up and down. He threw the oranges into the picnic basket which my mother held. Sometimes he missed and I chased the oranges and put them into the basket. My father went from tree to tree, yanking at the lower branches, throwing the oranges into the basket.
> "Daddy, we have enough," said my mother.
> "Like hell."
> He kept yanking.
> Then a man stepped forward, a very tall man. He held a shotgun.
> "All right, buddy, what do you think you're doing?"
> "I'm picking oranges. There are plenty of oranges."
> "These are my oranges. Now, listen to me, tell your woman to dump them."

"There are plenty of god-damned oranges. You're not going to miss a few god-damned oranges."

"I'm not going to miss any oranges. Tell your woman to dump them."

The man pointed his shotgun at my father.

"Dump them," my father told my mother.

The oranges rolled to the ground.

"Now," said the man, "get out of my orchard."

(14)

The father is humiliated, forced at the point of a gun and in front of his family to put back the few oranges he has taken from the orchard. (There is the suggestion that if the father had stopped when he had satisfied his own needs, the family would have been able to leave with the oranges and thus been spared the humiliating confrontation with the owner.) The father's anger and resentment are beyond his control and his anger inevitably comes back to haunt him, here in the person of the owner. Because the father can never manage to use his anger productively, he will never get anywhere and always ends by defeating himself. Since the incident takes place in the 1920s, before the Crash and the Depression and at a time when the father is employed, he is not taking the oranges out of need but purely out of resentment of the rich. He is not upset at the political system, only at his place in it. Hence, his act of individual "redistribution" is inevitably doomed to failure. Yet the father sees no alternative. Frustrated at every turn, resentful of his loss of status, he reacts by administering brutal beatings to his son, striking his wife, insulting complete strangers and generally making life miserable for anyone he comes into contact with, though in the end intimidating no one. Anger is all his father has and it is almost as if he is afraid of losing that, too, by allying himself with anyone else.

As part of an attempt to disassociate himself from his working-class environment, he refuses to allow his son to play with the neighborhood children: " 'They are bad children,' said my father, 'their parents are poor.' 'Yes,' agreed my mother. My parents wanted to be rich so they imagined themselves rich" (27). In typical petty-bourgeois fashion, the father's hopes for (vicarious) advancement are focused on the educational system:

That September I was scheduled to go into Woodhaven High but my father insisted I go to Chelsey High.

"Look," I told him, "Chelsey High is out of this district. It's too far away."

"You'll do as I tell you. You'll register at Chelsey High."

I knew why he wanted me to go to Chelsey. The rich kids went there. My father was crazy. He still thought about being rich. °

(125)

"I want you to be an engineer," he tells his son, at one point in the novel, hoping, somehow, to regain the wealth and status his own father had as head of a construction firm. Having scored well on a test himself, the father does finally get a job, as a museum guard, and throws himself whole-heartedly into this low-level position still hoping for his own "meritocratic" advancement:

My father's rule was that all lights were to be out by 8 p.m. He wanted to sleep so that he could be fresh and effective on the job the next day. His conversation at home was always about "the job." He talked to my mother about his "job" from the moment he entered the door in the evenings until they slept. He was determined to rise in the ranks.

(152)

This does not happen.

In fact, nothing ever succeeds for the father. When, early in the novel, his son is injured by a drunk hit-and-run driver, the father sees it as his chance to escape from a miserable existence:

"When they catch that son-of-bitch," he said, "I'll sue him! I'll sue him for his last penny! He'll support me for the rest of his life! I'm sick of that god-damned milk truck! *Golden State Creamery!!* Golden State, my hairy ass! We'll move to the South Seas. We'll live on coconuts and pineapples! . . ."

But my father's dream was not to be. They caught the man who hit me and put him in jail. He had a wife and three children and didn't have a job. He was a penniless drunkard. The man sat in jail for some time but my father didn't press charges. As he said, 'You can't get blood out of a fucking turnip!"

(59)

Such a negative portrayal of the elder Henry Chinaski and the rejection of his values and worldview reflect Chinaski's (as well as Bukowski's) refusal to espouse advancement for merit, a meritocratic circulation of elites, in short, the whole "petty-bourgeois ideological sub-ensemble." It is not of course, that such advancement doesn't occasionally happen. It is clearly going to happen for Chinaski's acquaintance, Abe Mortenson, with his nose-in-the-books, studying-civics-on-sunday attitude ("Civics, for chrissakes!" Chinaski remarks); it is just as clear, however, that this will not succeed for the vast majority because in the end there are only so many (and proportionally they are not many) desirable slots into which individuals may rise. Henry Chinaski, Sr. is one of those who have fallen prey to "the pervasive illusions of mobility without the reality." It clearly hasn't worked for him. In fact, the father is depicted as having become an almost inhuman villain owing to his economic insecurity and status anxiety. In any event, the sacrifices that one has to make, if one takes this path, are beyond Chinaski *fils*. °

The young Chinaski has accepted the fact that the family is not affluent and chosen, too, a working-class rather than a petty-bourgeois ethos; he refuses to try to graft himself onto the "rich kids" of Chelsey High in an attempt to achieve higher status through association. In fact, he is constantly identifying himself in opposition to such people, most vividly towards the end of the novel in the brutal fight on the roof of the "Mears-Starbuck" department store, where, having dropped out of junior college, he is working as a stockboy. There he sees "Jimmy Newhall. Halfback of our football team, undefeated for three years," whom Chinaski had seen "break off many 50 and 60 yard runs while I rooted for the other team." Newhall is with friends. Chinaski's antipathy towards them is almost instinctual:

> I didn't like them, never had. They might look glorious to others but not to me. There was something about their bodies that was like a woman's body. They were soft, they had never faced any fire. They were beautiful nothings. They made me sick. I hated them. They were part of the nightmare that always haunted me in one form or another.
>
> (212–13)

Chinaski has a visceral reaction against power and privilege; his "nightmare" is different from his father's, a dislike of either dominating or of being dominated, or more generally, of the injuries of class. This is clear in the first paragraph of this chapter, describing the social stratification of the department store staff:

> The caste system was an accepted fact. There wasn't a single salesclerk who spoke to a stockclerk outside of a perfunctory word or two. And it affected me. I thought about it as I pushed my cart about. Was it possible that the salesclerks were more intelligent than the stockclerks? They certainly dressed better. It bothered me that they assumed their station meant so much. Perhaps if I had been a salesclerk I would have felt the same way.
>
> (210)

Chinaski does not want status and yet, naturally enough, does not want to be looked down upon, either. He rejects such a system of superficial differences, yet recognizes that it's difficult not to be caught up in it. The clearest expression of class differences lies in work, and Jimmy Newhall and his buddies have provoked Chinaski by disparaging him because of his job ("HEY, SKI! SKI, YOU LOOK GREAT IN YOUR LITTLE OUTFIT!"; "Hey, look, the stockboy!"); he has to work while "[t]hey were trying on sweaters, hiking shorts, various items. . . . They stood around and tried on sweaters and laughed, waiting to go to U.S.C. or Stanford" (212).

Chinaski accepts the proletarianization that has befallen his family as, in his eyes, the lesser of two evils. As the weakest member of that unit he has borne the brunt of his father's resentment and anger which are in part his father's reaction to his own failure (in the "boom" years of the 1920s as well as in the Depression 1930s) to make a better life for himself and his family. Hence, having seen what society and its values have done to his father, the son has early on decided that such a life and such values are not for him.

4

SERGEANT: What they could use around here is a good war. What else can you expect with peace running wild all over the place? You know what the trouble with peace is? No organization. And when do you get organization? In a war. Peace is one big waste of equipment. . . . It takes a war to fix that. In a war, everyone registers, everyone's name's on a list. Their

shoes are stacked, their corn's in the bag, you count it all up—
cattle, men *et cetera*—and you take it away! That's the story:
no organization, no war!
RECRUITING OFFICER: It's the God's truth!

In *Ham on Rye*, and in his other novels, Bukowski has en-
dowed Henry Chinaski with a worldview that we might, following Hans Mayer in his essay on Brecht, call that of the "plebeian
tradition." Commenting on the discussion between the Sergeant
and the Recruiting Officer in the opening scene of *Mother
Courage*, where the two soldiers lament the deplorable effects
the absence of war is having on their own fortunes, Mayer
remarks:

> Thus someone speaks who only accepts pure self-interest—
> and if he accurately recognizes and can formulate this interest.
> Then there results a comic effect: for laughter is always tied
> to inappropriate behavior, to an offense against social conven-
> tions. Laughter represents the aftereffect of the shock that "one
> really mustn't speak or act like that!" . . .
> The logic of pure self-interest . . . cannot be denied.
>
> (8–9)

Meyer notes that "such an attitude, which we might designate
as the 'plebeian tradition' " appears frequently in Brecht's work
and that "each time the standpoint of the 'other side' is developed" (10). Brecht does not, of course, recommend such a position. He merely sees it as understandable under the circumstances
as "[the plebeian], too, was formed in a world that was split. Why
should he be naturally more high-minded than his superiors?"
(12).

It is this "logic of pure self-interest" underlying the plebeian
tradition that best characterizes the worldview of the young
Henry Chinaski in *Ham on Rye* and to some extent that of the
mature Chinaski in the earlier novels; it is also the source of much
of the humor of Bukowski's writing. While it clear that Chinaski
rejects the petty-bourgeois ethos of his déclassé father, and the
possibility of a bourgeois class-consciousness is slim for someone in his socio-economic position, it would be wrong, likewise,
to assign to him a working-class consciousness, pure and simple. Solidarity with other workers is not something one would
expect from a product of Chinaski's milieu and family. There are

clearly psychological reasons for this, but the lack is not owing to these alone.

Indeed, the absence of a strong working-class consciousness among many American workers has often been noted. Kolko has cited a number of possible explanations, among them: impermanent immigrants (internal and external), the escape hatch of the West, "personalism and numerous socially approved modes of escaping reality . . . [and] the pervasive illusions of mobility" (173). Yet there were also conditions specific to Los Angeles and Southern California. There had been no effective working-class movement in Southern California after the repression that followed the capital-labor violence of the first decade of the century (culminating in the bombing of the *Los Angeles Times* building in 1910) and the defeat of Job Harrison, the Socialist candidate for Mayor, in 1911. The crux of the conflict was the perceived need on the part of the elite to keep Los Angeles open shop, and the methods they used to do it.° This resulted in the singularly hostile attitude towards labor of the Los Angeles power structure, represented by the *Los Angeles Times* dynasty and the Merchants and Manufacturers Association. Crucial to the open shop was keeping labor disorganized and this was achieved in two ways. The tactical aspect was the terror, maintained by the L.A. "Red Squad," which, according to Carey McWilliams, "presided, like an S.S. Elite Guard, over the city of Los Angeles," making "a mockery of the right of free speech" (291) in the city from 1920 to 1934.

But the more important aspect was strategic and even more effective. Without the dream of homeownership luring more and more immigrants into the area (thus continually enlarging the pool of labor from which employers could draw) the workers already there might have been able to achieve some leverage in their struggle against the employers. Hence, the ideology of homeownership was extremely important for two reasons: first, because the city's primary "industry" was real estate and second, because of the constraints it placed on workers' freedom to manoeuver against employers. The phenomenon of private homeownership in Southern California also gave a tremendous boost to a petty-bourgeois individualism of the kind we see in Chinaski, Sr. Homeownership growth in the 1920s was such that by 1930 "a

staggering 94 percent of all dwellings" were single-family homes.°
Such an ideological (and spatial) arrangement militated against
the development of a traditional working class and indeed "[b]itter
union leaders . . . denounced the mortgage payments on the little
bungalows as a 'new serfdom' that made Los Angeles workers
timid in the face of their bosses" (*City*, 28). It is in this crucial ideological area that Bukowski focuses his critique in *Ham
on Rye*.

Chinaski's reaction (not all that different from the union leaders') to such an ideology surfaces, for example, in the references
(in poems, novels and stories) to mortgage-ridden co-workers. But
the most vivid response is the young Henry Chinaski's reaction
against his father's gradualism, as it is reflected in just this issue
of home-ownership:

> My father had a master plan. He told me, "My son, each man
> during his lifetime should buy a house. Finally he dies and
> leaves the house to his son. Then his son gets his own house
> and dies, leaves both houses to *his* son. That's two houses. That
> son get his own house, that's three houses . . ."
>
> The family structure. Victory over adversity through the
> family. He believed in it. Take the family, mix with God and
> Country, add the ten-hour day and you had what was needed.
>
> I looked at my father, at his hands, his face, his eyebrows,
> and I knew that this man had nothing to do with me. He was
> a stranger. My mother was non-existent. I was cursed. Looking
> at my father I saw nothing but indecent dullness. Worse, he was
> even more afraid to fail than most others. Centuries of peasant
> blood and peasant training. The Chinaski bloodline had been
> thinned by a series of peasant-servants who had surrendered
> their real lives for fractional and illusionary gains. Not a man
> in the line who said, "I don't want a house, I want a *thousand*
> houses, *now!*"
>
> (192–193)

Though couched in the tone of the Rimbaudian narrator of *A
Season in Hell* ("It's quite clear to me that I've always been
of an inferior race. I do not understand revolt"), the passage
reflects more than individual revolt; it is really a rejection of
a world-view which has reduced the father to something less
than human (as in the poem, "retired"), to a machine whose

176

only function is to reproduce itself. Chinaski criticizes his father for his small-mindedness and acceptance of the status quo. Yet the humor comes, I think, from the portentous way in which the father delivers himself of his homeowner homily, revealing only a blinkered vision that cannot see any meaning in life other than accumulation. The "finally" in the second sentence of his father's speech is masterful: it can be read as saying "at long last the individual has died and now the accumulation can continue," i.e., the individual is only there *in order* to accumulate, as the vessel through which the accumulation takes place. What mustn't be overlooked, though, is that Bukowski's critique is a serious one and the passage would also not be humorous if it lacked this underlying serious intent.

One point in the passage should be emphasized because it is easily overlooked in the humor and because it is an especially apt example of Bukowski's sophisticated critique of his father and the conditions in which he lives. Chinaski says that his father is one of those who have "surrendered their real lives for fractional and illusionary gains," like a house. I think this statement embodies a radical critique. After all, a large fraction—indeed it might even be seen as a whole number—of the American Dream was homeownership. What is illusionary about such an achievement? Chinaski says that it is illusionary, indeed, false (in that it has cost them "real" life) because it has not brought freedom, has, on the contrary, as the labor leaders said, led to a "new serfdom." Bukowski is questioning the whole concept of the American Dream, because for many it was and is a freestanding house that symbolizes the promise of the United States. Yet Bukowski, quite rightly, refuses to see that achievement undialectically—as an abstraction—but gives us the phenomenon within a totality that reveals its costs. It is also significant that Bukowski ties the whole house-accumulation mechanism to the family, thus emphasizing that institution's complicity in (if not its role as raison d'être for) the accumulative-exploitative process. Chinaski refuses to accept his father's collaboration with the system, his petty-bourgeois gradualism, rejecting, as well, the attempt to rise, seeing it only too well as a chimera: "He had sent me to that rich high school hoping that the ruler's attitude would rub off on me. . . . Instead I learned that the poor usually stay poor" (193).

The history of labor struggles in Los Angeles from the 1890s through the mid-1930s is the history of an extraordinary repression of the working class and the labor movement. Denied any organized radical response by this political repression *cum* mortgage-serfdom, Chinaski is thrown back on the "logic of plebeian self-interest," on the "plebeian tradition." In point of fact, Chinaski oscillates between the two poles of a proletarian *Weltanschauung*: that of pure self-interest (of which the demand, "I want a *thousand* houses, *now!*" is the most extreme expression) and that of a utopian change in social relations.

Let us look first at the more common expression of the Chinaskian worldview, the "logic of pure self-interest." As Mayer notes, this is bound up with the comic, inappropriate in such situations because it points to things which people would prefer left unsaid. Chinaski's humor is always inappropriate, stemming from his unveiling of the facts of life of class interests in a society which insists on its classlessness and that "one mustn't really speak or act like that."

When the young Henry Chinaski is undergoing a painful (and in the end, unsuccessful) treatment for a severe case of acne, administered by uninterested and uncaring doctors, he reflects: "They experimented on the poor and if that worked they used the treatment on the rich. And if it didn't work, there would still be more poor left over to experiment on" (136). As a result of his acne Henry Chinaski enrolls in R.O.T.C. as an alternative to gym (so that others won't see the boils on his back).

> There was something wrong with everybody enrolled in R.O.T.C. It almost entirely consisted of guys who didn't like sports or guys whose parents forced them to take R.O.T.C. because they thought it was patriotic. The parents of rich kids tended to be more patriotic because they had more to lose if the country went under. The poor parents were far less patriotic, and they often professed their patriotism only because it was expected or because it was the way they had been raised. Subconsciously they knew it wouldn't be any better or worse for *them* if the Russians or the Germans or the Chinese or the Japanese ran the country, especially if they had dark skin. Things might even improve. Anyhow, since many of the parents of Chelsey High were rich, we had one of the biggest R.O.T.C.'s in the city.°
>
> (170)

178

While one can argue with the particular logic here (would dark-skinned Americans really have been better off had the Germans —or for that matter the Japanese—run the country?), the basic, comic and "inappropriate" truth of class interests is revealed. While Chinaski doesn't particularly like "marching around in the sun" where "all you ever saw were the backs of some guy's ears and his buttocks,"

> On the other hand, I couldn't see myself crouched down in a football helmet, shoulder pads laced on, decked out in Blue and White, #69, trying to block some mean son-of-a-bitch from across town, trying to move out some brute with tacos on his breath so that the son of the district attorney could slant off left tackle for six yards.
>
> (174)

It is a recognition of the realities of class worthy of Mother Courage herself. That it is class, and not race or ethnicity, is suggested by the fact that his opposite number (and the high number indicates the low status of their position) is a Chicano but that this is not the important point. Anglo and Chicano are both "in the trenches."

The alternative plebeian reaction is expressed in the "rational utopian"° response of the adult Chinaski, who, at the end of *Factotum*, having been authorized to manage the employment office of the Hotel Sans on Sunday, becomes drunk, corners the Assistant Manager of the hotel and lectures him on how to run the hotel, suggesting, for example,

> "that prostitutes be registered on the first floor only and that they should be given regular examinations. . . . [and] that only two men were needed on the loading dock instead of ten, and that it would cut down on theft if each employee was given one live lobster to take home each night in a specially constructed cage that could be carried on buses and streetcars.
>
> (195)

In Henry Chinaski we have examples of both the plebeian tradition and the "rational utopian" response, the latter embodying a kind of pre-conscious socialist impulse in that it takes into consideration the welfare of more than the individual. It is a worldview that occasionally, as here in *Factotum*, goes beyond its own self-interest, but often does not because the plebeian "is shaped in a world that is split." It is, as Mayer points out with respect to the sergeant's confession, "an ethos; one might call it ethos from the bottom, perhaps, but it possesses an ethical logic" (12).

Take, for example, the detail of the overstaffed loading dock which is clearly important because this is the second time Chinaski has mentioned it. Pure self-interest is registered in the first mention: "I never touched anything," the rational utopian in his informing Mr. Pelvington, the Assistant Manager of the hotel, of the overstaffing. The humor is "inappropriate" because we don't expect the individual proletarian to a) go against his own self-interest and b) bring out into the open something that both labor and management (for different reasons) prefer to keep hidden. The same dynamic lies behind the humor of Chinaski's suggestion that the facts of life be admitted and prostitutes registered so that the practice can be controlled and the spread of venereal disease prevented. The funniest, and most utopian suggestion—Chinaski's special lobster cage—is brilliant because it combines several things. First, the sheer boldness of the suggested redistribution: *one lobster for each employee every night!*; second, again, the inappropriate (or perhaps unexpected would be a better word) acknowledgement by an employee that theft is going on; finally, the choice of lobster, that arch-symbol of the good life led by the rich, is a brilliant stroke, made even more effective by the suggested provision of the cage; after all, the proletarian, too, wants his seafood fresh. (It is reminiscent of the demand by the narrator of the poem "$$$$$$," who goes to the cafeteria manager and demands steaks, as well as of Chinaski's demand in *Ham on Rye* for "a *thousand* houses, *now!*") What is ultimately so powerful in this, and many, many other passages in Bukowski's novels, is how Bukowski weds social demands to humor. It is perhaps something that has caused him, unjustly, to be taken less seriously than he should be taken and it is another aspect of his work that bears comparison with Brecht, another writer who never shied away from using humor for social criticism.

One more point should be made, and it is something that we are especially liable to let slip by as well as something that is often lacking in socio-political exegesis. This is Chinaski's ambivalence, represented by his oscillating between the two poles of plebian

180

response. Ambivalence is something that political theory finds hard to deal with, and rightly so. In the end, theory deals with the ultimate choice we make, not our ambivalence in making that choice. But the best fiction is the appropriate tool for handling such a split and Bukowski handles it as admirably as any writer does. In fact, he is at his most effective when depicting such situations and it is when he tries to avoid such a profound element of the human condition that he is less than completely successful.

Bukowski wants to make clear the son's refusal of the father's gradualism. But because the character of Henry Chinaski is so vividly realized in the novels, we tend to take his actions and his "career" as being extremely idiosyncratic and forget the extent to which he is representative of millions of individuals in his response to the real chances of class advancement in the United States. Part of the reason for this oversight is that the vast majority of readers of serious fiction (and this is perhaps all the more true for readers of poetry) do not suffer a fate similar to Chinaski's. Though the routine and boredom of the jobs Chinaski holds in the course of Bukowski's first two novels may be shared in varying degrees by some readers (*Post Office* probably hits closest to home in this respect), there is still a tremendous distance, especially with respect to Chinaski's career in *Factotum*. On the other hand, the declining American economy of the last twenty years (the decline of the real wage beginning two years after *Post Office* was published) and its effect on the college educated may bring that novel a little too close for comfort. °

Bukowski's novels are valuable in several ways; as documents of one kind of American working-class life in the middle of the 20th Century, for their depiction of work and for their effective mixing of humor and social criticism; but I would not want to suggest that this exhausts their achievement. They are remarkably effective in their portrayal of one idiosyncratic yet at the same time representative persona; and their style, something I have barely touched on, constitutes an impressive achievement in its own right. (To take just one example, Bukowski's handling of dialogue, and speech is, especially in the novels after *Post Office*, extremely assured and effective.) Bukowski is, after all, a novelist and not a social theorist and were he not so effective a novelist, we would not be concerned with social comment in his work.

CHAPTER SEVEN:
SEX, WOMEN AND IRONY

"Why can't you be decent to people?" she asked.
"Fear," I said. (W 54)

No aspect of Bukowski's writing has been more sharply criticized than his portrayal of women. In response to his early work, one critic wrote (hyperbolically but with some justification):

> Bukowski's antics with women, his thoughts about them, are one vast and sniggering cliché. He has nothing to tell us about them because, I'm convinced, he knows nothing about them (e.g., "the ladies will always be the same.") and is determined at this point not to learn. They are a dirty joke to him, a dirty joke on him. Inside the web of his booze-bull-and-broad exploits lurks a demon sexual jingoist, erupting and irrupting in self-punishing concatenations; hostile, frustrated, pugilistic—fearful of the role into which (he thinks) one is cast by fate of genitalia.°

Although such a characterization is no longer valid, it represents an early (and continuing) response to Bukowski's work. However, his depiction of women has changed significantly over the third of a century in which he has been writing. The crucial period for this change was the 1970s and this essay focuses on the novels written during this period; just in the seven years between *Post Office* (1971) and *Women* (1978) there was an increased subtlety of characterization, a more nuanced treatment of psychological dynamics and less reliance on stereotypes.

While I will discuss Bukowski's undeniable male chauvinism, what has become significant in his writing is the irony with which he has come to treat his protagonist's machismo, something which distinguishes him from many male American novelists of his generation. Reading Fulton's comments after reading *Women*, it becomes clear how far Bukowski has moved from his earlier position.

Kate Millett's 1970 book *Sexual Politics* provides a useful background for such a discussion. There, she places the women's movement in a historical context and develops categories for the analysis of patriarchal society's views of women in literature. She convincingly argues that women were rarely depicted objectively by modern male authors who were the prisoners of myth and of a puritanical view of sexuality in which a woman, by virtue of her interest in and enjoyment of sex was seen as perverse or defiled. Her periodization of the liberation movement is also useful. She notes that the years 1930–1960 represented a counter-revolutionary period with respect to women's liberation. This is important in any discussion of Bukowski's work because it underlines the fact that part of his boyhood, all of his adolescence, and part of his maturity took place during an era of reaction against women's gains, while his novels were written and published in the middle of the "second wave" of women's liberation.

1

In his novels Bukowski has depicted a number of women through their relationships with Henry Chinaski; indeed, one of the reasons "thoughtful female readers find no chance whatsoever to positively identify with the female characters" is that women are rarely presented independent of their relationships with Chinaski. ° By the time Bukowski came to write *Women*, however, this had begun to change and his depiction of women and sexual relationships gradually shifted from crude descriptions of events and flat characterizations of women to fuller descriptions, more rounded characterizations and female characters who, it was suggested, had lives outside the orbit of Henry Chinaski.

In his first novel, *Post Office*, Bukowski depicts events that, but for their brevity, might suggest comparison with the most chauvinist scenes in Henry Miller:

> I think it was my second day as a Christmas temp that this big woman came out and walked around with me as I delivered letters. What I mean by big was that her ass was big and her tits were big and that she was big in all the right places. She seemed a bit crazy but I kept looking at her body and I didn't care.
>
> She talked and talked and talked. Then it came out. Her husband was an officer on an island far away and she got lonely, you know, and lived in this little house in back all by herself.
>
> "What little house?" I asked.
>
> She wrote the address on a piece of paper.
>
> "I'm lonely too," I said, "I'll come by and we'll talk tonight."
>
> I was shacked but the shackjob was gone half the time, off somewhere, and I was lonely all right. I was lonely for that big ass standing beside me.
>
> "All right," she said, "see you tonight."
>
> She was a good one all right, she was a good lay but like all lays after the 3rd or 4th night I began to lose interest and didn't go back.
>
> (9/13–14)

Here, on the first page of Bukowski's first novel, the woman is objectified in the crudest terms, presented as mentally problematic, the aggressor and unfaithful. But even in such a crude and simplistic depiction, there are hints of a subtler dynamic: along with the woman's seemingly unambiguous infidelity, a reason for her behavior is suggested: her husband is away (i.e., withholding his affection), behavior repeated by Chinaski who soon stops seeing the woman.

A few pages further along, Chinaski encounters a woman who grabs a registered letter (without signing for it) which he then attempts to retrieve, forcing his way into the house:

> "YOU HAVE NO RIGHT IN MY HOUSE! GET OUT!"
>
> "And you have no right to rob the mails! Either give me the letter back or sign for it. Then I'll leave."
>
> "All right! All right! I'll sign."
>
> I showed her where to sign and gave her a pen. I looked at her breasts and the rest of her and I thought, what a shame she's crazy, what a shame, what a shame.
>
> She handed back the pen and her signature—it was just scrawled. She opened the letter, began to read it as I turned to leave.
>
> Then she was in front of the door, arms spread across. The letter was on the floor.

"Evil evil evil man! You came here to rape me!"

"Look lady, let me by."

"THERE IS EVIL WRITTEN ALL OVER YOUR FACE!"

"Don't you think I know that? Now let me out of here!"

With one hand I tried to push her aside. She clawed one side of my face, good. I dropped my bag, my cap fell off, and as I held a handkerchief to the blood she came up and raked the other side.

"YOU CUNT! WHAT THE HELL'S WRONG WITH YOU!"

"See there? See there? You're evil!"

She was right up against me. I grabbed her by the ass and got my mouth on hers. Those breasts were against me, she was all up against me. She pulled her head back, away from me—

"Rapist! Rapist! Evil rapist!"

I reached down with my mouth, got one of her tits, then switched to the other.

"Rape! Rape! I'm being raped!"

She was right. I got her pants down, unzipped my fly, got it in, then walked her backwards to the couch. We fell down on top of it.

She lifted her legs high.

"RAPE!" she screamed.

I finished her off, zipped my fly, picked up my mail pouch and walked out leaving her staring quietly at the ceiling . . .

(23–24/37–38; ellipsis in original)

Once more a woman is depicted as disturbed and aggressive—although here it is a more complicated situation; indeed, although she cries "rape!", she is shown as partially complicit and when Chinaski agrees that it is rape, we feel he doesn't really believe it, that somehow her physical aggression sanctions his sexual violence.° But he does rape her, or at least I think most readers would see it that way, and such irony as there is in the passage is overshadowed by the protagonist's brutal actions and crude chauvinist language. Such language is especially evident in *Post Office* because Bukowski is nowhere near as effective in distancing himself from Chinaski as he became in the later novels.

If the writing is sometimes repetitive and unmediated in *Post Office*, this is no longer the case in *Factotum* (1975) . But although Bukowski's distance from his protagonist is more evident and the writing more skillful, the underlying dynamic remains the same. On the first page of the novel, soon after his arrival in

Miami, Henry Chinaski is assaulted by the siren call of a "high yellow": *"Hey, poor white trash!"* (11) and responding, is made a fool of. Twenty-odd pages later in the first explicit sexual encounter of the novel he is literally assaulted by Martha, a fellow-lodger in his rooming house. After some brief conversation and a dance-cum-strip-tease Martha attacks:

> Suddenly her eyes narrowed. I was sitting on the edge of the bed. She leapt on me before I could move. Her open mouth was pressed on mine. It tasted of spit and onions and stale wine and (I imagined) the sperm of four hundred men. She pushed her tongue into my mouth. It was thick with saliva, I gagged and pushed her off. She fell on her knees, tore open my zipper, and in a second my soft pecker was in her mouth. She sucked and bobbed. Martha had a small yellow ribbon in her short grey hair. There were warts and big brown moles on her neck and cheeks.
>
> My penis rose; she groaned, bit me. I screamed, grabbed her by the hair, pulled her off. I stood in the center of the room wounded and terrified. They were playing a Mahler symphony on the radio. Before I could move she was down on her knees and on me again. She gripped my balls mercilessly with both of her hands. Her mouth opened, she had me; her head bobbed, sucked, jerked. Giving my balls a tremendous yank while almost biting my pecker in half she forced me to the floor. Sucking sounds filled the room as my radio played Mahler. I felt as if I were being eaten by a pitiless animal. My pecker rose, covered with spittle and blood. The sight of it threw her into a frenzy. I felt as if I was being eaten alive.
>
> If I come, I thought desperately, I'll never forgive myself.
>
> (36–37)

The last sentence is one of the funniest in all of Bukowski's writings. Rarely has the mind-body split been presented so comically. The tactic Bukowski uses is reminiscent of the effective use of humor in his social criticism (noted in the last chapter) as he treats a subject of some (psychological) weight—Chinaski's reluctance to lose control—in a comic way.

Here the male has completely lost control; while the scene is comic, it is the comic transformation of the male's ultimate nightmare: he—or at least his penis—has fallen prey to a sexually devouring woman. The depiction of a wounded and terrified Chinaski radically contravenes our traditional expectations. To appreciate how radically, we need only try to imagine Henry Miller or Norman Mailer invoking such a protagonist. Both Miller and Mailer have too much invested in maintaining the male's power to allow this much loss of control or to present what is at bottom for them a serious issue—in fact, *the* issue, as a subject for jest.

Chinaski, in a tactic not unknown in Bukowski, gives the woman money afterwards, although she hasn't mentioned payment and, indeed, seems content with the pleasure she has derived from the act itself. Commodifying the act is the male's last-gasp attempt to maintain control and escape his victimization (inherent in his being treated as an object) by reversing the roles. This passage represents something quite unusual in the presentation of a male protagonist in American fiction. Though it does not depict the woman positively, indeed not even as fully human, neither is it the language of simple chauvinism, and its significance lies as much in what it reveals about men and the masculine role as in its degradation of women. The male's loss of control and the anxiety it provokes are clear in the language. The passage is comic, but the comedy is also a defense against the anxiety occasioned by the loss of control.

In *Factotum*, Bukowski develops Chinaski's passivity, even masochism, which, along with the theme of male victimization is the virtual signature of the protagonist. This becomes obvious in his relationship with Gertrude, a young woman he meets in his St. Louis roominghouse. They become emotionally involved (though not lovers).

> Whenever I went out into the hall of the roominghouse Gertrude seemed to be standing there. She was perfect, pure, maddening sex, and she knew it, and she played on it, dripped it, and allowed you to suffer for it. It made her happy. I didn't feel too bad either. Like most men in that situation I realized that I wouldn't get anything out of her—intimate talks, exciting roller-coaster rides, long Sunday afternoon walks—until after I had made some odd promises. (57)

Here the masochistic element, which runs like a red thread through Chinaski's relationships, appears explicitly for the first time, expressed in the passage: "She was sex . . . and allowed you to suffer for it. It made her happy. I didn't feel too bad either."

188

In one sense, Chinaski remains in control by denying women sex, or deeper involvement (thus expressing a sadism that we would also expect to be present), but this is not the whole story. The ambivalence of the situation is reflected in the odd construction: "allowed you to suffer." The more expected phrasing would be "made you suffer," but this is too straightforward and suggests the possibility of an open conflict whereas in the narrator's phrasing, the male is presented as totally powerless and the choice of "allowed" implies that something desireable, pleasurable, i.e., painful, is being granted, a projection of his own masochistic delight in the situation; indeed the tentativeness of Chinaski's language in the whole exchange is marked, as if he is almost pleading to be subjected to Gertrude's power.

However, this is only the opening gambit in a more complex interaction. Gertrude is interested in Chinaski and shows it. Yet Chinaski is obviously of two minds. In spite of his knowledge of the need for "some odd promises," he allows the relationship to progress, ostensibly grateful for her "allow[ing] him to be warmed by a glimpse of it." One night Chinaski takes Gertrude to a bar:

Gertrude turned her head and stared into the crowd of people. Then she looked at me.
"Isn't he *handsome?*"
"Who?"
"That soldier over there. He's sitting alone. He sits so *straight*. And he's got all his medals on."
"Come on, let's get out of here."
"But it's not late."
"You can stay."
"No, I want to go with *you.*"
"I don't care what you do."
"Is it the soldier? Are you mad because of the soldier?"
"Oh, shit!"
"It was the soldier!"
"I'm going."
I stood up at the table, left a tip and walked toward the door. I heard Gertrude behind me. I walked down the street in the snow. Soon she was walking at my side.
"You didn't even get a taxi. These high heels in the snow!"
I didn't answer. We walked the four or five blocks to the rooming house. I went up the steps with her beside me. Then I walked down to my room, opened the door, closed it, got

189

out of my clothes and went to bed. I heard her throw something against the wall of her room.

(59–60)

While Gertrude is interested in Chinaski, he, needing a reason
to end a difficult situation (difficult because his involvement en-
tails vulnerability), uses the pretext of her casual remarks about
the soldier to terminate the relationship. While the incident may
have been used to suggest the faithlessness of women (a theme
in Bukowski), the underlying cause of the break is the protagonist's failure to respond to a woman's emotional needs. What,
in fact, has happened? Gertrude has become involved with
Chinaski who, not interested in a deeper relationship, has
nevertheless allowed Gertrude to become involved and causes
her pain by his behavior. What has taken place is the reverse
of what had been described in the passage quoted earlier: he
has allowed her to become involved with him and makes her
suffer for it. Gertrude is obviously ambivalent, too; her attraction
to the soldier stems not so much from his physical attractiveness
as from his "straightness": he has played the game correctly, has
gotten medals to prove it, whereas the appeal of Chinaski is his
refusal to play the game (which also appeals to Gertrude).

This passivity is again evident in the relationship with Laura
(the first extended sexual relationship in the novel). While
Chinaski initiates it, it soon becomes clear who is in control.
Chinaski buys Laura four or five drinks, then tells her, "That
drink was it. I'm broke."

> "Are you serious?"
> "Yes."
> "Do you have a place to stay?"
> "An apartment, two or three days left on the rent."
> "And you don't have any money? Or anything to drink?"
> "No."
> "Come with me."
>
> (67–68)

Laura, along with two other women, Grace and Jerry, is living
with and being supported by Wilbur Oxnard, an eccentric millionaire who is writing an opera, *The Emperor of San Francisco*.
Chinaski is accepted into the fold, ostensibly to write the libret-
to. At one time or another, each of the women had been Wilbur's

lover, though "Grace is his main girl." Wilbur has a boat and on it, in one memorable chapter, Chinaski has sex, *seriatim*, with all three women, though Laura is *his* main woman. The situation as it develops is noteworthy because here he immediately moves in with (sort of) the first woman he meets who shows him the slightest bit of affection and who has sex with him and by virtue of his relationship with her winds up being supported by Wilbur. This complete "surrender" doesn't jibe with the independent loner image that Chinaski likes to project. That Chinaski himself recognizes this and is, momentarily, made uneasy by the developing structure of the relationship is apparent when, on the night of their first meeting they return to his apartment with liquor, food and cigarettes (charged to Wilbur): "I brought her drink and curled up next to her. I did feel foolish." It is the loss of control that is at the root of this feeling.°

Throughout the book women continue to initiate relationships. The most important such relationship, with Jan Meadows, begins somewhat as the relationship with Laura began:

> We had met at an open air lunch counter—I was spending my last fifty cents on a greasy hamburger—and we struck up a conversation. She bought me a beer, gave me her phone number, and three days later I moved into her apartment.
>
> (90)

The relationship is broken off, a good deal later there is a reconciliation, and then it ends for good. Jan precipitates both breakups, though the first time it is Chinaski who leaves. This occurs after a period in which Chinaski has been working regularly and also winning money at the track.

> The new life didn't sit well with Jan. She was used to her four fucks a day and also used to seeing me poor and humble. After a day at the warehouse, then the wild ride and finally sprinting across the parking lot and down through the tunnel, there wasn't much love left in me. When I came in each evening she'd be well into her wine.
>
> "Mr. Horseplayer," she'd say as I walked in. She'd be all dressed up; high heels, nylons, legs crossed high, swinging her foot. "Mr. Big Horseplayer. You know, when I first met you I liked the way you walked across a room. You didn't just *walk* across a room, you walked like you were going to walk through a wall, like you owned everything, like nothing mattered. Now

you get a few bucks in your pocket and you're not the same anymore. You act like a dental student or a plumber."

(108)

Whatever superficial cogency Chinaski's explanation might initially possess is demolished by the exchange that follows:

> "Don't give me any shit about plumbers, Jan."
> "You haven't made love to me in two weeks."
> "Love takes many forms. Mine has been more subtle."
> "You haven't fucked me for two weeks."

(108)

Surely Jan has a point in that the reduction in the incidence of lovemaking from about 28 times per week (!) to zero cannot be completely traced to the demands made on Chinaski's stamina by steady employment and the visits to the track (he is, after all, in his twenties); clearly Chinaski has begun to withdraw his affection from Jan, and her complaint, which his superficial riposte does nothing to answer, seems justified. Jan's focus is not so much on Chinaski's having money but on his going to the track which takes place after work and thus deprives her of his company. Chinaski, however, subtly changes the grounds of her complaint: "The arguments were always the same. I understood it too well now—that great lovers were always men of leisure. I fucked better as a bum than as a puncher of timeclocks" (109). Again, there is an element of projection here. It is Chinaski who resents having to work whereas Jan's objection merely expresses her resentment at his neglecting her for the track; he takes his resentment out on Jan because she is an easy target. Jan has said nothing at all about the quality of their lovemaking (indeed, how could she, since there hasn't been any), only wanted to make love. What has happened has been a replay of the relationship with Gertrude: the woman has become emotionally involved with Chinaski and Chinaski has begun to withdraw from her. The result is that Jan, naturally enough, begins to seek love and affection elsewhere:

> Most of the evenings fell into a pattern. She'd argue, grab her purse and be gone out the door. It was effective; we had lived and loved together for too many days. I had to feel it and feel it I did. But I always let her go as I sat helpless in my chair and drank my whiskey and tuned in the radio to a bit of

classical music. I knew she was out there, and I knew there would be somebody else. Yet I had to let it happen, I had to let events take their own course.

This particular evening I sat there and something just broke in me and I got up and walked down the four flights of stairs and into the street. I walked down from Third and Union Streets to Sixth Street and then West along Sixth toward Alvarado. I walked along past the bars and I knew she was in one of them. I made a guess, walked in, and there was Jan sitting at the far end of the bar. She had a green and white silk scarf spread across her lap. She was sitting between a thin man with a large wart on his nose, and another man who was a little humped mound of a thing wearing bifocals and dressed in an old black suit.

Jan saw me coming. She lifted her head and even in the gloom of the bar she seemed to pale. I walked up behind her, standing near her stool. "I tried to make a woman out of you but you'll never be anything but a goddamned whore!" I backhanded her and knocked her off the stool. She fell flat on the floor and screamed. I picked up her drink and finished it. Then I slowly walked towards the exit. When I got there I turned. "Now, if there's anybody here . . . who doesn't like what I just did . . . just say so."

There was no response. I guess they liked what I just did. I walked back out on Alvarado Street.

(109–10)

The portrayal of the male and of the psychological dynamics at work, in this passage, lies somewhere between the depictions of *Post Office* and those of *Women*. There is no irony here although there are obvious contradictions. Initially, it seems Bukowski wants the reader to see things from Chinaski's point of view. Jan's "infidelity" is being used to justify Chinaski's ending the relationship; once again, Chinaski is shown as victimized. Rhetorically, Bukowski gives Chinaski an edge (though calling Jan's behavior a "counterattack" implies that she is the original victim). He is "helpless," though this contradicts the assumption of control in "I always let her go," which is in turn trumped by "I had to let it happen . . . to let events take their own course"; this last is itself an ambivalent formulation, the redundant "own" perversely indicating the *protagonist's* control. But overall, the passage conjures up a victimized Chinaski, forced to be content with "a bit" of music. Given his unwillingness (or inability) to deal with his conflicts, Chinaski must view himself as betrayed. °

It is Chinaski's contention that all women are whores or at least all the women he becomes involved with. But in reality he is almost never involved with prostitutes and Jan is not a prostitute. Chinaski feels compelled to make women into whores (in his eyes) and here we can see one reason why. His own implication in terminating relationships is disguised and evaded if women can be presented as inherently unfaithful, like prostitutes. It seems obvious that what Jan most wants here is companionship. Clearly, were sex her intent, she would hardly have chosen "a thin man with a large wart on his nose" or "a little humped mound of a thing wearing bifocals and dressed in an old black suit." If it seemed at first that it was Bukowski's purpose to justify Chinaski's behavior, he concludes by letting us see that Chinaski's inability to sustain relationships is the issue, not Jan's, although it is a nice question as to how conscious a strategy this is in *Factotum*. (It is clearly so in *Women*.)

Not too long after the incident in the bar Jan and Henry separate in an unusually abrupt way. They are drinking in their apartment: "When Jan brought the drink I drank it straight down. 'You keep the car,' I said, 'and half the money I have left is yours'" (121). No reason is given for Chinaski's wanting to leave, but in the preceding chapter, five pages after the incident in the bar (the exact mid-point of the novel), Chinaski has a revealing dream, which forms all of chapter 51.

Though the entire chapter is printed in italics and, after the introductory paragraph, is one long paragraph, not even being indented for dialogue, the description is quite realistic and not very dream-like (it is only the violence and possible murder that suggest a lack of reality in the event); so realistic that we can believe that Henry Chinaski, on awakening, has trouble believing it was only a dream. (And not just Henry Chinaski. Readers, too, not infrequently ignore the italics and think a murder has been committed.) In the dream Henry and Jan go to the race track at Los Alamitos. On returning to their seats after placing their bets, they find that their places in the grandstand have been taken by a *"small gray-haired man."* They had previously placed newspapers there to indicate that the seats were taken. They explain to the man that this is the custom, but he simply says, *"These seats are NOT reserved."* After that they go for a drink and Jan taunts Chinaski, saying the old man had *"called your card."* Chinaski replies, *"What can a guy do with an old man?"* to which Jan responds, *"If he had been young you wouldn't have done anything either."* When they return to where they have squeezed in beside the old man, Jan begins to flirt:

> *Jan sat down next to him. Their legs were pressed together. "What do you do for a living?" Jan asked him. "Real estate. I make sixty thousand a year—after taxes." "Then why don't you buy a reserved seat?" I asked. "That's my prerogative." Jan pressed her flank against him. She smiled her most beautiful smile. "You know," she said, "you've got the nicest blue eyes?" "Uh huh." "What's your name?" "Tony Endicott." "My name is Jan Meadows. My nickname is Misty."*
>
> (116)

After this continues for a little while, Chinaski grabs the man by his shirt collar and, after a struggle, manages to push him down between the rows of the grandstand, a thirty-five foot drop.

It is, presumably, the emotions that caused such a dream, along with Jan's behavior, that prompt Chinaski to think that it's time to get out of the relationship, although we are told nothing of this. ° But while no explicit connection between the dream and the first break-up is made, there is an implicit connection between this dream and the final break-up between Jan and Henry at the end of the novel. After a gap of eighty pages, in which Jan has only been mentioned once, she reappears, only to disappear for good:

> The day before I had helped Jan move in with a fat real estate operator who lived on Kingsley drive. I'd stood back out of sight in the hall and watched him kiss her; then they'd gone into his apartment together and the door had closed. . . . We'd been evicted from our apartment. I had $2.08. Jan promised me she'd be waiting when my luck changed but I hardly believed that. The real estate operator's name was Jim Bemis, he had an office on Alvarado Street and plenty of cash. "I hate

it when he fucks me," Jan had said. She was now probably saying the same thing about me to him.

(196–197)

Chinaski suggests that Jan has left him because he's down on his luck. Yet that was his situation when they met: a man spending his "last fifty cents on a greasy hamburger," whom she had to buy a beer. Hence, lack of money isn't the issue. But it's important that it seem the issue in order to reinforce Chinaski's view of women as faithless and predatory creatures drawn only by wealth. Though Chinaski doesn't actually say that that's why she's leaving him, the implication is more effective than any explicit statement could be because it is presented "objectively," solely in terms of "facts": he has no money; the real estate "operator" does; the reader draws the conclusion. (We might also wonder why, if Jan does leave him because he has no money, Chinaski earlier asserted that she liked him best as a "bum.")

Because the reasons for this—as for the earlier—break-up are not explored (and because the scene recalls Jan's behavior towards the wealthy real-estate salesman in the dream), we can see that the function of this scene is to show Jan deserting Chinaski in his hour of need, clearly a false and self-serving construction of the events, aimed at justifying Chinaski's view of women. There is yet another attempt to create sympathy for the "victimized" Chinaski when, concealed, he is described as "watch[ing]" them kiss. Why he waits around to view this moment is not hard to guess: it represents both the actual confirmation of Jan's "unfaithfulness" as well as a masochistic gratification.

In summary, we can say that in these novels women are presented as aggressive and faithless, "allowing" men to suffer, "whores" attracted to men with money. Men are shown as "helpless" creatures who not infrequently, the moment a woman becomes interested in them, move in with her.° For the most part, relationships are synonymous with conflict and inevitably end in bitterness.

2

Bukowski's third novel, *Women* (1978), represents a change in his depiction of women and of relationships between men and women. Here such relations are the dominant theme of the novel which focuses on the interpersonal and the emotional (although fame and success are important sub-themes) as Bukowski treats such issues as the possibility of lasting relationships, sexuality and "what men want." While the protagonist of the novel continues to objectify women, it is an objectification that often subverts itself by depicting the male chauvinist ironically (this is *Women*'s real achievement). There is also, by the end of the novel an attempt to depict women sympathetically.

Historically, the novel came at the end of the second wave of women's liberation. Hence, fifteen years after its publication, *Women* can be seen as a product of the same era that saw the publication of novels like John Updike's *Couples* (1968) and Philip Roth's *Portnoy's Complaint* (1969) and as having come at the end of a twenty-year period of increased equality and sexual freedom for women. Bukowski (born in 1920, in Germany) was in a particularly ambivalent position vis-à-vis such a movement. On the one hand, he gained by the decrease in hypocrisy and the weakening of the Victorian moralism reinstituted during the reactionary period that had coincided with the formative years of his childhood and adolescence. Yet, irresistibly, the attitudes towards women and sex engendered during those years still played a role in the 1960s and 1970s, (Bukowski's forties and fifties). The two distinct dynamics produced both the chauvinism and its ironic treatment.

In the course of *Women*, according to one critic, Henry Chinaski has sex with "well over 20 women."° These relationships yield a representative sample with which to analyze Bukowski's depiction of women and relationships in the late 1970s, as the liberating effects of the 1960s made their way into the general population and as Bukowski approached his 60th birthday.

Octavio Paz's delineation of the *macho* is useful in revealing how Bukowski's portrayal of men and women has changed:

> The fact is that the essential attribute of the *macho*—power—
> almost always reveals itself as a capacity for wounding, hu-
> miliating, annihilating. . . . He is power isolated in its own
> potency, without relationship or compromise with the outside
> world. He is pure incommunication, a solitude that devours
> itself and everything it touches.
>
> (82)

While this is an apt characterization of the early Chinaski, it is
no longer valid for the protagonist of *Women.* One important
difference is Bukowski's attempt in *Women* to give us more of
the feelings of both his protagonist and the women with whom
he has relationships. *Women* is both an attempt to let his protagonist speak, to progress beyond the "pure incommunication
. . . that devours itself and everything it touches" as well as to
portray women as more than "wholly mechanical and one-
dimensional . . . exploitable objects."° While not always successful, the attempt itself represents a profound shift in his thinking. Equally important is the extent to which Bukowski has begun
consciously and consistently to treat his male protagonist ironically. Although the book is entitled *Women*, it is an ironic deconstruction of its womanizing protagonist.°

The most important relationship in *Women* is that between
Henry Chinaski and Lydia Vance, a sculptress. It is Bukowski's
most successful attempt at presenting such a relationship in depth
and (with the exception of Henry Chinaski, Sr. in *Ham On Rye*)
at creating a "round" character other than the protagonist. The
two meet at a poetry reading Chinaski is giving. Lydia approaches
Chinaski during the break, but is repelled by his crude response:
" 'I'd like to rip that fringe off your jacket—we could begin there!'
Lydia walked off. It hadn't worked. I never knew what to say
to the ladies" (8). At moments like these one gets the impression
that Chinaski is acting according to an image he has of how men
are expected to act rather than how he actually feels.° Chinaski,
having achieved some fame as a writer (and his writings having
been misinterpreted and distorted to present an image that is
more his readers' projections than the texts'), has now become
a prisoner of that distortion. But even here, there is a somewhat
ambivalent turn in that we would expect Chinaski, in his chauvinist mode, to want to rip off more than merely the *fringe* of

198

the jacket. It should also be noted that this is verbal, not physical, aggression, a not unimportant distinction.

Nevertheless, taking the initiative (as—true to form—do a number of the women in *Women*) Lydia tries again, coming over to Chinaski's apartment a few days later. After a brief visit, during which Chinaski's interest in her is evident, Lydia leaves and returns two days later and asks if she can sculpt his head. They agree on an appointment for the following morning. During the first session Chinaski plays the aggressor. He grabs Lydia and after two kisses she pushes him away. The sessions continue, however, and one morning he comes over and we see a new and surprising vulnerability in Chinaski:

> "Ooooh," she said, "you've got on a new shirt!"
> It was true. I had bought the shirt because I was thinking about her, about seeing her. I knew that she knew that, and was making fun of me, yet I didn't mind.
>
> (13)

Sometime later they consummate the relationship. Shortly before they make love, though, Lydia tells him about herself. Her father had left her some money that "had enabled Lydia to divorce her husband. She also told me she'd had some kind of breakdown and spent time in a madhouse. I kissed her and told her that was fine" (18). There is an irony in the last sentence of which Chinaski is not unaware. On one level, he is assuring Lydia that he is not judgmental. We are undoubtedly meant to see his response as evidence of tenderness and understanding—maturity —on his part. It may well be that. But "fine" is marked here. We would expect "all right," or something similar, a neutral and less positive characterization. On the other hand, anyone familiar with Chinaski's track record, could as easily take it to mean that it is "fine" because Chinaski needs a woman with emotional problems so that, viewing her as "crazy," there will be little chance for the real intimacy that would allow a relationship to develop. Suspicions as to Lydia's motivation (and ultimately as to her rationality) have been raised by an exchange that took place four pages earlier:

> "I've heard about you," she said.
> "Like what?"

"About how you throw guys off your front porch. That you beat your women."

"Beat my women?"

"Yes, somebody told me."

I grabbed Lydia and we went into our longest clinch ever.

(13–14)

Lydia's questionable mental state can also be seen as giving Chinaski (at least in his mind) some power in the relationship. Before they make love, Lydia warns him:

"Listen," she said, "after you stick that thing inside me, pull it out just before you come. O.K.?"

"I understand."

I climbed on top of her. It was good. It was something happening, something real, and with a girl 20 years younger than I was and really, after all, beautiful. I did about 10 strokes—and came inside of her.

She leaped up.

"You son-of-a-bitch! You came inside of me!"

"Lydia, it's been so *long* . . . it felt so good . . . I couldn't help it."

(18–19)

There are several things worth noting here. Foremost, perhaps, is the humor, and irony of the scene. Lydia's instructions about Chinaski's withdrawing before he ejaculates prepare us, as in a vaudeville routine, for what happens by telegraphing the reader that something *is* going to happen. This and the tenderness in the scene before they go to bed, where she speaks intimately to Chinaski lead up to the quick climax on Chinaski's part (followed immediately by Lydia's leaping out of bed, hardly the *post coitum triste* we might expect) which makes a mockery of everything that has gone before, just because it is so thoughtless and self-involved. The humor in Chinaski's half-hearted defense—"it sneaked up on me!"—is capped by their last exchange which opposes sharply different reactions:

"Lydia, I love you."

"Get the hell away from me!"

All of this contributes to making this depiction of seduction and love so distanced and *verfremdend* and the characters so pathetic that one can see just why Bukowski's writings have often

200

alienated readers. It is not the explicitness of his writing, since he is clearly within the boundaries of realist sexual *écriture* as it existed from the mid-1960s on in American fiction, but rather the lack of sentiment with which he handles such material. Perhaps even more than the ironic treatment of love, the ironic treatment of sex strikes a disquieting note at this point in our social history.

Yet more than simple irony is at work because in irony an identification with the character is preserved; we cannot fully appreciate the ironic situation of a protagonist unless we feel— at least to some extent—positively involved in his fate. Here, and in other passages in *Women*, the reader's identification with the protagonist is threatened. In the earlier novels there was no doubt as to whose side the implied author was taking and where the reader's sympathy was being directed. A simplistic view of "right" and "wrong" in such affairs had begun to break down in *Factotum* as, for example, the bar scene quoted earlier reveals. Now Bukowski is consciously questioning Chinaski's behavior and the male role in such situations and trying to present events from the woman's perspective as well.

The issue of fidelity has also been introduced. The view that women are inherently unfaithful, "whores," is confirmed by what Chinaski perceives as Lydia's flirtatious behavior at a party he throws where, on arriving, "she didn't speak to me but immediately sat down next to a handsome young bookstore clerk and began an intense conversation with him" (16). Chinaski tolerates this behavior, although it clearly upsets him and, again a masochistic trait is apparent. On their first formal date Lydia and Henry drive to Venice beach. They buy food at a delicatessen and then sit on a knoll of grass overlooking the sea where they see "a tall black man," shirtless, with "a very strong muscular body" who "appeared to be in his early twenties."

> "Did you see that guy?" she asked.
> "Yes."
> "Jesus Christ, here I am with you, you're twenty years older than I am. I could have something like that. What the hell's wrong with me?"
> "Look. Here are a couple of candy bars. Take one."
> She took one, ripped the paper off, took a bite and watched

the young black man as he walked along the shore.

"I'm tired of the beach," she said, "let's go back to my place."

(20)

(The depiction of) Chinaski placatingly offering Lydia the candy bar after she has crudely insulted him is the antithesis of what we would expect from a true representative of the patriarchy. Chinaski's behavior here is quite different from his reaction to Gertrude's comment about the soldier in the bar in *Factotum*. Bukowski's skill in depicting the nuances of behavior (and to a certain extent of character as well) has increased considerably. The male is no longer imprisoned in stereotypes and stock reactions but is revealed as vulnerable at times and, at other times, as downright unattractive. He has become something quite different from "power isolated in its own potency, without relationship or compromise with the outside world," as Paz described the *macho*.

The break-up with Lydia is revealing. Chinaski has returned from a reading in Houston where he has had a brief affair with another woman, Laura. He had injured his leg before the trip and it has still not healed on his return to L.A. Met at the airport by Lydia, who is "horny as usual," Chinaski wonders if he can "handle" sex with his injury:

> "*What?*"
> "It's true. I don't think I can fuck with my leg the way it is."
> "What the hell good are you then?"
> "Well, I can fry eggs and do magic tricks."
> "Don't be funny. I'm asking you, what the hell good are you?"
> "The leg will heal. If it doesn't they'll cut it off. Be patient."
> "If you hadn't been drunk, you wouldn't have fallen and cut your leg. It's *always* the bottle!"
> "It's not always the bottle, Lydia. We fuck about four times a week. For my age that's pretty good."
> "Sometimes I think you don't even enjoy it."
> "Lydia, sex isn't *everything!* You are obsessed. For Christ's sake, give it a rest."
> "A rest until your leg heals? How am I going to make it meanwhile?"
> "I'll play Scrabble with you."
> Lydia screamed. She literally screamed. The car began to

swerve all over the street. "YOU SON-OF-A-BITCH! I'LL KILL YOU!"

(90–91)

Clearly Chinaski is acting in bad faith. His injured leg has not prevented him from making love to Laura, so it cannot be the reason he doesn't make love to Lydia. Lydia is depicted as disturbed and obsessed with sex, Chinaski, as having a more balanced view. Chinaski's points are not those we associate with the typical male protagonist, who is again being subverted here. Bukowski uses Chinaski's eminently sane view of sex to gain the reader's sympathy while Lydia's compulsive demands puts her in a bad light. Yet both these positions are in turn undermined; it is clear that sex is not really the issue for either Chinaski or Lydia. The fact is, Chinaski's feelings have changed. It is a nice question, however, as to how much his bad faith causes the reader to withhold giving full credence to the otherwise sensible view he espouses of the place of sex in a relationship. But whatever we finally decide, the tone of Chinaski's argument, and the depiction of Lydia cut across our expectations in this 1970s Thurberesque "battle of the sexes."°

Bukowski has begun presenting the male as he is rarely presented in American fiction (especially in what might be termed "the chauvinist tradition"); indeed, he has begun to deconstruct that tradition as we have come to associate it with Hemingway, Miller and Mailer.° This is effected through a character who, while on one level attempting to maintain the older image of the unreconstructed male chauvinist, on another is aware of the contradictions involved. Right after the break-up with Lydia and about to enter another relationship, he is asked:

> "But, Hank. don't forget what you told me about your women."
> "Told you what?"
> "You said, 'They always come back.' "
> "That's just macho talk."

(92)

Chinaski doesn't want to have sex with Lydia, but Bukowski portrays him as feeling rejected by Lydia because he "can't" have sex. Lydia is presented as a "sexaholic," completely irrational, and relentless in her demands. Previously it had been Chinaski

203

who objectified women, saw them primarily in terms of their physical attractions, as potential objects of his sex drive, denied them mind and emotions. Here this view is projected onto Lydia, who is shown as rejecting companionship. Chinaski does not admit to the fact that it is he who makes the break here by denying her sex (as he had denied Jan sex in *Factotum*).

In the earlier novels Bukowski was content to let events speak for themselves without making much of an attempt to get at his characters' motivation. In *Women* he is trying to explain and to have his readers understand why his protagonist acts as he does, to make events intelligible. Laura (renamed "Katherine" by Chinaski for her resemblance to Katharine Hepburn), the woman with whom Chinaski *has* had sex during his trip to Houston for a poetry reading, figures in one of Chinaski's more significant relationships. Interested in understanding his protagonist, Bukowski has Chinaski trying to understand why that relationship ended. It seems to be going well when, as Chinaski puts it, he "loses her." He takes Laura to the fights and the track where she realizes that he is one of "them," "the racetrack people and the boxing crowd."

> That night she drank half a bottle of red wine, good red wine, and she was sad and quiet. I knew she was connecting me with the racetrack people and the boxing crowd, and it was true. I was with them, I was one of them. Katherine knew that there was something about me that was not wholesome in the sense of wholesome is as wholesome does. I was drawn to all the wrong things: I liked to drink, I was lazy, I didn't have a god, politics, ideas, ideals. I was settled into nothingness, a kind of non-being, and I accepted it. It didn't make for an interesting person. I didn't want to be interesting, it was too hard. What I really wanted was only a soft hazy space to live in, and to be left alone. On the other hand, when I got drunk I screamed, went crazy, got all out of hand. One kind of behavior didn't fit the other. I didn't care.
>
> The fucking was very good that night, but it was the night I lost her. There was nothing I could do about it. I rolled off and wiped myself on the sheet as she went into the bathroom. Overhead a police helicopter circled over Hollywood.
>
> (104)

Suggestive as this passage is, it really tells us almost nothing about the emotional states of Katherine and Chinaski. Most of what Chinaski says about himself is patently false and what isn't is clearly no news to Katherine who has read his books and must, on one level, be attracted to his life-style. To take but one example: to call someone lazy who has worked for decades to become a successful writer is misleading and disingenuous. Chinaski has organized his life efficiently and been extremely productive. And indeed, one might also wonder why Chinaski "loses" Laura in the very night when the lovemaking was "very good." One suspects that, at the very least, something has been elided here. The naturalist profession of faith: "There was nothing I could do about it," is ultimately more faithful to Chinaski's determinist world view, but it is not particularly enlightening.

It is clear that in *Women* Bukowski wants to create a certain depth to his characters, and depicting their thoughts and feelings is one way to do this. He succeeds in this to a greater extent than he had previously. Yet, in the end, he cannot get outside the narrator, and even then rarely goes beyond superficial analysis. The first sentence of the above passage is good because it relies on description but the repetition of "wine" hints at the felt limits of description alone, because here repetition is substituting for development or qualification. There is the feeling that something more should be said to prepare us for or explain "Katherine's" mood; Bukowski senses this, otherwise there would be no impulse to repeat the fact of the wine; but owing to the limits Bukowski has—consciously or unconsciously—placed on himself, he is at a loss as to how to proceed. Giving us the Volkswagen license plate number—"TRV 469"—in the passage quoted below reflects the same dynamic. As soon as Bukowski tries to go further he inevitably has to revert to the protagonist: "I knew she was connecting me with . . ."

Once again, Chinaski implies that it is the woman who terminates the affair. Yet they continue to enjoy making love and Laura wants to continue the relationship. After the above-mentioned night of lovemaking and after the fights

> Katherine stayed 4 or 5 more days. We had reached the
> time of the month when it was risky for Katherine to fuck.
> I couldn't stand rubbers. Katherine got some contraceptive

foam. Meanwhile the police had recovered my Volks. We went down to where it was impounded. It was intact and in good shape except for a dead battery. I had it hauled to a Hollywood garage where they put it in order. After a last goodbye in bed I drove Katherine to the airport in the blue Volks. TRV 469.

It wasn't a happy day for me. We sat not saying much. Then they called her flight and we kissed.

"Hey, they all saw this young girl kissing this old man."

"I don't give a damn . . ."

Katherine kissed me again.

"You're going to miss your flight," I said.

"Come see me, Hank. I have a nice house. I live alone. Come see me."

"I will."

"Write!"

"I will. . . . "

Katherine walked into the boarding tunnel and was gone.

I walked back to the parking lot, got in the Volks, thinking, I've still got this. What the hell, I haven't lost anything.

It started.

(107)

The odd juxtaposition of the last days of sex with the recovered car, implied in the last sentence of the first paragraph, where a kind of identity is effected between the sex and the car, and then explicitly (if perhaps a bit ironically) stated in the next-to-last paragraph, underline Chinaski's dilemma when humans are objectified. Clearly there are pressures here that remain unexamined; once again Chinaski has rejected the woman but tried to hide that fact from himself. (It is more than a little reminiscent of "Bukowski's" equating the death of his first real love with the "death" of his first automobile in the poem "I didn't want to," discussed above.)

3

After the relationship with Laura ends, a good part of *Women* concerns itself with Chinaski's string of relatively casual affairs, with no one relationship depicted as having any great significance (with the obvious exception of the relationship with Sara and with the possible exception of the relationship with Tammie) although the narrator is almost always shown as at least somewhat involved emotionally. While the depiction of intense emotional involvements is foregone, we do have a picture of sex and the American male in the 1970s, the full flowering of the "second phase" of Women's Liberation. Here again, Bukowski has done something noteworthy, not to mention out of "character." In the way that Henry Miller can be taken as representative of male attitudes of an earlier era (and Miller, too, came to a writing career late and represents attitudes characteristic of an earlier generation than the one in which he wrote, while that in which he wrote immediately succeeds an era of increased freedom for women), so Bukowski reflects those of his own era by revealing in his descriptions of sex the changes that have taken place in (sexual) relations between men and women. Miller's "I slipped it in and gave her what's what" (language that reflects the attitude of a murderer, not a lover) has been significantly transformed.

As early as *Post Office*, sexual intercourse had sometimes been depicted as problematic:

> In bed I had something in front of me but I couldn't do anything with it. I whaled and I whaled and I whaled. Vi was very patient. I kept striving and banging but I'd had too much to drink.
> "Sorry, baby," I said. Then I rolled off. And went to sleep.
> (72/121)

The inability to perform, often because of drink, comes up frequently. It is the pendant to the theme of the sexually assertive woman. Indeed, the traditional view that men have more interest in sex than women is often reversed in these novels: in *Post Office*, "Joyce, my wife, was a nymph" (35/56); in *Factotum*, "You haven't fucked me for two weeks" (108); and in *Women*, "Lydia liked to fuck at least five times a week. I preferred three" (40).

When Chinaski is met at the Houston airport by Joanna Dover, a woman whom he is visiting to escape from Tammie, there is no beating about the bush:

> ". . . Did I interrupt anything?"
> "No. There was a garage mechanic. But he petered out. He couldn't stand the pace."
> "Be kind to me, Joanna, sucking and fucking aren't everything."
> (126)

Later, after dinner out and drinking, and then more drinking back at Joanna's place, she says:

> "Let's fuck."
> "I've drunk too much."
> "Let's go to bed."
> "I want to drink some more."
> "You won't be able to . . ."
> "I know. I hope you'll let me stay four or five days."
> "It will depend on your performance," she said.
> "That's fair enough."
> By the time we finished the wine I could barely make it to the bed. I was asleep by the time Joanna came out of the bathroom . . .
>
> (128, ellipsis in original)

The affair runs its course: "I lasted five days and nights. Then I couldn't get it up anymore. Joanna drove me to the airport" (130). The roles have been reversed; the woman is sexually the aggressor. The man, sensing his loss of control, feels exploited and resists at first by drinking himself into incapacity, and then is put out to pasture when his usefulness is gone. Looked at realistically, the reasons for the end of the relationship scarcely seem credible. Are we to believe that Chinaski only had it in him to perform for "four or five nights" and then, the first night he can't (or doesn't want to?) make love, Joanna asks him to leave? That she could go at least one night without sex was proven by her having somehow survived the first night without sex. But that is irrelevant. What is important is the way Bukowski has chosen to present the episode, his using it to undermine the traditional male role.

Chinaski's drinking had also interfered in the relationship with Lydia: "She loved sex and my drinking got in the way of our lovemaking. 'Either you're too drunk to do it at night or too sick to do it in the morning' " (33); later in the novel, with Cassie: "Her body was amazing, glorious, Playboy style, but unfortunately I was drunk" (202); or with Lilly:

> I switched off the bed lamp fast. I kissed her some more, played with her breasts and body, then went down on her. I was drunk, but I think I did O.K. But after that I couldn't do it the other way. I rode and rode and rode. I was hard but I couldn't come. Finally I rolled off exhausted and went to sleep . . .
>
> (31, ellipsis in text)

and Mindy: "Mindy and I finished the bottle and then went to bed. I kissed her for a while, then apologized, and drew away. I was too drunk to perform. One hell of a great lover" (77); and Liza:

> Without foreplay it was much more difficult but finally I got it in. I began to work. I worked and I worked. It was another hot night. It was like a recurring bad dream. I began sweating. I humped and I pumped. It wouldn't go down, it wouldn't come off. I pumped and I humped. Finally I rolled off. "Sorry, baby, too much to drink."
>
> (192)

With Mercedes (after having "dr[u]nk and smoked [marijuana] quite a long time"):

> I pumped on and on. Five minutes. Ten minutes more. I couldn't come. I began to fail. I was getting soft. Mercedes got worried. "Make it!" she demanded. "Oh, *make* it, baby!" That didn't help at all. I rolled off. It was an unbearably hot night. I took the sheet and wiped off the sweat. I could hear my heart pounding as I lay there. It sounded sad. I wondered what Mercedes was thinking. I lay dying, my cock limp.
>
> (156–157)

With Iris: "We drank another hour and then went to bed. I ate her up but when I mounted I just stroked and stroked without effect. Too bad" (234).

Not infrequently sex is just work, and hard labor at that: "I began to work. I worked and I worked . . . I began sweating. I humped and I pumped. . . . I pumped and I humped" (192); "I pumped on and on" (156); "I worked and worked" (198). And in perhaps the most excruciating sexual moment in the novel:

> I worked and I worked . . . I began to sweat. My back ached. I was dizzy, sick . . . It was agony, it was relentless work without a reward. I felt damned . . . I desperately wanted to come . . . My heart began to pound loudly. I heard my heart. I felt my heart. I felt it in my chest. I felt it in my throat. I felt it in my head. I couldn't bear it. I rolled off with a gasp.
>
> (78)

I don't want to give the impression that this is the sole image of sex presented in the novel because it isn't. Sex is often satisfying with the same women with whom sex has been less than satisfying. But it can't be denied that all of this constitutes a distinctly unmacho (not to mention unromantic) depiction of lovemaking. The drinking can be viewed as a means of allaying Chinaski's underlying anxiety, or as a hostile, sadistic way of hurting women by denying them the full pleasure, and intimacy, of successful lovemaking. In any event, there has been a significant amount of slippage in how much control the man has—the decision to have sex, for example, is often the woman's. It cannot be argued that it is not a different image of the male that Bukowski is giving us. The distinctly unromantic, at times alienated, light in which sex is shown offers a different picture of the man and the male role, a part of the larger change in Bukowski's depiction of men.

It is in this larger change that the primary significance of the novel lies. What has happened is that the male protagonist is now being treated ironically. This irony manifests itself both generally and in small, self-deprecating comments by Chinaski, as, for example, when he remarks of himself: "Not a very well-known writer, of course, but I managed to pay the rent and that was astonishing" (70) where the remark also serves to distance the reader from the sexual description. The male has been problematized as the protagonists of Lawrence, Miller and Hemingway had not been.

4

This deconstruction of the male protagonist in *Women,* as male, is clear from the first paragraph, indeed, from the first sentence, of the novel:

> I was fifty years old and hadn't been to bed with a woman for four years. I had no women friends. I looked at them as I passed them on the streets or wherever I saw them, but I looked at them without yearning and with a sense of futility. I masturbated regularly, but the idea of having a relationship with a woman—even on non-sexual terms—was beyond my imagination. I had a 6 year old daughter born out of wedlock. She lived with her mother and I paid child support. I had been married years before at the age of 35. That marriage lasted two and one half years. My wife divorced me. I had been in love only once.
>
> (7)

Relationships with women have become problematic for Henry Chinaski. Although he has sexual relationships with twenty-odd women in the roughly six-year span of the novel, these are rarely devoid of involvement. Indeed, the depths of Chinaski's needs, the overdetermined nature of his involvement (where his complete avoidance of relationships with women then causes him to overvalue any woman, causes him, indeed, to immediately think of marriage) are often ironically mocked, as, for example, with "Katherine," with whom he had spent a night in Houston. She then visits him in L.A. In the evening of the day of her arrival, after they have made love—"It was glorious" (99)—and before falling asleep, Chinaski muses on the day's and evening's events:

> For the first time I thought of marriage. I knew that there certainly were flaws in her that had not surfaced. The beginning of a relationship was always the easiest. After that the unveiling began, never to stop. Still, I thought of marriage. I thought of a house, a dog and a cat, of shopping in supermarkets. Henry Chinaski was losing his balls. And didn't care.
>
> At last I slept. When I awakened in the morning Katherine was sitting on the edge of the bed brushing those yards of red-brown hair. Her large dark eyes looked at me as I awakened. "Hello, Katherine," I said, "will you marry me?"
>
> "Please don't," she said, "I don't like it."
>
> "I mean it."
>
> "Oh, *shit*, Hank!"
>
> "What?"
>
> "I said, 'shit,' and if you talk that way I'm taking the first plane out."
>
> "All right."
>
> "Hank?"
>
> "Yes?"
>
> I looked at Katherine. She kept brushing her long hair. Her large brown eyes looked at me, and she was smiling. She said, "It's just *sex*, Hank, it's *just sex!*" Then she laughed. It wasn't a sardonic laugh, it was really joyful. She brushed her hair and I put my arm around her waist and rested my head against her leg. I wasn't quite sure of anything.°

It is clear that Chinaski's behavior arises to a much greater extent than is usual from various "historical" psychic factors rather than from a just appreciation of the real person. Indeed, the fact that he can't use her real name, but renames her after a movie star long past *her* viability as a sex symbol, i.e., she, too, is not being viewed as she is, but as a memorial to some idealized image, indicates the extent to which Chinaski is here operating at a remove from reality.

Such scenes as this one with Katherine have an additional significance. (It is worth noting that this scene is an identical repetition—dynamically—of the scene of the beginning of his relationship with Lydia Vance.) Similar scenes, and there are more than a few in the novel, have, in Bukowski's phrase, a "comic edge" to them, but there is also an underlying seriousness present. Here we have an absolute reversal of the scene where the woman (traditionally viewed as the romantic in such situations) falls in love and it is the man who makes (or thinks) the distinction between love and sex. Thus *Women* hardly presents a traditional male protagonist, let alone a *macho*. Surely the image of Chinaski, his head resting against Laura's leg, "not quite sure of anything," is a far cry from Henry Miller's descriptions, who to the best of my knowledge has never written a scene of such calm intimacy and whose descriptions of alienated sex and objectified women are too well known to require quotation. In fact, whenever, in *Women*, Chinaski attempts such a role, attempts, that is, to act "in character," he is unsuccessful. At one point in the novel, after a fight with Lydia, he goes to the track and has a good night, drinking and betting, leaving "$950 ahead." He calls Lydia from a phone booth:

> "Listen," I said, "listen, you bitch. I went to the harness races tonight and won $950. I'm a winner! I'll always be a winner! You don't deserve me, bitch! You've been playing with me! Well, it's over! I want out!. This is it! I don't need you and your goddamned games! Do you understand me? Do you get the message? Or is your head thicker than your ankles?"
>
> "Hank . . ."
>
> "Yes?"
>
> "This isn't Lydia. This is Bonnie. I'm baby sitting for Lydia. She went out tonight."
>
> I hung up and walked back to my car.
>
> (44)

Here Chinaski and his "macho talk" are ridiculed. Such passages sabotaging the traditional male role are important evidence of a change. Moreover, Lydia's having gone out that night, rather than sitting around in her apartment, depressed, adds a nice touch, revealing her as independent. She doesn't need to rely on Chinaski for a social life.

If, in *Factotum*, the women usually initiated relationships, in *Women* they are even more assertive and not content to play their traditional roles in other ways. This reversal of traditional sexual roles and its ironic effect on the male image appear in the sphere of sexual practices as well. Traditionally, the man has been viewed as the more adventurous, the more willing to experiment, perhaps because he has also been—or at least been seen as—the more experienced. The reason for a woman's supposed lesser interest in sexual variety and experimentation might be that such an interest would suggest more prior sexual experience than society feels comfortable with her having. Here, too, things have changed in *Women*:

> We remained apart a week. Then one afternoon I was over at Lydia's place and we were on her bed, kissing. Lydia pulled away.
> "You don't know anything about women, do you?"
> "What do you mean?"
> "I mean, I can tell by reading your poems and stories that you just don't know anything about women."
> "Tell me more."
> "Well, I mean for a man to interest me he's got to eat my pussy. Have you ever eaten pussy?"
> "No."
> "You're over 50 years old and you've never eaten pussy?"
> "No."
> "It's too late."
> "Why?"
> "You can't teach an old dog new tricks."
> "Sure you can."
> "No, it's too late for you."
> "I've always been a slow starter."
> Lydia got up and walked into the other room. She came back with a pencil and a piece of paper. "Now, look, I want to show you something." She began to draw carefully on the paper. "Now, this is a cunt, and here is something you probably don't know about—the clit. That's where the feeling is. The clit hides, you see, it comes out now and then, it's pink and very *sensitive*. Sometimes it will hide from you and you have to find it, you just touch it with the tip of your tongue . . ."
> "O.K.," I said, "I've got it."○

(20–21)

Once again Bukowski humorously undermines a traditional image of the male: as aggressive, adventurous, experienced—that is, powerful. The scene is also effective for suggesting one reason for Lydia's attraction to Chinaski, a reason that is in direct contradiction to her statement: "Jeez, I thought you were a man, all your books . . . . " What she has sensed in him is a vulnerability and insecurity vis-à-vis women.

The effect of Bukowski's depiction of women, chauvinist though it can be, is quite different from what his predecessors and contemporaries produced. Although depicting Chinaski as sexist, Bukowski at the same time, and more tellingly, goes to great pains to undermine this position. Indeed, it would be more accurate to characterize Chinaski as "pseudo-macho." In the light of this it is useful to return to the earlier criticisms. Huffzky had written:

> In his underground society he describes a purely masculine world, in which women are hardly more than splashes of a puddle through which hardy fellows traipse, mostly drunk, or in which they wallow. Then afterwards: wipe off & away! Also most of the times drunk. . . . almost everything in his head is reduced to the magical actions: fuck, drink, fight: beating women . . ."

> (22).

It should be clear by now that this and similar critiques concerning Bukowski's portrayal of women don't do justice to what are really complex texts. It is not a purely masculine world that Bukowski depicts. The women and relationships presented in *Women* are more than simplistic stereotypes. For example, the women presented almost always have jobs and sometimes have careers. Huffzky is, however, more justified in her criticism that "there are no women in his novels with whom a thoughtful female reader can identify positively." But this must be seen in a larger context. While Huffzky is correct in what she says about the absence of positive women characters (though there are exceptions, such as Laura in *Women*), what has to be grasped is that there are few characters generally, male or female, with whom an intelligent reader, male or female, can identify. As Bukowski remarked to Sean Penn: "Sure I make women look bad sometimes, but I make men look bad too. I make *myself* look bad"

214

(96). At times we may identify with certain aspects of Henry Chinaski: his anti-authoritarian stance vis-à-vis bosses and bureaucracy and his self-deprecation and irony are attractive qualities. But those are, especially in *Women,* only moments. We do not identify with Henry Chinaski in his behavior towards women.

What Bukowski has achieved here is a kind of Brechtian "Verfremdung," the "playing in quotation marks" (17). As Brecht explained in "A Dialogue About Acting":

> Oughtn't the actor then try to make the man he is representing understandable? Not so much the man as what takes place. What I mean is: if I choose to see Richard III I don't want to feel myself to be Richard III, but to glimpse this phenomenon in all its strangeness and incomprehensibility.
>
> (27)

In Bukowski, the reader's subjectivity has not been captured through empathy but is rather alienated and this facilitates a critical analysis of the protagonist's behavior. Reading Bukowski in this way, without any preconceptions based on a reputation that he has long outgrown, I think we can see him questioning (sometimes, granted, in spite of himself) rather than advocating, the attitudes and behavior with which he has long been (mistakenly) identified.

CHAPTER EIGHT:
CONNECTIONS:
FANTE—HAMSUN—MAHLER

The critic Harold Bloom's ideas in *The Anxiety of Influence* concerning specific aspects of a poet's relation to his predecessors are useful in that they suggest a number of ways in which writers may actively engage earlier texts. But although Bloom's ignoring of history seems misguided, his suggestion that a later writer can use a specific text of an earlier writer but change its thrust ("swerve") as well as the idea that both earlier and later writers can share an impulse, a stance towards society ("daimon") are useful for framing Bukowski's relation to predecessors. Bukowski has used specific texts of earlier novelists but changed the thrust of those texts because history required such changes; his impulse, his "daimon," was similar to that of the earlier writers but changed historical circumstances forced him to realize that impulse in a radically different way.

In numerous passages in his writings, both in his own person and through his alter ego Henry Chinaski, as well as in interviews, Bukowski has enumerated influences on his writing. The most extended such list comes in a letter to Loss Glazier:

> I'm not all that isolated. I've had my crutches: F. Dos, Turgenev, some of Celine, some of Hamsun, most of John Fante, a great deal of Sherwood Anderson, very early Hemingway, all of Carson McCullers, the longer poems of Jeffers; Nietzsche and Schopenhauer; the style of Saroyan without the content; Mozart, Mahler, Bach, Wagner, Eric Coates; Mondrian; e.e.

cummings and the whores of east Hollywood; Jack Nicholson; Jackie Gleason; Charlie Chaplin, early, Baron Manfred von Richthofen; Leslie Howard; Bette Davis; Max Schmeling; Hitler . . . D. H. Lawrence, A. Huxley and the old bartender with the cadmium red face in Philly . . . And there was a particular actress whose name I can no longer think of, who I consider to be, has been the most beautiful woman of our times. She drank herself to death . . .

(109–110)

This is a fascinating list. A detailed analysis would reveal how accurate a summation it is, that is, how wide and varied have been the cultural practices upon which Bukowski has drawn, and would also lay to rest any notion of Bukowski as a "naive" artist, as well as the occasionally stated characterization of him as anti- intellectual. The linking together of disparate categories (novelists, short-story writers, poets, philosophers, composers, musicians, artists, movie actors, TV actors, athletes, politicians and anonymous individuals) as well as the modulations from one category to another reflect Bukowski's aversion to conceptual pigeon-holing. While some of the references might seem facetious or exaggerated and, in the case of Hitler, thrown in to shock, this is not really the case (with the possible partial exception of this last). Some of the names mentioned, such as Dostoyevsky, Anderson and Hemingway, seem obvious and, in the case of the last two, hard to escape in an American writer born in 1920; others, like Turgenev, Celine, McCullers, Nietzsche, Jeffers, Schopenhauer and Lawrence are no surprise either; but among the writers John Fante and Knut Hamsun stand out, not just, as here, for being mentioned, but also for the many times Bukowski refers to them positively.

Fante

Of the two, surely the mention of Fante is the most striking, the writer the general reader is least likely to know. Yet to readers of Bukowski there is no surprise. While Dostoyevsky, for example, may be mentioned more often than either Hamsun or Fante, the latter is the author most passionately praised. Bukowski told William Packard, "John Fante had the line too and he was the first who knew how to let passion enter in, emotion, in without letting it destroy the concept" (323). When Henry Chinaski, the protagonist of Bukowski's third novel, *Women* is asked in an interview, "Who was your favorite author?" he replies

> "Fante."
> "Who?"
> "John F-a-n-t-e. *Ask the Dust, Wait Until Spring, Bandini.*"
> "Where can we find his books?"
> "I found them in the main library, downtown, Fifth and Olive, isn't it?"
> "Why did you like him?"
> "Total emotion. A very brave man."
>
> (200)

The poem "the passing of a great one," commemorating Fante's death in 1983, begins, "he was the only living writer I ever met who I truly / admired . . ." (Y 147) and much of the poem "suggestion for an arrangement" is about Fante and makes reference to his dying diabetic and blind:

> I told him one time that
> the gods were punishing him because
> he wrote so
> well.
>
> I hope I never write that
> well . . . .
>
> (WT, 158–59)

"The wine of forever," another poem in the same collection, remarked on "Fante's pure and magic / emotions" (149). Bukowski dedicated his 1981 collection, *Dangling in the Tournefortia*, to Fante and wrote a preface to the 1980 reissue of Fante's second novel, *Ask the Dust* (first published in 1939). Indeed, the revival of interest in Fante's work is in part owing to Bukowski's advocacy.° Although everyone may not share Bukowski's enthusiasm for Fante, his positive response needs to be analyzed, not only because of the working-class sensibility that informs that response but because of Bukowski's claim of the great influence Fante's writing had on his own work.°

Fante (1909–1983), like Bukowski, dealt with the problems of first-generation Americans: the American Dream, generational conflict, class and race, as well as with the issues of women and sex. But Fante's general acceptance of conventional values (in one sense an understandable result of the hard times of the 30s, where material survival was a pressing problem) and his inability to sufficiently distance himself from his alter ego protagonist resulted in problematic and at times overwrought books, while Bukowski's more dialectical treatment produced a more distanced and subtle work.

In a sense, Bukowski has willfully "misread" (to use Bloom's term) Fante and set about "correcting" him because at first glance Fante would seem an unappealing writer for Bukowski to emulate. The most striking difference is the difference in values between the two writers' creations. Arturo Bandini, Fante's alter-ego protagonist of the early novels expressed the same values that were later reflected in Fante's own career where the lure of screenplay money proved too great for him. (For thirty years, from 1940 to 1970, Fante published no fiction with the exception of the short novel *Full of Life.* °) Bukowski/Chinaski, on the other hand, refused to accept a conventional middle-class existence, preferring the "freedom" of the Post Office while establishing himself as a writer. Yet the intensity of Bukowski's positive response in the face of the marked differences in the two authors' values and careers suggests that it is worthwhile examining the connection between them and it is in comparing them that one becomes aware of Bukowski's achievements in "rewriting" Fante.

In his "Preface" to the reissue of *Ask the Dust* Bukowski relates that as "a young man, starving and drinking and trying to be a writer . . . nothing that I read related to me or the streets or the people about me" (5). Finally, after trying a number of books in different areas: religion ("a vast bog"), philosophy ("a couple of bitter Germans who cheered me for a while"), mathematics, geology and surgery and not being sustained, he found *Ask the Dust* and he was

> like a man who had found gold in the city dump . . . here, at last, was a man who was not afraid of emotion. The humor and the pain were intermixed with a superb simplicity. The beginning of that book was a wild and enormous miracle to me. . . . [John Fante] was to be a lifetime influence on my writing. . . .
> Yes, Fante had a mighty effect on me . . .Fante was my God.
> (6)°

Bukowski's positive response to a novel whose protagonist is in a plight similar to his own at the time he read it—jobless, woman-less and with a few days left on the rent—is not hard to understand. While the real source of the appeal lies deeper than any similarities in the immediate situations of protagonist and reader, the similarity in roots only underscores the difference in destination.

What Bukowski said he found in Fante, and what he himself actually achieved in similar areas, bear examination. The "total emotion," the "pure and magic / emotions" that he so admired in the older writer, he carefully side-stepped in his own fiction and in doing so also for the most part avoided a sentimentality that mars Fante's writing; on the other hand, the humor he found in Fante he heightened so successfully in his own novels (and this would not have been possible without the lack of sentimentality) that it constitutes one of his primary achievements. But these changes are the result of the changed historical conditions in which Bukowski wrote. The effects of the social changes of the 1960s, noted in the last chapter, resulted in Henry Chinaski being very different from Arturo Bandini; Chinaski's emotions are distinctly "impure" in that they have been socially mediated as Bandini's "pure" (really, solipsistic) emotions have not. Bukowski has also made of Chinaski a working stiff, but a working stiff of a very different sort than Bandini feared becoming in the 1930s.

Ask the Dust is Fante's second novel. Written in a relatively plain, realist style, it deals with the attempts of a young, working-class Italian-American to establish himself as a writer, and to establish a relationship with a woman. The plot is slight and the interest of the novel comes from the depiction of the psyche of the novel's protagonist and his reaction to his rather circumscribed life and straitened circumstances. Arturo Bandini is the son of immigrants. (A similar situation exists in Bukowski's novels, as Henry Chinaski's father is native-born but his mother is German.) Both Fante's Italian-American and Bukowski's German-American families are Roman Catholic but the sexual guilt so pervasive in Fante is mostly lacking in Bukowski. In both writers there are tremendous Oedipal conflicts which in Fante results from the son's ambivalence toward the father (indeed, Bandini's desire for his father's affection and approval seems almost a symbol for a larger acceptance by society, a dynamic absent from Bukowski's work) and ends in reconciliation; in Bukowski the intensity of this conflict is heightened and reconciliation ruled out.

The acceptance of his traditional nuclear family—in spite of its clearly disastrous effects in his own case—in much of Fante's work mirrors Bandini's capitulation to conventional values. ° For Henry Chinaski, on the other hand, the family appears as the root of all evil and while, for instance, the protagonist of *Post Office* marries, and fathers a child, it is with different women and the child is born out of wedlock. In the subsequent novels marriage and/or fatherhood are sometimes presented positively and sometimes not but the family as a whole is never characterized positively and in fact (with the exception of *Ham on Rye*) families are rarely depicted. °

Both Fante and Bukowski portray protagonists who want to become writers and who undergo a period of suffering for their art. But Fante and his fictional alter ego seem to have been betrayed by succumbing to the appeal of the American Dream while Bukowski and Chinaski, with their close to fifteen years at the Post Office, were not. This becomes evident when Bandini unreservedly embraces the culture of consumption and status. In the first chapter of *Ask the Dust*, he thinks to himself: "I have seen golf clubs on Sixth Street in the Spalding window that make me hungry just to grip them. I have grieved for a necktie like a holy man for indulgences," a longing it would be hard to imagine Henry Chinaski cherishing, for whom clothes are one among many "cons." "You know," he remarks in an unusually direct address to the reader in *Factotum*, "I'm not a clothes man. Clothes bore me. They are terrible things, cons . . . " (132). In Bukowski's work, wearing a tie is the authorial kiss of death. ° The extent to which Bandini is held prisoner to convention is in stark contrast to Chinaski's rejection of it. When one reads such statements of Bandini's as those just quoted, one wonders where the appeal lay for the future creator of Henry Chinaski.

Both Fante and Bukowski treat the issue of class, and here, too, their responses diverged greatly. Fante, of the working-class and starting out in the 30s, might have taken to writing proletariat fiction. "Helen, Thy beauty is to me—," one of Fante's best stories, treats Filipino working-class life in and around Los Angeles and he "often thought of writing a longer work about the Filipino experience in California" (F/M, 145). An ambivalence—when not outright refusal—with respect to working-class solidarity, is sometimes evident in his novels. At one point in *Ask the Dust*, Bandini visits an acquaintance, Benny Cohen:

> He had a wooden leg with a little door in it. Inside the door were marijuana cigarettes. He sold them for fifteen cents apiece. He also sold newspapers, the *Examiner* and the *Times*. He had a room piled high with copies of *The New Masses*. Maybe he saddened me as always with his grim horrible vision of the world tomorrow. Maybe he poked his stained fingers under my nose and cursed me for betraying the proletariat from which I came. Maybe, as always, he sent me trembling out of his room and down the dusty stairs to the fog-dimmed street, my fingers itching for the throat of an imperialist. Maybe, and maybe not; I don't remember.
>
> (37–38)

While the purposeful vagueness reflects Bandini's ambivalence, the presentation of the "radical" as something of a freak leaves little doubt as to where Bandini's ultimate sympathies lie (though he has a bad conscience about it). There is, at times, a strong impulse in Fante (as also in Henry Miller and perhaps for similar reasons) to avoid history completely. There is the implication that by narrowly focussing on the individual, his thoughts, impulses, feelings, the historical can somehow be eluded. This impulse is present in Bukowski, too; however, it not only became weaker in the course of his development as a writer but because of his focus on a distinctly historical category—work—it never had the effect on his writing that it does in *Ask the Dust*.

In part, the lack of class solidarity in that novel results from the prominence given to the protagonist's attempts to succeed as a writer. Bukowski, too, does not depict a protagonist in solidarity with his class. Yet the important thing to note is that Bukowski, (though also "apolitical"), in his emphasis on work in *Post Office* and *Factotum,* as well as in the lesser importance he gives to his protagonist's struggle for artistic success, presented, *malgré lui,* a critical representation of social life from a working-class perspective—wrote, in one sense, socialist problem novels—whereas Fante's avoidance of this topic in *Ask the Dust* serves to isolate his character even further than his own desires already do. All these issues had an appeal, especially for the young Bukowski. (Had he written novels in his twenties they might well have had more in common with Fante's than did the novels he eventually wrote in his fifties.) But they are issues which he treated differently than Fante did by substantially rewriting Fante. In another respect, however, the relationship is more complex.

The primary attraction of the older author lay in two closely related areas, one formal, the other related to content. First was the fact that *Ask the Dust* was written in the first person; the second receives added impetus from the first: the detailed depiction of a young man's confused and ambivalent attempts to establish a relationship with a woman and Fante's unusual (for the times) frankness in the portrayal of sex. In several ways Fante was breaking new ground in the American novel and thus had no predecessors to serve as guide or model.° Like the young Bukowski a few years later, Fante may well have felt that nothing he was reading was applicable to his own situation, that his experience was not being depicted in contemporary fiction.° Although writers like Dreiser and Lewis did reflect some of what Fante undoubtedly felt about American society, they were of a previous generation, handicapped by the morality of their times in depicting sexuality and unappealing, also, by virtue of the "objectivity" implicit in their choice of the third person for their narratives.

Fante's novel is noteworthy for several reasons (not the least of which is the way in which it runs so counter to its times). There is not only no suggestion of working-class solidarity or even sympathy but there is also very little in the way of ordinary human contact. The solitary man alone in his room, a recurrent image in Bukowski's writings, appears in Fante as well. This isolation and the first-person narrative produce the novel's extreme subjectivity, and connect it to Hamsun's *Hunger* as well as *Factotum*. At times, it barely seems anchored in an actual social world, held there only by Fante's realist style and Bandini's attempts to form a relationship with the waitress Camilla Lopez. The intensity that the solitary and insecure Bandini brings to this

224

relationship (or would-be relationship, since it is a relationship shaped by his inability to relate) is striking. Yet another noteworthy aspect of the novel is its treatment of women and male-female relationships. Along with Bandini's desire for a relationship with a woman there is also a hostility to women so extreme as to border on misogyny, manifested in the relationship with Camilla.

It is clear that Bandini hates Camilla because she is a woman, since his antipathy arises almost before he has even spoken to her. Indeed, the intensity of his emotions is almost infantile. The "total emotion" that Bukowski so admired results from Fante's inability to treat a conflict productively by achieving some distance through mediating his character's reactions, while the avoidance of this pitfall is one of Bukowski's major achievements. Bukowski is drawn to Bandini because Bandini seems to be acting with no regard for the consequences of his behavior, as if he is unconstrained by the world. For reasons that Bukowski's novel *Ham on Rye* made clear, the young Chinaski harbored similar emotions. Women embodied all that he could not have, not just by virtue of their sexuality but because the "acquisition" of that sexuality represented an achievement by the male, a sign of power, almost an existential status, that continually eluded Chinaski. The desire for these things, but also the recognition of what the lure of women involved, the loss of independence (something precious to the young Chinaski who had little of it in his life, especially his family life), find an outlet in denigrating the object that is both desired and feared. At the same time, the mature Bukowski recognizes that things are no longer that simple. The very different social era in which Bukowski wrote his novels did not permit of a protagonist like Bandini. History, in the form of the women's movement, had changed the ground rules. As a result the hint of irony that is occasionally present in Fante, undergoes a quantum leap in Bukowski as will be made clear in a moment by comparing two episodes. History caused Bukowski's "daimon" to veer quite abruptly in rewriting Fante's book.

Bandini feels threatened by women at the same time that he is attracted to them, and thus the issue of control—of power—becomes primary. Himself a poor first-generation American,

225

Bandini projects his feelings of inferiority onto Camilla and manages to achieve some leverage in terms of race and economic status, thus reinforcing her "inherent" inferiority as a woman.° When Bandini first meets Camilla in the Columbia Buffet, he tries to get her attention to complain about the coffee she has served him. After a glance, she ignores him, "looks at him vaguely," and then suddenly laughs, "mysteriously," but, Bandini assumes, at him:

> But I understood her laughter. It was for me. She was laughing at me. There was something about my appearance, my face, my posture, something about me sitting there that had amused her, and as I thought of it I clenched my fist and considered myself with angry humiliation.
>
> (35)

He cannot really understand why she is laughing at him. He "began to sneer, watched her closely and sneered" and is soon "grateful" to have something to sneer about:

> The girl moved like a dancer, her strong silk legs gathering bits of sawdust as her tattered shoes glided over the marble floor.
>   Those shoes, they were huaraches, the leather thongs wrapped several times around her ankles. They were desperately ragged huaraches; the woven leather had become unraveled. When I saw them I was very grateful, for it was a defect about her that deserved criticism. She was tall and straight-shouldered, a girl of perhaps twenty, faultless in her way, except for her tattered huaraches. And so I fastened my stare on them. . . . This had a powerful effect upon her. Gradually her pirouetting and dancing subsided. . . . She was embarrassed, and once I saw her glance down quickly and examine her feet, so that in a few minutes she no longer laughed; instead there was grimness in her face, and finally she was glancing at me with bitter hatred.
>
> (35–36)

The tattered huaraches are the perfect metonym for her inferiority because they represent both her race and her low economic status. (Later, they become strictly synecdochic in the letter where Bandini addresses Camilla as "Dear Ragged Shoes.") They function to stigmatize her. When Camilla finally comes over to Bandini's table, he says, "Maybe this isn't coffee after all. . . .

Maybe it's just water after they boiled your filthy shoes in it"
(36–37). The extent to which Bandini is prey to a diffuse hostility
in no way related to Camilla (note the quasi-reflexive: "I . . .
pleased me very much") becomes clear at the end of the incident:

> Before I left I did something that pleased me very much. I took
> the five cents from my pocket and placed it on the table. Then
> I spilled half the coffee over it. She would have to mop up the
> mess with her towel. . . . At the door . . . I nodded at the spilled
> coffee. Then I tossed my fingers in a salute of farewell and
> walked into the street. Once more I had a good feeling.
>
> (37)

In passages such as these we can see the appeal that Fante had
for the young, bitter and alienated Charles Bukowski: "Here at
last was a man who was not afraid of emotion," and to the writer
Henry Chinaski who liked Fante for his "total emotion." It is the
self-destructive, consequences-be-damned attitude that appeals
to Bukowski.

Yet Bandini's infantile, at times pre-verbal, responses to
women are precisely what Bukowski has in most cases been able
to overcome in his own novels. In Fante very little is worked
through, mediated, treated ironically; there is almost no distance
between protagonist and implied author. The almost paralysing
fear of women that runs through *Ask the Dust*, and may perhaps
be said to constitute its theme (as, though less intensely, it does
of *Women*) and that produces its exaggerations has in Bukowski,
been transformed, treated with humor and irony, in *Factotum*,
and above all in *Women*. It should also be noted that Bukowski
is both with respect to women and generally speaking, remarkably free of racism.°

Bandini returns early the next morning and leaves a copy
of a magazine containing his first published story. He had first
autographed the story, then erased the autograph and substituted
the inscription: "To a Mayan Princess, from a worthless Gringo,"
then erased that and finally left the book for her at the Buffet
with:

> Dear Ragged Shoes,
> You may not know it, but last night you insulted the author
> of this story. Can you read? If so, invest fifteen minutes of your

time and treat yourself to a masterpiece. And next time, be careful. Not everyone who comes into this dive is a bum.

Arturo Bandini

(39)

When he returns the following day, Camilla apologizes for the bad coffee and buys him a beer, which Bandini proceeds to pour into a spittoon; then, in full view of the saloon she rips up the pages of the magazine with his story. He leaves the buffet and she rushes out after him, apologizes and asks him for a date for the next night. After a momentary "reconciliation," he calls her back and says, "[t]hose huaraches—do you have to wear them, Camilla? Do you have to emphasize the fact that you always were and always will be a filthy little greaser?" (44). Bandini's relentless racism underlines the extent to which the issue of power is *the* issue for Fante in the novel: the protagonist, feeling powerless in society (for reasons of class, it might be noted) needs a scapegoat and the more ways that the scapegoat allows him to claim superiority, the better.

At those moments when some kind of equilibrium—if only that of a truce—has been achieved, the need to assert himself by denigrating Camilla reasserts itself. Though Fante occasionally tries—after such scenes—to achieve some distance from his character, it is without much success. The emotional intensity of such scenes is too great and we are left with the impression that the narrator, the implied author, and perhaps even the historical author are not sufficiently differentiated. Though some efforts are made to explain Bandini's shifts in mood, it is not finally clear to him nor the reader why he acts as he does. The reasons for his behavior seem uniquely determined by his own complex history and relate little, if at all, to their object, Camilla, and being unmotivated in a literary sense, they are an indication of Fante's lack of control over his material. What Bukowski saw as "total"and "pure" emotion seems merely unmediated subjectivity.

This is especially clear in Fante's depiction of sex, because within the relationship sex provides an especially vivid field on which Bandini can play out his various fears and insecurities; indeed, it may have been this aspect of his work that led Henry Chinaski to characterize him as "a totally brave man." Yet it is also here where Bukowski has been successful in going beyond

228

Fante. One night, after Arturo and Camilla have gone for a swim and are lying nude on the beach:

> she kissed me, her lips wet and cool. We lay a long time and I was worried and afraid and without passion . . . I felt her waiting. I drew my hands over her belly and legs, felt my own desire, searched foolishly for my passion, strained for it while she waited, rolled and tore my hair and begged for it, but there was none, there was none at all . . . no lust, only fear of her, and shame and humiliation.
>
> (68)

Later in the novel Camilla tries again but with the same result. Upset at Bandini's rejection of her, Camilla pushes him away. Bandini then becomes angry and then, finally, aroused and so has

> the rapturous self-satisfaction, the delight to know that I could possess her now if I wished. But I did not wish it, for I had had my love. Dazzled I had been by the power and joy of Arturo Bandini. I released her, took my hand from her mouth, and jumped off the bed. . . . The big thing was proved. I could have had her. . . .
>
> (124–25)

In Fante, as in Bukowski, we have the denial of sexual pleasure to women as a source of the man's gratification (indeed even more gratifying than consummation), i.e., the use of sex as control. The oddly solipsistic situation in the scene just quoted where it is sufficient for Bandini to have an erection to feel himself a man is striking. The pleasure is as great as it is for Bandini because it is a sadistic pleasure more in tune with what he actually wants, to hurt and degrade Camilla. Twice, Bandini arouses and refuses to satisfy Camilla, only himself becoming aroused when angry at her. His eventual arousal is significant because it makes clear that Bandini could gratify Camilla if he wanted to.

I don't want, however, to deny either the power of such scenes, their originality, or their success in treating sex in ways that Henry Miller, for example, did not allow himself. The raw, exposed quality of Bandini is effectively depicted. Yet the novel as a whole suffers because Bandini is rarely as unself-conscious as here and ultimately lacks psychological awareness in such a way that we are sometimes tempted to assume that that lack is also the author's.

Another episode in the novel warrants discussion because of its striking similarities to and significant difference from Bukowski's work and as an extremely vivid example of just how Bukowski has achieved what his predecessor did not. Here a sexual consummation does take place, with a woman named Vera Rivken. (Although when Bandini finally consummates the relationship with Vera, he can do so only by pretending she is Camilla.) Vera, who virtually assaults Bandini, is presented as stigmatized, half crazy and Jewish (which from Fante's perspective may be seen as reinforcing the previous two stigmas).° Thus Martha, the fat woman who assaults Chinaski in *Factotum* and whose breath is described as "tast[ing] of onions and stale wine" (36), has been preceded by Vera Rivken whose mouth is described as "tasting of liverwurst on rye (82)" and just as Martha has "warts and big brown moles on her neck and cheeks" so Vera has "a birthmark or something, a burn, a seared place (88)" on her thighs. Vera aggressively pursues Arturo Bandini and provides him (as Martha does Chinaski) with his first sexual experience in the novel and, as in the later novel, the protagonist commodifies the interaction by leaving the woman money, although she had not solicited any.

While the dynamics of the two writers are similar, depicting the male protagonists' social and sexual anxieties, Bukowski, more aware of the source of the conflict, has achieved an ironic and humorous depiction of his protagonist. His subjectivity—shaped by the socio-historical pressures of the intervening years—is of a different order than Fante's. The thirty-five years that separate *Ask the Dust* from *Factotum,* have had their effect on the American male psyche. Perhaps the most dramatic instance of the change this psyche has undergone is in the difference in the depiction of the two protagonists' handling of their sexual anxiety. Bandini, after getting an erection, "jumps off the bed." Whereas Henry Chinaski, on being assaulted by Martha, though upset at losing control ("If I come, I thought desperately, I'll never forgive myself"), ejaculates and, it seems safe to conclude, forgives himself.

Hamsun

I was not Hamsun eating his own flesh in order to continue writing but I had a fair amount of travail.°

Bukowski's fiction intersects interestingly at a number of points with that of Knut Hamsun and, once again, Bukowski rewrites the earlier author in interesting ways. The extreme subjectivity of the protagonists of Hamsun's novels of the 1890s finds its echo in Henry Chinaski and the negative depiction of women that we find in Hamsun is not lacking in Bukowski. Yet, as with his rewriting of Fante, Bukowski's relationship to the earlier novelist—in spite of his enthusiasm for him—is more than unmitigated acceptance. In a specific, formal sense, and more generally, as well, Hamsun's first novel, *Hunger,* is extremely important for Bukowski. It provided the form for *Factotum* (the single most important book in Bukowski's career). At the same time, Bukowski significantly changed the content of that form and in so doing produced the unique novel that *Factotum* is in post-War American literature. Bukowski found in *Hunger* a model for his own second novel as, in Ian Watt's terms, "a kind of narrative metaphor which assists the imagination of the writer to find a pattern for his own observation of life" (255).

Hunger was published in Norway in 1890. According to Robert Ferguson, Hamsun's biographer, it "drew on the experiences he underwent during his two most desperate periods in Christiania in the winters of 1880–1881 and 1885–86, and probably also drew on the experiences of his winter in Chicago in 1886–87" (110). The protagonist is a young man living in Christiania (now Oslo) trying to become a successful writer. He is impoverished when the novel begins and the novel charts his further material and emotional decline, interrupted by a few relatively brief moments of minor financial and literary success. In the course of the novel he pawns some of his clothes, tries to pawn a ratty blanket and cuts off the buttons on his jacket in an attempt to pawn *them.* His days are spent walking around the city while carrying all his worldly possessions in a blanket, writing in public gardens and trying to stave off hunger by sucking on wood-shavings. Occasionally he sleeps in a forest outside the city; one night he manages to sleep in the city jail on the pretext of having lost the key to his room. Towards the end of the novel he lives gratis above a stable and tinsmith's shop. Once or twice an article he has written is accepted by a newspaper, or he manages a small loan from friends. At the end, having failed to make a go of it, he gets a job on a boat and ships out. Because the protagonist is so isolated from his surroundings, history plays only a small role in the novel and there is something of a timeless quality to it (even natural time is almost completely excluded—though mention is made of the increasing cold as the seasons change) and the starkness of the narrator's life, stripped of so much that typically informs the life of a novel's protagonist, especially a nineteenth-century novel, stands out as in relief.

Both a downward trajectory and an ahistorical quality are also important aspects of *Factotum*. Although Bukowski's novel takes place over a much greater span of time, the temporal feel of the two novels is similar. In no other novel of Bukowski's is history so little in evidence. *Factotum*, too, feels as if it's outside of time. Its attitude to history is so muted and subjective that it produced Bukowski's classic expression of the subjectivity of history: "At some point during one of our hellish nights World War II ended" (100).

The major similarity between the two novels is their protagonists' alienation—although perhaps marginalization is a better word because it suggests that the protagonists are still a part of, if peripheral to, society. What both Hamsun and Bukowski emphasize, and it is surely something that Bukowski responded to in the earlier novel, is the ambivalence that their protagonists feel vis-à-vis bourgeois society. Much of the power of Bukowski's writing in general stems from this ambivalence, from the fact that he does not completely reject American society. Were this not the case, the sympathy that the reader feels for Henry Chinaski would be significantly diminished. Such sympathy exists because—to varying degrees—many readers share Chinaski's attitude. The attempt of the protagonists of both *Hunger* and *Factotum* to keep up appearances helps to retain the reader's interest in them; it is the thin thread by which they maintain their social tie. Neither Hamsun nor Bukowski allows his protagonist to descend to the level of the protagonist of, for example, Jean Genet's *Thief's Journal*, who cares not at all what society thinks of him, indeed finds his definition in its rejection. Both protagonists are close to the sidelines, but still on the playing field. They make their criticism from within—not outside of—society. Yet neither do these characters want the consumerist life held out as the ultimate reward (as well as the ultimate justification) of their societies (in this being markedly different from Fante's Arturo Bandini). Chinaski and the protagonist of *Hunger* want to live their own lives, but as a part of society. The ambivalence that results from this bind is comically presented on the first page of *Factotum*:

> I had a cardboard suitcase that was falling apart. It had once been black but the black coating had peeled off and yellow cardboard was exposed. I had tried to solve that by putting black shoepolish over the exposed cardboard. As I walked along in the rain the shoepolish on the suitcase ran and unwittingly I rubbed black streaks on both legs of my pants as I switched the suitcase from hand to hand.
>
> (11)

As Chinaski tries to "solve" the problem of the worn cardboard suitcase, so Hamsun's hero buttons his coat so that people will not see that he has no vest (having pawned it) and has his bundle of meager possessions wrapped at a department store so people will not realize what it is he is carrying around with him. It would be hard to characterize the behavior of either as stemming from pride; to a certain extent they are bowing to convention, something neither completely rejects. The crucial dynamic, though, is ambivalence.

While the protagonists' refusal to accept the world of conventional careers results in their increasing marginalization, there is an important difference in how each author presents his protagonist's situation. In Hamsun, the narrator's refusal is tightly connected to an art-for art's sake moralism, a privileging of the artist's role in society not unusual in fin-de-siècle European literature. Hamsun's first book, *The Cultural Life of Modern America* (published while he was working on *Hunger*) reveals the moralism that underlies Hamsun's position. As *Hunger* was written shortly after his return from his second trip to the United States, Hamsun may even have been strengthened in his views by his American experiences. In *Cultural Life* much of his critique of the United States focuses on the unabashed materialism he finds rampant there, a common European criticism:

> The Americans are a commercial nation devoted to buying and selling, not an artistic or art-loving nation. Their minds respond immediately to any kind of sale or money transaction that comes their way; the spirit of art, on the other hand lies completely beyond their ken. . . . A true Yankee, one with the right national tastes, would much rather amuse himself with a patent report at the atheneum than attend a Wagner opera.
>
> (78)

In *Hunger*, this aestheticism results in Hamsun's emphasizing his protagonist's position as a writer to a far greater extent than Bukowski does in *Factotum*. This separates him from society and it is no accident that this is so. The protagonist's literary aspirations are emphasized to the point where we are told some of the things he is working on: "Crimes of the Future," a "consideration in three parts of philosophical Consciousness" or an essay on "freedom of the will" or a play on Jesus. In the end *Hunger* is an idealist novel and an (admittedly somewhat backhanded) plea for art for art's sake. In fact, the novel is about a man literally starving for his art.

Chinaski, on the other hand, is never in danger of starving, always has a roof over his head and spends most of the novel working. Indeed, the striking difference between the two novels is Chinaski's continued attachment to the labor market. In *Factotum*, though we are aware that Chinaski writes, and even gets a story published, this is quite peripheral to the all-engulfing problem of alienated labor. It is Bukowki's achievement to have created a novel in which the protagonist's despair is more extreme—and convincingly so—than that of Hamsun's protagonist, although his material existence is nowhere near as desperate. This is so because the despair of *Hunger*'s protagonist is remediable by a job while Chinaski's is not. Chinaski can get jobs, Hamsun's protagonist, for whatever reason, cannot. He makes very little effort to find a job and the one example we have—his attempt ot land a job as a bookkeeper with a grocery—fails through his own lack of persistence as well as because he misdates his letter of application, an ordinal and thus (for a bookkeeper) a cardinal sin. *Hunger* is a powerful novel but remains, for all its emphasis on the hard material fact of hunger, in the end, idealist, an (unusual, to be sure) expression of the *l'art pour l'art* world of the European fin de siècle as well as, in Ferguson's words, "one of the great novels of urban alienation, on a par with Kafka's *Castle*, Dostoyevsky's *Notes from the Underground*, and Rilke's *Notebooks of Malte Laurids Brigge*" (110). Hamsun said that he wanted to show how each person starves in a unique way and it is this emphasis on the individual detached from his social condition that is the strongest difference between the two novels.

The differences are underlined by the differences in the endings of *Hunger* and *Factotum*. Hamsun's protagonist's dilemma is solvable in one of two ways: either he can succeed as a writer, or he can get a job, and *Hunger* ends on a positive note with the protagonist getting a job on a ship. His hunger has ended for the present and for the immediate future and so his overall physical decline is arrested and his spiritual depression, if not at an end, seems to have bottomed out. The protagonist of *Hunger* had it within his power to end his marginalization by accepting society's terms. This is not true for the materialist Chinaski. At the end of *Factotum* Henry Chinaski is at his lowest spiritual and material ebb in the novel, with no sign of improvement in sight. He never seriously contemplates supporting himself as a writer and yet he cannot "accept" the jobs he gets. *His* demands are ultimately much more radical (because social in nature) than those of Hamsun's protagonist: he wants nothing less than a changed society:

> How in the hell could a man enjoy being awakened at 6:30 a.m. by an alarm clock, leap out of bed, dress, force-feed, shit, piss, brush teeth and hair, and fight traffic to get to a place where essentially you made lots of money for somebody else and were asked to be grateful for the opportunity to do so.
>
> (127)

Bukowski's genius was to take over Hamsun's "disinterested subject," strip him of his idealism and make him—however tenuously and unwillingly—a member of the working class. In *Factotum*, Bukowski materialized Hamsun's spiritual marginality of the 1890s into a material refusal of the 1970s.

Note on Orwell

While Hamsun's *Hunger* provided the frame for Bukowski's F*actotum*, George Orwell's *Down and Out in Paris and London* (1933) was the immediate impetus. As Bukowski told Robert Wennersten:

> "Now I can have the everyday humdrum thing of the alcohol-ic, low-class, as they call them, workers trying to make it. I got the idea, kind of, from *Down and Out in Paris and London*. I read that book and said, 'This guy thinks something has hap-pened to him? Compared to me, he just got scratched.' Not that it wasn't a good book, but it made me think that I might have something interesting to say along those same lines."
>
> (53–54)

Orwell's book of reportage forms a kind of middle term between *Hunger* and *Factotum*. In common with Hamsun's novel, the nar-rator suffers hunger, something Chinaski never does. The issue of the problem of appearances is something that runs through all three books, a function of their urban setting where the differ-ent social classes were increasingly mixing in public and thus the issue of status was introduced, and hence of appearance, at a more intense level than had been the case earlier. Orwell, describing his friend Boris, a white-Russian refugee looking for a job as a waiter in the Paris of the late 1920s (in a scene that may have been somewhere in Bukowski's mind as he wrote the opening scene of *Factotum*, quoted above), wrote that he

> tied his tie so that the holes did not show, and carefully stuffed the soles of his shoes with newspaper. Finally, when he was dressed, he produced an ink-bottle and inked the skin of his ankles where it showed through his socks.
>
> (23)

But what connects Orwell's book to Bukowski's most strongly and differentiates it from Hamsun's is the issue of work, of the job (and of finding a job). Perhaps the most interesting part of Orwell's book is the section narrating the one job he does get (and it is a job of the type that Chinaski might have gotten): dish-washer in a cheap restaurant. It is a horrible job, paying so little and consuming so much time that the dishwashers can barely attain to a conscious life outside of work, so much is their day engulfed by the job or recuperating from it. But this was the connection for Bukowski. He can be said, in *Factotum*, to have taken the horror of *Hunger*'s hunger and wedded it to the horror of the job in *Down and Out in Paris and London*.

Indeed, this explains an otherwise puzzling aspect of Bukowski's statement to Wennersten. He says that " '[t]his guy thinks something has happened to him? Compared to me, he just got scratched,' " and that he "kind of" "got the idea" from Orwell. He "*kind of* got the idea" because Orwell's focus was primarily on the down-and-out experience, of *not* working, whereas Bukowski's was on the work experience; on the other hand Orwell "just got scratched" because he only had the one horrible job whereas Bukowski had many. For Bukowski, it is almost as if work is worse than starving.

The material forces of society have become so productive that *Hunger*'s hunger and the travails of the tramps in *Down and Out in Paris and London* are not issues for the first-world proletariat with which Bukowski was concerned; along with the rise in productive capacity has come a rise in expectations. But Bukowski's novel is significant for having highlighted the alienation that remains, though the physical immiseration is rarely present.

Mahler

> My penis rose; she groaned, bit me. I screamed, grabbed her by the hair, pulled her off. I stood in the center of the room wounded and terrified. They were playing a Mahler symphony on the radio. Before I could move she was down on her knees and on me again. She gripped my balls mercilessly with both of her hands. Her mouth opened, she had me; her head bobbed, sucked, jerked. Giving my balls a tremendous yank while almost biting my pecker in half she forced me to the floor. Sucking sounds filled the room as my radio played Mahler.

Readers of Bukowski are aware of the many references to Western classical music in his writings: Bach, Mozart, Beethoven, Brahms, Mahler, Wagner, Shostakovich are all mentioned with some frequency.° Such mention figured in his writing as early as his first publication, the short story "Aftermath of a Lengthy Rejection Slip," which appeared in *Story* magazine in 1944 and contained a reference to Tchaikowsky's *Sixth Symphony*. Although other composers, and smaller-scale works, are occasionally mentioned, the emphasis is on symphonic music in the Austro-German tradition, the mainstay of western concert halls of the last one hundred and fifty years and of the classical recording industry, especially since the development of the long-playing record, and then stereo, both of which were especially conducive to the large scale, multi-movement works that form the core of this tradition.

As with his citation of writers, Bukowski does not often make reference to specific works or passages, but rather cites only the name, as a metonym: Mozart, Mahler, Beethoven etc. Hence, unlike in conventional citation, we are not meant to think of specific correspondences or analogies between the work cited and the context in which it is cited.° Rather, in Bukowski, the citation is meant to be no more than vaguely suggestive. Still, the very fact of a reference to high culture in what is often a marginalized, proletarian existence takes the reader aback.

In the passage from *Factotum* quoted above, a comico-vulgar scene is described, and twice in one paragraph we are told that the radio was playing Mahler. The effect is to distance the reader (and the protagonist) from the raw reality of the event described. These casual citations are not leitmotifs which suggest another, specific association which then adds a layer of meaning to the passage where they appear. They are peripheral, always heard on a small radio, never the sole focus of attention but always accompanying another activity.° The citations serve to *distract*, to prevent a suggestion of depth, rather than, as with traditional citation to deepen the meaning of what is going on by connecting it to another text.

There are reasons for the modest technology beyond Henry Chinaski's early poverty. In the first place, a more impressive device would suggest a stable middle-class existence for Henry Chinaski which would be in strong contrast to his semi-nomadic marginality. Even in *Women,* a depiction of a materially more settled and successful era in Chinaski's life, no mention is made of his possessing a stereo system: it may be anything from Haydn to Mahler; no matter, Henry Chinaski hears it over a small radio. Nor, in the roughly fifty-five years covered by the four novels does he ever attend a symphony concert, not even the cheap

238

and accessible Hollywood Bowl. This is another expression of Chinaski's aversion to the group, be it even the collective reception of an artwork.°

In Bukowski's writings the three most frequently mentioned composers are Beethoven (48), Mozart (25) and Mahler (24).° The mention of the first two comes as no surprise. Mozart and Beethoven (along with Bach, whom Bukowski mentions nine times) would certainly be expected and any surprise the many mentions of Beethoven cause is owing only to the clichéd aura, that, at this late date, almost inevitably attaches to the name, so complete in the public mind is its identification with "high-brow" music.

But the references to Mahler are decidedly marked, especially here in *Factotum*. In the first place, it seems anachronistic in the context of a novel which takes place in the 1940s. (The passage above takes place during World War II.) Mahler's reputation was then at a low-point and, although the chauvinism that had resulted in the banning of German music from American concert halls during World War I was nothing like as extreme during World War II, it was unlikely that Mahler's music would have been performed at that time.° For that reason, and also because the extreme length of Mahler's music did not lend itself to 78 rpm recordings, it is also unlikely that Henry Chinaski or Bukowski in the actual events that somewhere underlie the fictional account would have been listening to a recording of a Mahler symphony. Hence it is a fair assumption that Bukowski, writing in the 1970s, is projecting the composer's huge contemporaneous critical and popular success back into the milieu of his protagonist in the early 1940s.

While I would not say that Mahler was directly an influence on Bukowski, there are some interesting ways in which the Mahler *Gestalt* connects with Bukowski's work; much that is written about Mahler's music might also be said of Bukowski's writing with respect to both form and content. It is not accidental that Mahler is mentioned far more often than one would expect in Bukowski's writings and that there is an underlying sympathy in the two artists that—elucidated—throws an interesting light on Bukowski's work.

Mahler, I suggest, functions as a metonym, embodying a whole

239

range of connotations. He is the neurotic, deracinated, ethnic (Jewish) outsider. He is both the end of the Viennese symphonic tradition that began with Haydn, and also distinctly a modern whose achievement was not completely recognized until a half century after his death. With Bruckner, he is the only major composer who almost completely devoted his artistic efforts to the symphony, whose development he completed. He is both the culmination of that form and the beginning of its decline; after him it had nothing like the prominence in the works of major composers that it had before. He changed it radically by emphasizing its programmatic nature—its "narrative" possibilities—(four of his nine completed symphonies have choral and/or vocal sections), in a sense making it less "pure" a form.

One of the aspects of both Mahler and his music that a number of writers on the subject note is their concern with the outsider. (Lea entitled his book, *Gustav Mahler: Man on the Margin*.) A Jew who later converted to Roman Catholicism, Mahler grew up in a culturally and linguistically German city in Bohemia, one of the Czech Historic Lands. As his family were assimilated Jews, there was no national or ethnic tradition with which he could specifically identify, though all these aspects influenced his work. As a result, as Burnett James wrote: "All his life Gustav Mahler felt himself an alien and an outcast, an outsider in all senses of the term" (19). Adorno suggested that "The instinct of the pedler's grandson, even if despairing and illusory, was . . . on the side of those on the margins of society" and that "Mahler's music sympathized with the asocial."° His political actions as an adult revealed sympathy with the oppressed. According to Lea, "two rare recorded political actions are his vote for Viktor Adler [Viennese socialist leader] in 1901 and his accompanying a workers' procession on May Day in 1905" (27). While it is hard to imagine Bukowski not being aware of at least some of these aspects of Mahler's biography, the primary question is what it is about Mahler's music that appeals to Bukowski?°

It is, I think the extreme subjectivity expressed in Mahler's music that fascinates Bukowski: the split between subject and object, society and individual. Adorno, though a Hegelian, did not agree with the identity principle and neither (in Adorno's view) did Mahler. As he wrote: "All the breaches are the inscription of truth." Mahler's symphonizing "nowhere patches

240

together the split between subject and object; rather it falls to pieces itself rather than present the illusion of a successful reconciliation" (15). In Mahler "the split becomes a formal law" (24) and this *parti pris* for the individual, as opposed to the totality, appears in the increased prominence given to individual orchestral voices; instrumental voices that, in Haydn, Mozart or Beethoven "knew their place" forget it in Mahler.° In part, this accounted for the great length of Mahler's symphonies. (Mahler substituted duration for intensification and condensation," a procedure strikingly similar to Bukowski's own poetic practice.°) The great length of his symphonies was potentially a problem because too prominent a role for the individual would destroy the form of the whole, and thus the whole itself. This "formal destruction" results from the content of the music:

> He who admits the lower as a stratum of composition is composing from the bottom to the top. This type of symphonic composition does not recognize a command of any totality, except one arising from the chronological layers of its individual fields.
>
> ("Gedenkrede," 123)

This dilemma was solved by Mahler in that he "either experimented with the individual at such great length that a whole came out of it. Or he consciously, artfully avoided the rounded whole" (*Mahler*, 72).

Both these devices aptly characterize Bukowski's procedure in his successful works, both poetry and prose,° where the refusal to deny the break, to assume the existence of a totality that doesn't exist inevitably results in a recognition, at times a privileging, of the marginal, the outside(r). Bukowski refuses any totality, and it would be hard to conceive of a more apt description of his poetic process than "experimenting with the individual. . . ." This lack of a constructed meaning, the refusal to paper over the split between subject and society (and thus the a priori construction of the marginal) resulted for Mahler in what has been viewed as a predisposition to "banality."

This charge of triviality or banality was often levelled against Mahler (as it has been against Bukowski and Hamsun, too.) But, as James wrote, "Mahler's 'banalities' were conscious, deliberate,

241

put in for specific purposes" (37). "Banality" functions in a similar way in Bukowski. In one sense a novel like *Factotum* can be seen to consist almost solely of "banalities." Certainly the events are ordinary enough. Both Mahler and Bukowski refuse to accept the seamless identity of subject and object in an antagonistic and split society and thereby acknowledge the individual and the outsider. Mahler's music can be viewed as being in "bad taste" only because he introduced elements into the "society" of symphonic tradition that hadn't been there before, and thus the architectonic, overarching and clearly delineated form of the symphony—the sonata form—was drastically altered; so, too, did Bukowski refuse the rounded form in both his poetry (the organic poem of the New Critics) and his novels, although Bukowski (especially in his fiction) was less the formal innovator than Mahler.

Mahler, the complex composer, full of ambivalence, mixture of romantic irony and modernist (and even post-modernist) techniques, an artist who (like Bukowski) is drawn to the sentimental and unmediated, to the naive and the raw in life and who refuses to deny the split not only between the individual and society but also within the individual himself between the material and the spiritual, but who also can rarely prevent himself from parodying it and distancing himself from it is here the composer whom Henry Chinaski is listening to on the radio while unmediated life unfolds and he, too, is unable to mediate a (psychical) split.° The scene would be less successful—less comic, less subtle —were there no mention of the classical music, and the specific mention of Mahler, emphasized by the second, metonymic reference, is especially apt because it is Mahler, and not a more predictable choice.

EXCURSUS:
GLEASON

Speech is one of the most important aspects of a novel. The speech of Bukowski's characters works as much as any other single factor to create the impression of realism that they possess. Speech and dialogue are surely one of Bukowski's most impressive achievements; yet in and of itself the language his characters speak is unremarkable, not, indeed, very marked linguistically. Bukowski rarely uses speech, as for example Dickens does, either dialectically or idiolectically, to give us an idea of a character's social environment or personality. In fact speech in the novels is almost completely free of slang and its strongest colloquial elements are its vulgarisms. What is most striking in Bukowski's use of speech, specifically dialogue, is the dramatic concision it undergoes in what I call "the routine," the humorous, formulaic, stereotyped, dialogic interaction derived from some classic American comedians.

On more than one occasion, Bukowski has indicated that one of his influences was Jackie Gleason,° most emphatically in a remark to Neeli Cherkovski:

> "I always liked Gleason's comedy, the truthful, long slow murder of humanity, filled with a Brooklynese madness of poor people pitted against the bosses, always about to be fired. Jesus, how could I help but identify?"°

Such an influence is particularly visible in the form of the routines that were a large part of *The Honeymooners* and that play an important role in the dialogue of Bukowski's novels. In the classic American comic routines (deriving from vaudeville) of

Groucho and Chico Marx, Bud Abbott and Lou Costello, Ralph Kramden and Ed Norton, and Ralph and Alice Kramden, there are certain unvarying structural aspects. (Otherwise they wouldn't be "routines.") There is always one character who is naive and views things in a narrower context than his or her more sophisticated partner who sees the larger picture. While the viewer perceives the ironic nature of the relationship and is aware of where the exchange is heading, he is caught up in the procedure; the foreordained resolution only adds the reassuring pleasure of the familiar. At the same time, if we know, generally, where it is heading, we never really know specifically how we (they) will get there. Hence there is an element of discovery and the pleasure of surprise.

Another appealing feature of the routine is that not only is the audience implicated through its superior knowledge but it bonds the speakers as well; it presupposes a community of interests. It could not exist without the (tacit) agreement of the "straight man" to be a part of, and party to it and because of this it has an air of camaraderie about it: whatever differences may exist, there is also basic agreement. But the routine is fundamentally constraining. It cannot last very long and thus the very interchanges which compose it have to be short lest it become too diffuse and amorphous (and thus complex) to control. An essential part of its structure precludes any kind of serious dialogue in the sense of an open-ended investigation of a topic. It is the triumph of form over content. It is just this constraint, the determined quality of the individuals caught in the meshes of the routine that constitutes the appeal for Bukowski and allows him to use it to such advantage in the novels. Two examples of how Bukowski uses this popular form to deal with a serious issue while at the same time limiting its treatment occur in the middle of *Factotum*. Henry Chinaski and Manny, a fellow employee at an auto parts warehouse, are racing through traffic immediately after work to try to get to Hollywood Park in time to place bets on the last race.

> "Shit, a red light!"
> "Fuck it. Go on through."
> "I'm going to hang a right." Manny abruptly switched lanes and cut right at the signal. "Watch out for squad cars."

> "Right." Manny could really tool that thing. If he could bet
> horses like he drove, Manny was a winner.
> "You married, Manny?"
> "No way."
> "Women?"
> "Sometimes. But it never lasts."
> "What's the problem?"
> "A woman is a full-time job. You have to choose your
> profession."
> "I suppose there is an emotional strain."
> "Physical too. They want to fuck night and day."
> "Get one you like to fuck."
> "Yes, but if you drink or gamble they think it's a put-down
> of their love."
> "Get one who likes to drink, gamble and fuck."
> "Who wants a woman like that?"
>
> (104–05)

Serious issues are being treated here, if somewhat defensively.
The routine's form helps disguise what is going on, and part of
the ideological-novelistic raison d'être for the routine's use is to
facilitate the acceptance of the routine's (not to mention the novel's) latent content.

The surface content of the exchange is that of a casual, light-
hearted treatment of relationships between men and women;
but while its form, especially its punchline-like ending, aims to
persuade us to accept its content with something less than complete seriousness, allows us to shrug it off if we want to, there
are indications in the language that Bukowski is quite serious
here. This and the routine that follows in the novel (quoted below) treat several themes of importance in Bukowski's writing:
human relationships, masculinity and work. Here the theme is
relationships between men and women (and between men) and
what it means to be a man. Certainly the name of the partner
in the routine is not accidental nor is the choice of the verb:
"Manny could really tool that thing . . . Manny was a winner."
As a noun "tool" is a common enough slang word for penis. What
is being talked about here is what it takes to be a successful man
in our society. This is reinforced by Chinaski's next questions
about Manny's marital status and sexual interests.

In the second routine, two pages later, it is relationships
among men and work relationships that are the subject of the

exchange. Manny and Chinaski have succeeded in getting to the race track in time to place their bets on the last race. The next day, after finding out where they went, their co-workers ask them to place bets for them.

> Some of the guys asked if we would take bets out for them. I said I didn't know. At noon Manny and I went to a bar for lunch.
> "Hank, we take their bets."
> "Those guys don't have any money—all they have is the coffee and chewing gum money their wives give them and we don't have time to mess around with the two dollar windows."
> "We don't bet their money, we keep their money."
> "Suppose they win?"
> "They won't win. They always pick the wrong horse. They have a way of always picking the wrong horse."
> "Suppose they bet our horse."
> "Then we know we've got the wrong horse."
> "Manny, what are you doing working in auto parts?"
> "Resting. My ambition is handicapped by laziness."
>
> (106–7)

Interestingly, Chinaski plays the role of the naive figure: Chico, Costello, Norton vis-à-vis Ralph, Ralph vis-à-vis Alice. This bears on how the exchange functions in the novel. Perhaps most important is the question of whether we are meant to identify with Manny and the views he expresses. It would seem that Henry Chinaski does so, or at least admires Manny for his shrewdness. The surface moral of the two dialogues is the proposition that to be a (successful) man means objectifying others in order to exploit them. Such a view—openly stated—would hold little attraction for most readers. The appeal of Bukowski, and of what is going on here, is subtler. It is important that this worldview be projected onto Manny, the other, while Chinaski is depicted as harboring doubts about its morality. It is consonant with Chinaski's generally passive stance towards people and the world that he would never initiate such a project on his own. Secondly, Bukowski has taken a complex issue about which he (and not only he) is ambivalent and "resolved" this ambivalence, at least in terms of the novel, by splitting up the two positions and projecting the one onto Manny while leaving the other, more socially acceptable view to Chinaski; *Chinaski* is concerned, not exploitative.

The form of the routine is useful in two ways. First, the snappy back-and-forth rhythm straitjackets the reader, making it easy for him to forego analyzing the constituent premises and the logic involved. For instance, in the earlier exchange, when Manny refers to the "physical" demands (although one suspects it is rather the emotional demands that are at issue) of women and remarks: "Who wants a woman like that?" there are a number of questions that could be asked, as, for example, if such a woman is unattractive, what is attractive to a woman about a man with the same combination of characteristics? But we are not meant to ask such questions, just as we are not meant to examine the exploitative nature of the proposition in the second interchange. Secondly, the distancing from the content that the very formulaic and stylized quality of the routine affords permits Bukowski to more easily incorporate ideological material into the novel, making of such routines more than just a routine.

CHAPTER NINE:
THE FASCINATION OF
THE (EXTRA)ORDINARY:
THE SHORT STORIES OF
CHARLES BUKOWSKI

I started with the short story, starving in little rooms around the country and drinking too much cheap wine, and I'd mail the things out to THE ATLANTIC MONTHLY or HARPERS and when they came back I tore them up. I used to write 8 or 10 stories a week. All I'd do was write these stories and drink as much as possible.°

Bukowski has published about two hundred short stories. He began almost compulsively writing short stories in early adolescence and broke into print in *Story* magazine in the mid-1940s.° After several additional publications, he abandoned the form for almost twenty years. Although he returned to it with some chapbook publications in the mid-1960s, the impetus for an enduring return was the offer of a column to write virtually anything he wanted by John Bryan (the founder of the Los Angeles alternative paper *Open City*).° These columns subsequently included opinion pieces, non-fiction sketches, and fiction, often, but not exclusively, of an autobiographical nature, and appeared in a context where Bukowski's "fiction took its place alongside coverage of student unrest, the New Left, black power, civic and police corruption, the draft resistance, drug information, and adverts for sexual contacts and services."° The fiction was of two sorts: narratives

of a sometimes fantastic nature and fictional reworkings of autobiographical material.° Bukowski continued writing stories, and
while as a whole there is some variation in the quality, he has
developed and evolved as a short story writer to the point where
his two most recent collections, *Hot Water Music* (1983) and *Septuagenarian Stew* (1990) contain his best stories.

Although his serious short story production began in the late
1960s, and his best stories have been written in the 1980s,
Bukowski's acknowledged influences are the American writers
of the 1920s and 1930s: Anderson, Hemingway, Saroyan, Fante,
McCullers.° In terms of his contemporaries, there is some similarity to the work of Raymond Carver but the striking difference
in their acceptance suggests significant differences in their work.°

As in the poetry, a noticeable change appeared in the stories
in the 1970s, evident with the third collection, *South of No North*.
Bukowski began to achieve a distance from his material, formal
evidence of which was his increased use of the third person.
Another indication was the fact that the content of the stories
(even when written in the first person) became less frequently
autobiographical. An objective point of view and an increasingly distanced stance towards his characters and material are continued in the two subsequent collections where Bukowski uses
the third person even more frequently; indeed, in the most recent collection, more than three-quarters of the stories are third-
person narratives.°

There is a remarkable difference in quality and style between
the first two collections and the two most recent collections (with
South of No North forming a transition). This essay briefly looks
at the early stories to provide a background for a discussion of
Bukowski's achievement in the later ones. However, the first two
collections remain important for several reasons: because they
are the prose on the basis of which Bukowski first achieved a
broader American audience as well as an international reputation (and for a long time influenced Bukowski's reception here
and abroad); because both collections have their redeeming moments (e.g., the "frozen man" essays in *Notes*, the prison realism
of "Doing Time with Public Enemy No. 1" and the Hemingwayesque amoralism of "All the Pussy We Want" in *Erections*);
and finally, because much of this material was re-used later in

the novels, the differing treatments of the same material allow us to see Bukowski's progress as a writer.

Not surprisingly, in light of Bukowski's early success in Germany, one of the most comprehensive and scholarly evaluations of the early stories was undertaken by two German scholars, Armin Geraths and Kurt Herget.° Although their analysis of the stories' shortcomings is somewhat misguided (and suffers from ignoring the collection *South of No North*), it is an intelligent and useful attempt to come to grips with Bukowski's early prose and provides a basis for discussing the later stories.

Geraths' and Herget's criticisms fall into three areas: language, subject matter and ideas. They write that Bukowski's

> language is without intellectual pretension. It is the trivial language of everyday life, with a limited vocabulary and enriched by the most lavish use of argot. Linguistic and intellectual structures are of great simplicity. The subjects often appear banal. The insights gathered in the stories seldom go beyond the level of tired clichés.
>
> (176)

With one exception, this is an accurate generalization but in and of themselves, such reproaches are limited: simplicity of language as manifested in the limited vocabulary of everyday speech had been an integral part of many of Hemingway's best stories. Argot, except for the stories dealing with horse-racing, is not in evidence: rather an emphatic colloquialism is probably what the authors were remarking upon, something that has been a hallmark of American fiction since the late nineteenth century, and for which it makes little sense to censure Bukowski. Again, Bukowski's linguistic structures are no simpler than Hemingway's and not all that much simpler than Anderson's or Saroyan's. Given the "pragmatic" American tradition, the emphasis on experience and distrust of intellectualism that is a primary trait of 20th century American literature (one example of which found its most concise expression in Williams' statement in *Paterson*: "no ideas but in things"), Bukowski's position, and the resultant stories, are not unusual in this respect. And it should also be borne in mind that ideas can be presented in a number of ways and that Bukowski's presentation of them often hides behind apparently trivial content.

251

But the authors do note one element of these early stories (though they overemphasize it) which has continued to appear in his short fiction, but which has never been a part of his novels:

> The orbit of the subject proves to be completely ordinary, trivial, banal. Yet an element of the sensational lies hidden in everything . . . one is always proceeding as if the exceptional were the ordinary. It is just at this point that Bukowski places his simple tactic. The unusual and the sensational modulate seamlessly into the familiar and the common thereby producing a banalization of the incredible and at the same time the all too familiar is given a new dimension.
>
> (181)

There is some truth in this, but it suffers greatly from an attempt to bring all sixty-four stories collected in *Erections* under one rubric. They do, also, accurately note a failing of the early stories which Bukowski has subsequently overcome, a

> lack of an ability to abstract, the meagerly developed conceptual language. Always, at the point where in the course of a narration a summary imposes itself, the flatness of the thought becomes revealed in a cliché, through which complex facts are simplified. Also a sentimental streak in the manner of the dime novel often makes its presence felt.
>
> (194)

Although their premises are false and their judgments sometimes questionable, some of the particular criticism is valid and useful in analyzing the difference between the early and late stories. Issues such as "a low level of abstraction," clichéd content (which lends the stories a formulaic quality) and a tendency towards sentimentality are all legitimate criticisms of Bukowski's early stories. The status of "the sensational" also underwent a change from the early to the late stories. A discussion of these issues reveals that the more recent stories represent a significant advance over the first two collections, even as they retain and transform certain "suspect" elements.

Bukowski was able to distance himself from his material, through an increased control of language (most noticeable with respect to diction and sentence structure). His handling of plot also became more assured. The clearest measure of his increased confidence, however, was his increased use of the third person. There was no longer the need to "vouch" for the authenticity of his material by writing in the first person. In the end this reflects a confidence in the nature of the material itself, even though the content often remained ordinary and the sensational never completely disappeared. Indeed, this is part of Bukowski's achievement.

Perhaps nowhere is this increased distance more obvious than in Bukowski's treatment of relations between the sexes, most particularly in his explicit descriptions of sex, a topic that is more prominent in the stories than in the novels (with the exception of *Women*). The "absence of an ability to abstract, a meagerly developed conceptual language" had resulted in a formulaic quality with respect to action and motivation as well as clichéd language. Although the number of stories that contain explicit descriptions of sex remained about the same from *Erections* through *Hot Water Music*, the treatment changed. While none of Bukowski's stories seems to me pornographic in the sense of sexually arousing, the sexual scenes in the early stories were repetitious and simplistic:

> I rather went crazy and began clawing at her dress—what there was of it. I saw a bit of underslip and panties; then I ripped the dress at the top, ripped the brassiere; I got a tit. I got a tit. It was fat. I kissed and sucked at the thing. Then I twisted it in my hand until she screamed, and as she did I pushed my mouth against hers, gagging the screams.
> I ripped the dress back—nylon, nylon legs knees flesh. And I picked her up out of the chair and ripped those chickenshit panties off and rammed it home.
> "Andre," she said. "*Oh*, Andre!"
> I looked over and the guy was watching us and jacking off in his chair.
> ("The Day We Talked about James Thurber," E 145–46)

This is all too close to, if it is not actually, the language of pulp fiction. When it is not brutally formulaic, it is inflated and clichéd:

> "We kissed again. Cass was crying without sound. I could feel the tears. That long black hair lay behind me like a flag

253

of death. We enjoined and made slow and sombre and won-
derful love."

("The Most Beautiful Woman in Town," E 6)

"Rammed it home" on the one hand and "enjoined" on the other
are sentimental and clichéd. Both seem written with one eye
clearly on an audience.

In the later stories the descriptions of sex, though equally
explicit, indeed sometimes even more so, have become more
mediated. In several of the stories sex is not reported first hand
and in one particularly artful passage is almost proleptic. Most
important, sex in the later stories is often funny. This is not true
of the earlier stories because of the violence (as in the scene just
quoted). In "Have You Read Pirandello?," in *Hot Water Music*, the
narrator, speaking on the phone to a woman he has never met
and from whom he is thinking of renting a room, tells her how
he performs cunnilingus:

> "How do you begin?" "With a brush stroke, lightly." "Of
> course, of course. Then, after you begin?" "Yes, well, there are
> techniques . . ." "What techniques?" "The first touch usually
> dulls the sensitivity in that area so that you can't return to it
> with the same effectiveness." "What the hell do you mean?"
> "You know what I mean." "You're making me hot." "This is clin-
> ical." "This is sexual. You're making me hot." "I don't know what
> else to say." "What does a man do then?" "You let your own
> enjoyment guide your exploration. It's different each time."
> "What do you mean?" "I mean sometimes it's a bit gross, some-
> times it's tender, whichever way you feel."
>
> "Tell me." "Well, everything ends up at the clit." "Say that
> word again." "What?" "Clit." "Clit, clit, clit . . ." "Do you suck
> it? Nibble it?" "Of course." "You're making me hot." "Sorry."
> "You can have the master bedroom. You like privacy?" "Like
> I told you." "Tell me about my clit." "All clits are different."
> "It's not private here right now. They're building a retaining
> wall. But they'll be through in a couple of days. You'll like it
> here."

(64–65)

Here playful humor replaces the violence and whatever coarse
humor exists in the earlier story. The fact that we are reading
a phone conversation, which is itself somewhat distanced by the
interspersing of ordinary, even "trivial" details, and the slight
reluctance of the narrator to go into a detailed description of

254

the act convey the impression of an author in control of his material, and of an explicit sexual description that is the opposite of formulaic, neither brutal nor sentimental. Yet the irony is that the description is not explicit because no actual (if fictional) act is being described. Such irony is worlds away from the unmediated physicality of the earlier stories. Sexual arousal, Bukowski is saying, while not just in one's head, is not merely physical either.° The narrator's statement that "it's different each time" might well be taken as a recognition that the formulaic and clichéd—in any sphere—are only hindrances to creativity; that variety and change—perhaps even the unexpected—are pleasurable. One final point should not be overlooked: the whole passage concerns the woman's pleasure and how a man can best provide that. This is a far cry from the situation in a number of the early stories where women function only as objects of the man's gratification. It would be hard to imagine a character in those stories averring that "everything ends at the clit."°

Geraths and Herget characterized the early stories as "naive," "elementary," and "spontaneous." This is valid for a good deal of the writing in *Notes* and *Erections* (although it should also be noted that many of the stories have moments where they overcome these failings). It is the last element, however, "spontaneity"—a lack of mediation—that resulted in the stories' most problematic aspects. The repetitive, sometimes sloppy, writing is a result of an aesthetic credo that marred a fair amount of Bukowski's early work, especially the prose. For Bukowski this appearance of spontaneity was something to be valued because it was important not to seem "literary." The result was described by Julian Smith as

> a deliberately disorderly syntax, a "spontaneous" typewriterese that creates its effect by a radical difference from smoother, more literary writing. . . . Bukowski flavors the lexical stew of *Notes* with misspellings, ungrammatical constructions, sentences with no verbs, repetitions, split infinitives, much slang and swearing, sexual innuendo and other linguistic ambiguities that enable him to splice sexuality, violence, nastiness and humor. By deliberately leaving in the text the sort of grammatical confusions common in speech but usually suppressed in written English, Bukowski is indicating that he wants to align writing with *spoken* rather than *written* conventions.
>
> (57)

Such writing, however, while not "literary," is not "natural," either. With its repetitions, redundancies and choices of the not-quite-right word it is as mannered as consciously literary prose, though in a different way (an important difference for Bukowski). Such writing calls attention to itself as much as the writing it reacts to, "loaded" in Roland Barthes' words, "with the most spectacular signs of fabrication."° One result of such a stance is the "banality" of the writing because, as Smith wrote (though viewing this positively), it involved "no recourse to . . . intellectual concepts."

One of the best earlier stories is "A Couple of Winos" from the collection *South of No North* (1973). It suggests something of what Bukowski was later to succeed in achieving more consistently as well as manifesting some of the weaknesses that flaw the early stories. The first-person narrator is a drifter in his 20s and the events described in the story take place over a few days in the California desert. He and an older man are hired to stack discarded railroad ties for someone who is later going to resell them:

> We drove along not talking, the truck rocking back and forth. There was nothing but dust, dust and desert. The guy didn't have much of a face, he didn't have much of anything. But sometimes small people who stay in the same place for a long time achieve minor prestige and power. He had the truck and he was hiring. Sometimes you have to go along with that.
>
> (44)

The repetitions in the second and third sentences are weaknesses in the paragraph, adding nothing to the descriptions and probably deriving from the author's feeling that the description is lacking in some way. But the fourth sentence is effective and assured, content to present a minor insight from the world of ordinary work. It is something we might find in *Factotum*, for example. The last two sentences of the paragraph are also effective, unvarnished representations of a fact of life.

Bukowki's description of the job's function in a broader context is an effective summary and reaches to a criticism of the uneconomic practice:

> Every now and then the railroad company would rip up the old ties and replace them with new ones. They left the old ties laying beside the tracks. There wasn't much wrong with the old ties but

the railroad left them laying around and Burkhart had guys like us stack them into ricks which he toted off in his truck and sold.

(45)

Here the repetition (of "left . . . laying") seems justified, effectively (even poetically) emphasizing a point the narrator is making. Even more effective is his description of the feelings such work arouses:

It was like any other impossible job, you got tired and you wanted to quit and then you got more tired and forgot to quit, and the minutes didn't move, you lived forever inside of one minute, no hope, no out, trapped, too dumb to quit and nowhere to go if you did quit.

(45)

Phrases like "the minutes didn't move, you lived forever inside of one minute" are impressive, extraordinarily vivid representations of the feelings created by such work and though there is repetition, again it is such that it adds the weight of rhythm *and* develops the description.

But ultimately Bukowski didn't yet have quite enough confidence in the simple force of his experience. This is clear in the ending of "A Couple of Winos":

Some nights earlier I had found that when it got cold the slivers in my hand began to throb. I could feel where each one was. It began to get cold. I can't say that I hated the world of men and women, but I felt a certain disgust that separated me from the craftsmen and tradesmen and liars and lovers, and now decades later I feel that same disgust. Of course, this is only one man's story or one man's view of reality. If you'll keep reading maybe the next story will be happier. I hope so.

(48)

It would have been better to end the paragraph (and story) with a period after "disgust." With every additional thought after that point he weakens the force of what has come before: first condemning humanity, then heightening the condemnation, then taking it back, apologizing and so on. Endings are difficult, but what seems to have been particularly injurious to some of the early stories (and poems) was Bukowski's feeling that somehow his description of the experience itself was not enough; it was almost as if Bukowski himself did not appreciate the force of those experiences and what they said about the world. Subsequently, Bukowski never questioned the validity of his experience and the authority of individual experience became more powerful with the increasing objectivity of its depiction.

In the later stories Bukowski has replaced the "lexical stew" with an illusion of ordinary discourse, achieved through formal and structural techniques. One reviewer perceptively noted that the principal character

> is mediated not only through its actions, but more through its manner of verbal expression. Bukowski's dialogues are not merely the result of a good ear for a specific scene. Rather, in their purposive abruptness and concise diction, they are the consequence of a formal intention.°

An increase in conceptualization is evident in the ability to summarize an individual and a situation—one form of an ability to abstract—in a paragraph or two, as in "Head Job," about a widow who finds interest in pianoplaying, drinking and little else:

> She'd had two lovers since the death of her husband but both affairs had been desultory and short-lived. Men seemed to lack magic, most of them were bad lovers, sexually and spiritually. Their interests seemed to center on new cars, sports and television. At least Harry, her late husband, had taken her to an occasional symphony. God knows, Mehta was a very bad conductor but he beat watching Laverne and Shirley. Margie had simply resigned herself to an existence without the male animal. She lived a quiet life with her piano and her brandy and her scotch. And when the sun went down she needed her piano very much, and her Chopin, and her scotch and/or brandy. She would begin to light one cigarette after another as the evening arrived.

> (113)

Cliché has been replaced by a nuanced language capable of effectively reflecting mood. Indeed, here we have a narrative passage which at times employs free indirect speech, a particularly effective way to get into a character's mind while retaining an objective tone, but a technique Bukowski rarely used in his early stories. In such sentences as "Men seemed to lack magic," and "God knows, Mehta was a very bad conductor but he beat watching Laverne and Shirley" we have entered another person's mind

258

and the assumption that we can do such a thing is a marked change from Bukowski's earlier views. It is not the easiest technique to use as it requires an ability to create differentiated characters. It is also a sign of Bukowski's increasing skill and technical confidence that he uses it so effectively. Bukowski has developed an apparently unexceptional prose that doesn't call attention to itself (though it is clearly an artistic prose, with its many conjunctions and poetic repetitions).

The subtle changes in context and the ironic humor of the sexual descriptions preclude any suggestion of the formulaic. The "banality" of the events described does not differ all that much from the subjects of the early stories, but they are no longer "naive" and "spontaneous" in their presentation. The stories have been pared down as well. Those in *Hot Water Music* are almost a third shorter than the stories in *Erections*. The titles are shorter as well and less "flippant," because more often ironic, as in "Head Job." Any ideas that Bukowski wants to impart are imparted obliquely, through concise description, or short effective dialogue, (in marked contrast to some of the dialogues in the earlier stories). In general, the loose, sprawling awkwardness of the early stories is no longer evident. As Bukowski remarked: "My style keeps adjusting and changing as my life does. . . . "°

The sensational is also handled better, toned down and domesticated (in some instances quite literally). This is illustrated through one of its more frequent manifestations, the theme of human mutilation. It appears in "The Fuck Machine" in *Erections* and in "Maja Thurup" in *South of No North*. In the latter, Bukowski had begun to put such extreme events in a quotidian context—less removed from his middle-class readers' milieu— and in this way sharpened the humor of his depiction by making the situations more credible. In "Decline and Fall," in *Hot Water Music*, he has perfected this type of story by placing depravity in an everyday context of "ordinary" people. Here Bukowski uses successfully what Geraths and Herget had identified as one strategy of the stories though they had questioned its efficacy: "one is always proceeding as if the exceptional were the ordinary. . . . The unusual and the sensational modulate seamlessly into the familiar and the common thereby producing a banalization of the incredible." Though the technique is the same, the effect is far more successful in the later stories because Bukowski has made his characters far less marginal or self-consciously alienated, less eccentric (in both senses of that word). At the same time, Bukowski has downshifted from the incredible to the improbable. Whereas in the early stories, the characters had been in their own private worlds, indeed, had even included a mad German scientist in "Fuck Machine," here the characters are no longer marginal, but middle American and Bukowski uses minor, inconsequential, details to increase the credibility of the events.

In "Decline and Fall," Mel is telling a bartender about an unusual experience he had.° He has visited a couple he knows and while playing cards and watching a football game, the man tells him that his wife likes to have sex with him while somebody else is watching. Mel doesn't reply, but the couple proceed to have sex:

> "He picks her up and kisses her, then throws her on the couch. He's all over her, kissing her and ripping at her clothes. Then he's got her panties off and he's at work. While he's doing this she's looking out from underneath to see if I'm watching. She sees that I'm watching and she starts squirming like a mad snake. They really go to it, finish it off; she gets up and goes to the bathroom and Al goes into the kitchen for more beers. 'Thanks,' he says when he comes out, 'you were a big help.' "
> "Then what happens?" asked the barkeep.
> "Well, then the Rams finally scored, and there was a lot of noise on the tv, and she comes out of the bathroom and goes into the kitchen. . . ."
>
> (58)

Then they have dinner:

> "Then Erica calls us into the breakfast nook where the table is all set and we sit down. It smells good—a roast. There are slices of pineapple on top of it. It looks like an upper shank; I can see what almost looks like a knee. 'Al,' I say, 'that thing really looks like a human leg from the knee up.' 'That,' says Al, 'is exactly what it is.' "

Mel thinks Al is joking and says, "Great, cut me a nice slice."

> " 'Listen Al,' I said, 'this isn't really bad. What is it?' 'It's like I told you, Mel,' he answers, 'it's a human leg, the upper flank. It's a 14-year-old boy we found hitchhiking on Hollywood Boulevard. We took him in and fed him and he watched Erica

and me do the thing for three or four days and then we got tired of doing that, so we slaughtered him, cleaned out the innards, ran that down the garbage disposal and dropped him into the freezer. It's a hell of a lot better than chicken, though actually I don't prefer it to porterhouse.' "

"He said that?" asked the barkeep, reaching for another drink under the bar.

"He said that," answered Mel. "Give me another beer."

The barkeep gave Mel another beer. Mel said, "Well, I still thought that he was joking, you know, so I said, 'All right, let me see your freezer.' And Al says, 'Sure —over here.' And he pulls back the lid and there's the torso in there, a leg and a half, two arms and the head. It's chopped up like that. It looks very sanitary, but it still doesn't look so good to me. The head is looking up at us and the eyes are open and blue, and the tongue is sticking out of the head—it's frozen to the lower lip.

" 'Jesus Christ, Al,' I say to him, 'you're a killer—this is unbelievable, this is sickening!'

" 'Grow up,' he says, 'they kill people by the millions in wars and give out medals for it. Half the people in the world are gonna starve to death while we sit around and watch it on tv.' "

(59–60)

Mel tries to leave, but is prevented by Al whose wife then forces herself upon him: "The Rams are still on tv. I step back from the door and then his wife runs up, she grabs me and starts to kiss me. I don't know what to do. She's a powerfully built woman. She knows all these nurses' tricks" (60). Mel and Erica then have sex while Al watches. Afterwards Mel drinks a beer and smokes a cigarette, then leaves. Carl, the bartender, is upset that Mel didn't go to the police:

"The way I look at it is that you're an accessory to a murder."

"But what I got to thinking, Carl, is that those people really didn't seem to be *bad* people. I've seen people I disliked a lot more who never killed anything. I don't know, it's really confusing. I even think of that guy in the freezer as some kind of big frozen rabbit . . ."

(61)

Carl pulls a gun on Mel and is about to call the police. Mel then says he was making the whole thing up, that "it was just bullshit." Carl is unconvinced:

"You mean what you just told me?"

"Yeah, it was just bullshit. One big joke. I sucked you in. Now put your gun away and pour us both a scotch and water."

"That story wasn't bullshit."

"I just told you it was."

"That was no bullshit story—there was too much detail. Nobody tells a story like that. That's no joke. Nobody jokes that way."

"I tell you it was *bullshit*, Carl."

"There's no way I can believe that."

As Carl reaches for the phone Mel hits him with the beer bottle,

> picked up the Luger, aimed carefully, squeezed the trigger once, then put the gun in a brown paper bag, jumped back over the bar, walked out the entrance and he was on the boulevard. The parking meter read "expired" in front of his car, but there was no ticket. He got in and drove off.
>
> (61)

The story's power stems from the deadpan humor and the detailed realism with which it treats the sensational content. As Carl says, "there was too much detail" for the story not to be true. The humor results from Mel's absurd literalness. When Mel replies to Carl's question, "Well, then what happened?" with "Well, then the Rams scored," we see one type of mindset. In the most literal sense the Rams scoring *is* what happened next, but of course Carl did not mean his question literally. Yet the Rams scoring is what a mind focussed on the concrete would see, a mind incapable of viewing "the big picture"; and this directly relates to another level of the story, also suggested by the title, which this literalness counterpoints.

At the beginning of the story Mel tells the bartender: "Al says something about Reagan and something about unemployment but I can't respond; it all bores me. You see, I don't give a damn if the country is rotten or not, so long as *I* make it" (57–58). These people (with the exception of Carl, who is, significantly, a bartender) are profoundly asocial individuals. While Reagan, unemployment, even starvation have no meaning, a football game (something meaningless except in its own arbitrary terms) does. The very concept of the social world has disappeared from their lives and so, logically, must the private world. This is paradoxically underlined by their making the most private relations, sex,

262

public. At the end of the story Mel is relieved that he hasn't been ticketed—this just after he has shot someone. (The identification of the gun as a Luger perhaps also suggests a Nazi mentality: the complete absence of any remorse in the murderers.) Yet his reaction is humorous in much the same way that Bukowski's sexual chauvinism is humorous because it implicates (some of) us. The humor is based on the fact that these characters are completely in their own, narrow, private world: when Al says: "half the people in the world are gonna starve to death while we sit around and watch it on tv," he is getting a little too close for comfort.

The story operates on a number of levels, all of them disturbing. What solidifies the disturbance is the ending. In one sense the ending is problematic in that it heaps one extraordinary killing on another. Given the various mass murders, serial killings, instances of child abuse and just plain perverse murders of the last two decades we cannot say that a single instance of cannibalism is all that implausible. What strains credulity, of course, is that Al and Erica so casually reveal their crime to a friend, and not a particularly close friend at that.° That Mel then kills Carl, making for two murders within the confines of a four-and-one-half page story—while not at all unbelievable—begins to push the events more towards the incredible. Yet if the story were to have ended earlier, before Mel kills Carl, with Mel's recanting, saying "it's all bullshit," while allowing for ambiguity, it would detract from Bukowski's point which rests on the "truth" of the events within the context of the story. The story says that such things happen and such people exist and, once again in Bukowski, the message is made palatable by the humor. Mel's coolness—now that he is himself a killer—is essential to Bukowski's point which can be somewhat tritely summarized as the "banality of evil." Were the ending ambiguous the story's morality would vanish. While on the one hand the lack of ambiguity may make the story seem a little "retro," the humor and the banality lend it a post-modern touch.

One final point is of interest. In both "Decline and Fall" and "The Day We Talked about James Thurber," (quoted above) there are scenes in which two people have sex while a third watches. The scene in "Decline and Fall" is far more effective for two reasons. First of all, Bukowski has placed it in a context where it relates to other aspects of the story in a rather subtle fashion; he has also increased the distance between the reader and the event: the story is told in the third person by an omniscient narrator; yet within that narration the story is being told by one of the characters in long passages of direct speech in which *he* at times quotes the speech of others. In this way we have both the effect of immediacy and the objectivity distance provides. It would be simplistic to say that Bukowski's growing preference for the third person in his stories has produced better stories. The decision to change narrative techniques has come about as a result of deeper shifts of feeling; at the same time, though, the formal change undoubtedly helped crystallize what was at first, perhaps, a somewhat inchoate shift in authorial worldview.

The issue of child abuse appears in another story in *Hot Water Music*. In "Some Hangover," a married couple, Gwen and Kevin, are discussing the fact that the husband may have sexually abused the children of friends while drunk at a party. Gwen is preparing breakfast.

> Gwen had the bacon on. She poured him a cup of coffee.
> "Thanks."
> "Scrambled?"
> "Scrambled."
> "Married ten years and you always say 'scrambled.'"
> "More amazing than that, you always ask."
> "Kevin, if this gets around, you are out of a job. The bank does not need a branch manager who is a child molester."
> "I guess not."
> "Kevin, we've got to have a meeting with the families involved. We've got to sit down and talk this thing out."
> "You sound like a scene from *The Godfather*."
> "Kevin, you're in big trouble. There's no way of getting around it. You're in trouble. Put your toast in. Push it in slow or it will pop right up, there is something wrong with the spring."
> Kevin put the toast in. Gwen dished out the bacon and eggs.
> (95)

Here the situation, though dramatic, is less sensational than in "Decline and Fall."° Yet Kevin, too, is a character in his own world with very little ability to put things in a broader context: the faulty toaster is on a par with the possible child abuse. The skill in such a story is Bukowski's delicate balancing of the humorous interplay between the husband and wife with the serious nature of the possible offence. Each is necessary for the success of the story. This ability to hold different elements in solution underlies the success of a number of the stories and, once again, testifies to Bukowski's aesthetic distance from his material.

While it would be forcing it to say that we are complicit with these characters, yet we are not all that far removed. Indeed, here the child abuser is married and middle-class; Martin Blanchard in "The Fiend," was an alienated loner. The ordinariness of the people in these stories is reflected in their names: Mel, Al, Carl, Erica, Kevin, Gwen, names as unmarked as possible. Bukowski has constructed these stories in such a way that we are enmeshed in the same solipsistic detail as the characters. The dilemma that Bukowski's characters had confronted in the early poetry and novels: how to respond to the legitimate demands of the social world while at the same time maintaining one's self is here ratcheted up several notches. Now the question is: is there a social world?

2

In *Hot Water Music* and *Septuagenarian Stew* Bukowski's stories broaden their social horizons. A worldview of a certain scope is effectively dramatized without recourse to abstract philosophizing (which was actually more prominent in the early stories, perhaps owing to the appearance of some of them as columns and the marked use of the first person). In "The Death of the Father II" from *Hot Water Music* and "The Life of a Bum" (Bukowski's masterpiece in the genre) from *Septuagenarian Stew*, Bukowski redramatizes a view of the solitary nature of existence as well as the individual's inextricable connection to a predatory society.

"The Death of the Father II" is a small masterpiece that deals with these themes by examining an individual's relationship to his family, to his history. In one sense, it is a story about coming to terms with the death of a parent. At the same time, and in only three pages, it contains the core of Bukowski's views on authority, the individual and society, and the American Dream.

It is a story of final separation from the family and about the impossibility of that separation, about the power of personal history.

The story opens: "My mother had died a year earlier. A week after my father's death I stood in his house alone" (HWM 167). The narrator of the story hasn't seen his father "in some time" and the neighbors don't know him. Although his parents are dead, their broader social world remains: "Curtains drew back as I stood on the front lawn. Then they began coming out of their houses." Not "people" or "neighbors" but rather the vague, ill-defined and slightly ominous "they." Given Bukowski's skill at dialogue (and Chinaski's facility with speech), it is marked that to the neighbor Nellie Miller's direct question: "Are you Henry?" Bukowski does not have him answer in direct speech: "I told her that I was Henry." The slightly mocking, ironic repetition of her words nicely reflects the distance that he feels towards these people, their values and, most important, his father's values. The narrator feels ambivalent about talking to the neighbors but wants to adhere to the routine forms of politeness and civility (Chinaski is rarely boorish in such situations) though these *are* impositions, even physical ones: "I bent over and shut off the hose." (The key element becomes the uncomfortable physical activity.) The social world has again impinged—and thus imposed—on him, stopped him from doing what he had been doing, and forced him into politeness and direct speech: "'Won't you come in?' I asked." "We sat and looked at each other." The narrator doesn't give an inch: "'You look just like your father.' 'Yes, so they tell me,'" not genuinely responding to the Millers. Even when he does respond directly, he quickly whips the ball back into their court: "'He must have liked pictures.' 'Yes, he did, didn't he?'" (168).

The real motive for the neighbor's visit then becomes clear ("I just love that painting of the windmill in the sunset") along with Chinaski's further attempt at separating himself from his father through the deadpan comment on his father's taste in art reflected in Mrs. Miller's speech. We're left in no doubt on this score when another neighbor says:

"Oh, I just *love* this frame, but I don't like the picture.
"Take the frame."
"But what should I do with the picture?"
"Throw it in the trash."

(168)

The narrator remains passive-aggressive throughout the story. The ultimate aggression is the story itself which extends the neighbors more and more rope with which to hang themselves while their actions condemn the world of contention that was his father('s).

The neighbors pillage the house, denuding it of almost everything of value. But lest they be shown as unrelievedly predatory and the story lack credibility, Bukowski gives us one altruistic soul: "'You better save this vacuum cleaner, Henry. You can use it for your apartment.' 'All right, I'll keep it.'" The exchange is also evidence of Chinaski's passivity (which the implied author would like us to see as a victimization). But in reality Chinaski is in control of events. When something he values is threatened, he exerts himself: "Leave the whiskey"; "I'll keep the car."

The tone throughout is objective in its "absence of modals and of words of feeling,"° though occasionally a judgment is passed: "Passersby were coming in from the street, and not even bothering to introduce themselves." Then there is a slight—but, as so often in Bukowski, all the more powerful because it is foregrounded against an otherwise customary absence—moralizing (to little effect, however):

> One of the ladies opened a cupboard on the back porch. "What about all these preserved fruits? You'll never be able to eat all of these."
>
> "All right, everybody, take some. But try to divide them equally."
>
> "Oh, I want the strawberries!"
> "Oh, I want the figs!"
> "Oh, I want the marmalade!"

(169)

After everybody has left and all that remains is "the garden hose, the bed, the refrigerator and stove and a roll of toilet paper" (a nice list in that three basic needs are provided for) Chinaski leaves the house:

I walked outside and locked the garage door. Two small boys came by on roller skates. They stopped as I was locking the garage doors.

"See that man?"

"Yes."

"His father died."

They skated on. I picked up the hose, turned the faucet on and began to water the roses.

(169–70)

The ending is muted, yet nicely points the meaning: try as we will, we can't get rid of the father. The world won't let us.

Stylistically, "The Death of the Father II" gives us a side of Bukowski that became prominent in the stories in *Hot Water Music* and *Septuagenarian Stew*, that part of his sensibility which finds expression in a Hemingwayesque minimalism. In this respect "The Death of the Father II" is something of an ideal-type. Such stories are short and focus on a brief, sometimes quite mundane, moment in someone's life, and take off from that to present larger truths about people and society. In "Beer at the Corner Bar" a perfectly innocuous conversation about a newspaper story turns into near violence; in "It's a Dirty World," a (literally and figuratively) pedestrian incident does escalate into violence. Thus, it is clear that it was not the ordinariness of the content, per se, that marred a number of the early stories, but, at least in part, Bukowski's defensive stance. One basis for the shift in style, then, was a confidence in the material itself, a confidence that the lack of discipline of the earlier stories undermined, rather than supported.

Hot Water Music was published when Bukowski was 63 and he might well have stayed with a form he had mastered and that was serving him well. Yet the stories of his most recent collection, *Septuagenarian Stew*, show continued changes, supporting what he had said on the relationship of style to life.° In this collection Bukowski has continued to—not so much develop as—evolve. *Hot Water Music* had brought one kind of short story to a culmination: short, controlled, off-hand. In *Septuagenarian Stew* Bukowski expands his view. The stories are more carefully constructed and even in some cases, e.g., "The Vengeance of the Damned," consciously dramatize a political idea. Indeed, in that story Bukowski has, for the first time in his fiction, presented

268

a truly collective subject attempting to radically change existing social relations, never mind that it's a bunch of winos as stand-ins for a return of the consumerist repressed. The collective subject that appeared in the poems of the 1980s has continued into the 1990s. Thus, in respect to both subject matter, form and ideology, Bukowski's short stories have continued to change in significant ways, something true of the poetry, but less true of the novels.

The stories in *Septuagenarian Stew* are on average somewhat longer than in the preceding collections, but more important is the fact that Bukowski has written individual stories longer than anything he had attempted in twenty years. The long stories of the early collections reflected Bukowski's anti-formalist ethos of that period. In such stories as "Confessions of a Man Insane Enough to Live with Beasts," "All the Assholes of the World and Mine" and "The Birth, Life and Death of an Underground News-paper" the formal dynamic is a picaresque subjectivity. This is especially true of "Confessions of a Man Insane Enough to Live with Beasts," a dry run for the autobiographical novels. The other two stories focus more narrowly on specific episodes and are thus more unified but, unlike "The Life of A Bum," are motivated by an attempt to limit the scope of any possible meaning. More important, though, is the fact that in this late story Bukowski has written about his usual themes differently and achieved some-thing different: he has made the banal and trivial representa-tive, indeed, meaningful. Here Bukowski approaches Beckett and Joyce, the latter in his privileging of ordinary life, and the former in those moments when Beckett uses repetitive and simplified syntactic structures to highlight the banal and the routine, for example, when the narrator of *Molloy* tries to get a grasp on things through a simplification of syntax:

> I went upstairs again. My son was dressing. He was crying. Everybody was crying. I helped him put on his knapsack. I told him not to forget his raincoat. He began to put it in his knap-sack. I told him to carry it over his arm, for the moment. It was nearly midnight. I picked up my umbrella.
>
> (127)

There is something of this reductionism in the syntax of "The Life of a Bum" though Bukowski's language remains referential. In the way that certain passages in Mahler prefigure atonal music, while yet remaining within the traditional key structure of classical music, Bukowski here at times verges on a minimalism which without much alteration could emphasize linguistic structures themselves to the extent that they become the subject of the story. But referentiality, in the form of a plot and a focus on the objects of everyday existence was as strong an anchor for him as it was, in the form of melody, for Mahler.

"The Life of a Bum," narrated in the third person, is about Harry, an alcoholic, and the events of one afternoon in Los Angeles in 1943. Harry awakes in his rented room, walks to a park where he briefly dozes off, has a short encounter with another alcoholic, walks to a bar where he is bought drinks, first by one acquaintance, then by another, Monk, whom he then accompanies for a haircut for which he receives another two drinks. On the way back Harry (on purpose, though he makes it look like an accident) bumps Monk into the path of an oncoming bus. Monk is injured, though how seriously is not clear. Harry takes Monk's wallet, which has fallen out of his pocket, and goes to a restaurant where he twice orders the same large meal. He then leaves the restaurant and continues walking. With the exception of the assault on Monk the story is the quintessence of the routine. Yet it is one of Bukowski's most fascinating stories, its fourteen pages a veritable *summa* of his concerns.

Its tone reflects a low-key, but all-pervasive weariness with existence:

> Christ, he thought, people have intestines, mouths, lungs, ears, bellybuttons, sexual parts, and . . . hair, tongues, sometimes teeth, and all the other parts . . . fingernails, eyelashes, toes, knees, stomachs . . .
>
> There was something so *weary* about all that. Why didn't anybody complain?
>
> (SS 56, ellipsis in original.)

It is already clear that Bukowski is presenting one of the cornerstones of his worldview—the overwhelmingly tedious routine of so much of what passes for life—in a prosaic, if somewhat anomalous, context: as he says, the life of a bum. A bum is not everyman, but who is? Though low on the social scale, the bum is not beyond the pale, not, for instance, a criminal. He is someone who, if not at one with society's values, at least recognizes a certain social decorum.

Harry is a bum who cadges subtly, by his presence, rather than begging outright and in so doing performs a socially useful, or at least desired, role within the small community of bar habitués. As Harry remarks further on: "They noticed Harry because he was a bum. He made them feel superior. They needed that." They may need Harry, but Harry is aware of the power relationship: "As a professional bummer of drinks Harry knew the first rule: you never asked for one. His thirst was their joke and any demand by him subtracted from their joy of giving" (61). Once again, Bukowski is something of a Hegelian, recognizing the mutual necessity of Lord and Bondsman. But as we shall see later, Chinaski does his best to wrench the dialectic out of shape. For the others Harry represents passivity and suffering and any breach of his role is threatening. This is made clear when Harry, "in agony for another drink," suggests getting that drink *while* Monk is having his haircut: "Monk's eyes fixed on Harry, 'No, we'll get a beer after I'm finished here'" (63).

The bum's role as the victim of society's inherent and insistent need to find an object for its members' mindless hostility and violence towards anything different from themselves is evident in several incidents during Harry's peregrinations. The larger the group, the more extreme the violence and the hostility:

> A car came driving by swiftly. It was filled with four young men.
> "HEY, YOU OLD FART! DIE!" one of them screamed at Harry.
> The others laughed. Then they were gone.
>
> (56–57)

A little later an army convoy passes:

> The convoy moved slowly. The soldiers saw Harry sitting on the park bench. Then it began. It was an admixture of hissing, booing and cursing. They were screaming at him.
> "HEY, YOU SON OF A BITCH!"
> "SLACKER!"
> As each truck of the convoy passed, the next truck picked it up:
> "GET YOUR ASS OFF THAT BENCH!"
> "COWARD!"
> "FUCKING FAGGOT!"
> "YELLOW BELLY!"

It was a very long and a very slow convoy.
"COME ON AND JOIN US!"
"WE'LL TEACH YOU HOW TO FIGHT, FREAK!"
The faces were white and brown and black, flowers of
hatred.

(58)

The prominence of the group diminishes the individual's value. Excepting the protagonist, characters are almost always seen as members of a group, without much in the way of psychological detail. Even Harry's thought processes have been stripped of the personal. Harry thinks, but his thinking is never presented in the traditional forms that we associate with psychological characterization. At times it verges on a kind of meta-thinking: "He walked along in the warm sun thinking, I am walking and I am smoking a cigarette" (56–57). Looking up at the sky while lying down on the grass, Harry briefly muses about life, "trying to get something straight." But this is not a good thing to do: "Harry didn't like heavy thoughts. Heavy thoughts could lead to heavy errors." Of Harry's subsequent victim, Monk, the narrator notes: "He thought that gave him an edge. He wasn't good at thinking."

Bukowski has no interest in understanding Harry's character, merely in presenting it. In one sense, "The Life of a Bum" is Bukowski in his most determinist mode. The subject as free-willed agent is severely circumscribed. This diminution results from the emphasis on the group and Harry's passivity. We have already noted the soldiers; continuing on his way to the bar

Harry came to a vacant lot. A bunch of middle-aged men were playing softball. They were out of shape. Most had pot bellies, were small of stature, had large butts, almost like women. They were all 4-F or too old for the draft.
Harry stood and watched the game. There were many strikeouts, wild pitches, hit batters, errors, badly hit balls, but they kept playing. Almost as a ritual, a duty. And they were angry. The one thing they were good at was anger. The energy of their anger dominated.

(59)

The suggestion that these men feel obligated to engage in their softball-game activity by a ritual beyond their control, that their individuality is being overridden by a group ethos (against which their anger is an expression), goes hand-in-hand with the reduction of psychological characterization. There is no need to delineate the fine points of character when psychology is virtually irrelevant. The individuals in the story lead unexamined lives bound by routine, convention, habit and the anger they feel at this determines their lives just as his "thirst" does Harry's.

Yet, it is just the routineness of the characters and their lives that results in one of the story's most impressive achievements, its skillful characterization. (Evident earlier, nowhere has this skill been handled with as much precision as here. In "Some Hangover" and "The Death of the Father II," for example, the characterization was achieved through dialogue, of which there is significantly less in "The Life of a Bum.") With a few brief strokes Bukowski places a character, for example McDuff, whom Harry meets on his way to the bar.

> It was old thin McDuff, puffing his pipe. McDuff was around 62, he always looked straight forward, he never looked *at* you but he saw you anyhow from behind those rimless glasses. And he was always dressed in a black suit and a blue necktie. He came into the bar each day about noon, had two beers, then left. And you couldn't hate him and you couldn't like him. He was like a calendar or a pen holder.
>
> (59–60)

The similes are striking in themselves and also because Bukowski uses metaphor and simile sparingly. They emphasize the routine (temporal) aspect of life as well as that of duty (the pen-holder as associated with routinized, bureaucratic work) and pick up McDuff's dark suit and tie as well as other elements of routine ("weariness") which buttress one theme of the story.

> So Harry walked along with old thin McDuff and old thin McDuff puffed on his pipe. McDuff always kept that pipe *lit*. That was his thing. McDuff *was* his pipe. Why not?
> They walked along, not talking. There was nothing to say. They stopped at traffic lights, McDuff puffing at his pipe.
> McDuff had saved his money. He had never married. He lived in a two room apartment and didn't do much. . . . McDuff was neither happy nor unhappy. Once in a while he became a bit of a fidget, something would appear to bother him and for a tiny moment terror would fill his eyes. Then it left quickly

> . . . like a fly that had landed . . . then zoomed away for more
> promising territory.
>
> (60, ellipses in original.)

The marvelous simile of the fly with its suggestion that McDuff is so far gone as to be beyond even the province of terror implies that Harry has the advantage in that he is not without emotion; where there is the promise of terror, there is the possibility (however slight) of change.

McDuff is depicted as paradigmatically unexceptional, amazingly ordinary. Everyone at the bar is ordinary but McDuff is extraordinarily ordinary. The world of "The Life of a Bum" is as ordinary and unexceptional a world as one could meet and in this lies one part of its meaning. For it is exemplary not just of a bum's life. Syntax emphasizes this pervasive ordinariness. After meeting Monk, a window-washer, at the bar, Harry takes him up on his offer of a couple of drinks in exchange for accompanying him for a haircut: "Then Harry followed Monk out the door. They were together and Monk was going to get a haircut." The diction and sentence structure are that of someone trying to put things in the simplest possible terms, to get a handle on reality, to find a meaning because something in him is still hoping against hope for this. As with his earlier remark, "I am walking and I am smoking a cigarette," it is almost as if Harry feels that the best way to get a handle on what is happening is to state in the simplest possible terms what he is doing, or better yet, what is happening to him. Harry is like someone turning a shell over and over in their hands, trying to find a purchase from which to prise it open, hoping that there's some small pearl of meaning inside.

Yet sometimes, even this level of reduction may be too complex and Harry reduces it even further. At the barbershop, Monk introduces Harry to the barber:

> Then he heard Monk speaking to the barber, "By the way,
> Paul, this is Harry. Harry, this is Paul."
> Paul and Harry and Monk.
> Monk and Harry and Paul.
> Harry, Monk, Paul.
>
> (63)

The world is reduced to people as things: just names, no verbs, no relationships between the things other than the happenstance of contiguity, no action. And people become their things in a "metonymic" vision that transforms itself into metaphor: "McDuff *was* his pipe."

Harry, "in agony for another drink," tries to make the time pass while waiting for Monk to finish his haircut:

> Harry was conscious of his feet, of his feet in his shoes, then of his toes . . . on the feet . . . in his shoes.
>
> He wiggled his toes. His all-consuming life going nowhere like a snail crawling toward the fire.
>
> Leaves were growing upon stems. Antelopes raised their heads from grazing. A butcher in Birmingham raised his cleaver. And Harry sat waiting in a barbershop, hoping for a beer.
>
> He was without honor, a dog without a day.
>
> It went on, it went by, it went on and on, and then it was over.
>
> (64, ellipsis in original)

This is extraordinarily effective writing. Bukowski has maintained the horror of Harry's existence without sensationalizing or sentimentalizing it. With the mention of the animal, vegetable and human world and the geographic spread of the moments, not as explicit, but as implied comparisons, there is the suggestion that this is existence, *tout court*. Neither the comparisons nor their order is accidental: leaves grow, animals eat them, and are then in turn consumed by humans. It is the order of things, though not a particularly appealing one. The mechanism of the world grinds on. The relentless cycle that is existence was suggested in the fourth paragraph of the story: "Harry got up, relieved himself in the sink, washed it away with the spigot, then he stuck his head under there and drank some water." Living becomes akin to one of those statue-fountains endlessly recycling water through itself. The one attempt to break out of all this, to short-circuit the cycle, is Harry's assault on Monk, not quite the *acte gratuit* it appears to be at first glance.

Monk epitomizes all that Harry dislikes: "How he sat there! A *man's man*. And a comfortable one at that. He never thought about death, at least not his own"; and later: "Monk laughed. His laugh was like linoleum being sliced by a dull knife. Or maybe it was a death-cry." For Harry, Monk and Monk's life are death. On the way back to the bar Harry tries to realize this identification:

> Monk was walking next to the curb and it was like a dream. A yellow dream. It just happened. And Harry didn't know where the compulsion came from. But he allowed the compulsion. He pretended to trip and lunged into Monk. And Monk, like a top-heavy circus of flesh, fell in front of the bus. As the driver hit the brakes there was a thud, not too loud, but a thud.
>
> (65)

Monk is breathing and there is no sign of blood, but he is unconscious. Harry takes the wallet, which had "leaped out of Monk's back pocket on impact," and leaves. The wallet is full, apparently with Monk's pay.

Thus the element of the sensational is introduced into the story. While it is motivated in terms of Harry's dislike for Monk, and the feeling that he has been humiliated by him, it is still a slightly unrealistic element in the context of the overall tone and style of the story, although the incident has, typically, been made more credible by the description of the wallet's landing "like a little pyramid." Bukowski wants this incident in the story in this way because the incident shows Harry as, in fact, aggressive, although that aggression is somewhat subtly phrased: "But he allowed the compulsion." We see Harry taking control in a way he had not done before. In the bar, during the walk and haircut he had been passive, controlling only in manipulating his flunky position to get free drinks. His previous behavior had an element of economic rationality in it but here something else is at work because Harry doesn't know Monk is carrying a lot of cash and therefore doesn't push him into the path of the bus for that reason. He does so because Monk's existence is anathema to him and because Monk has humiliated him. Monk had also humiliated Harry in the bar by "offering" him a demeaning "job" (holding the ladder for Monk while he washes windows). His assault on Monk marks a decisive shift in the story. Harry is no longer an innocuous victim.

Harry chooses Monk as his victim for a number of reasons. In one sense everything about Monk irritates Harry but above all Monk had provoked Harry by offering him (a "bum") a job. It hadn't been a serious offer but Monk had attacked Harry in what is both Harry's most sensitive point and yet the crux of his ("bum's") existence: the refusal to work.

Earlier in the story Harry had characterized himself as a "dog without a day." Here, Harry gets his day. Monk has lost the fight for "recognition" while Harry has advanced to "Lordship" status (though he loses that soon enough in his conflict with the chef). But Harry is trying to get outside the whole tight conflictual circle organized around work and hierarchical work relations (cp. the primary definition of "bum": "a person who avoids work and sponges on others"). As he reflects to himself on being offered a job by the chef: "Why the hell is everybody trying to put me to work?" (64). Harry will not accept the wage/work relationship which (with Monk's money) he successfully, if momentarily, escapes.

Later in the day Harry goes to have a good meal with Monk's money. Because he looks so shabby, the chef is reluctant to serve him, then angrily relents.

> "Now," said Harry, 'I want a porterhouse steak, medium well-done, with french fries, and go easy on the grease. And bring me another beer, now.
> The chef loomed before him like an angry cloud, then he cleared off, went back to the refrigerator, repeated his act, which included bringing the bottle and slamming it down.
>
> (66–67)

Harry eats his meal and then orders the same meal all over again. After finishing the second meal:

> "I'll have it once more," Harry told the chef. "Another porterhouse and fries and another beer, please."
> "YOU WILL NOT!" the chef screamed. "YOU WILL PAY UP AND GET THE HELL OUT OF HERE!"
>
> (68)

This Harry does.

The chef's reaction is surprising and, at first glance, inexplicable. When Harry first entered the restaurant, the chef thought he was applying for the dishwasher's job advertised in the window. The reason for the chef's anger may be his disappointment that he can't fill the job (which could mean that *he*

277

is washing the dishes) as well as that subtle and irritating discomfort we feel when someone is not playing their role. While the habitués of the bar can maintain a sense of superiority over Harry by buying him drinks, and therefore his refusal of Monk's offer of a job doesn't particularly offend them, such is not the case with the chef. All he sees is a bum who somehow doesn't have to work. Twice in the story Harry refuses a job, a refusal justified by the horror of such an existence: the existence of McDuff, Monk, the chef.

After he pays, he leaves the restaurant and continues his Bloom-like odyssey.

> Early evening traffic was beginning to clog the avenues with cars. The sun slanted down behind him. Harry glanced at the drivers of the cars. They seemed unhappy. The world was unhappy. People were in the dark. People were terrified and disappointed. People were caught in traps. People were defensive and frantic. They felt as if their lives were being wasted. And they were right.
>
> Harry walked along. He stopped for a traffic signal. And, in that moment, he had a very strange feeling. He felt as if he was the only person alive in the world.
>
> As the light turned green, he forgot all about that. He crossed the street to the other side and continued on.
>
> (69)

With that the story ends. The ending is especially effective in that Harry's brief epiphany is taken back in the next sentence.

"The Life of a Bum" seems to me the best story Bukowski has ever written. The language is extremely impressive with truly not a word wasted. The metaphors and similes are strikingly effective. Impressive also, is how he has worked a number of his major concerns into its relatively small confines: the gnawingly deadening routine of everyday life and the quiet and not-so-quiet desperation of much of humanity, the irrational aggression of individual and group, and the refusal of work are all nicely delineated.

Generally speaking, Bukowski's stories fit quite well into what one critic has termed "the debunking rhythm of the American short story" which

> challenge[s] the character's, and the audience's, assumptions about the world without substituting any more-authoritative

knowledge, so that such stories constitute not a form of knowledge but a challenge to knowledge. . . . °

While this nicely provides a framework within which to view such stories as "Decline and Fall," "Some Hangover" and "The Life of a Bum," it does not quite capture the specific stamp of a Bukowski story. Bukowski not only questions the concept of a stable individual personality (though he sometimes does that) but often suggests as well the extent to which the individual is at the mercy of the surrounding social world, almost always represented as a hostile group.

Bukowski's short stories are a major achievement. They span almost his entire publishing career, from 1944 to 1990, almost a half century. Had he produced nothing but these stories his achievement would have been impressive. But almost as impressive as the achievement itself is his continuing evolution as a short story writer. While his mastery of the form has become complete over the years, the impulse behind that achievement has remained remarkably consistent: to reveal the ordinary's extraordinary aspect.

NOTES

Introduction

11: *"Indeed, because Bukowski is so unmistakably American . . ."* Bukowski himself certainly appreciates his "representative" quality. Cp. his comment to Neeli Cherkovski: "They tried to get me on Johnny Carson. I said no. They wanted me on those other shows, too: '20–20,' '60 minutes.' I turned them all down. But pick up a copy of *People* magazine. I'm in it. I let them do a story because they're just corny enough. Besides, you can buy it in any supermarket." Neeli Cherkovski, *Whitman's Wild Children*, 35.

12: *"Their work may even . . ."* It seems little short of amazing that as of 1992 not a single poem or short story of Bukowski's had appeared in any of the anthologies of poetry or short fiction regularly produced and revised for college literature courses; amazing indeed, is his omission from the anthology *Working Classics*, a collection devoted to poems of and/or by the working class.

12: *"Americans don't like . . ."* For a detailed reminder and analysis of this phenomenon by a traditional conservative, see Kevin Phillips, *The Politics of Rich and Poor* (1990) and from the left, Bennett Harrison and Barry Bluestone *The Great U-Turn* (1990).

13: *"Benjamin Franklin's Autobiography . . ."* J. A. Leo Lemay, "Franklin's Autobiography and the American Dream," in *Benjamin Franklin's Autobiography* ed. by J. A. Leo Lemay and P. M. Zall, 350.

14: *"An analysis of Chinaski's decision-making . . ."* Cp. Bukowski's own, more nuanced assessment: "The factories, the slaughterhouses, the warehouses were not exactly a choice and then they were a choice, and so were the women and so was the drinking. Yes and no." Charles Bukowski, "He Beats His Women."

16: *"The more general critique of the status quo . . ."* Cp. Noam Chomsky: "The United States . . . is . . . unusual in the narrowness of choice afforded within the political system" (117); "The right of free expression is vigorously maintained in the United States, in that state controls are very weak by comparative standards. On the other hand, the ideological system operates within very narrow constraints and those who do not accept them are effectively excluded" (123). Noam Chomsky, *On Power and Ideology.*

17: *"Moreover, politics . . ."* The repeated mention of Chinaski/"Bukowski's" refusal to vote is one clear indication of the political content of Bukowski's work, a rejection expressing a desire for something more than "the banal, vague ideological model of American political power and purpose described in elementary school 'civics' courses [which] retains a fundamental influence." See Gabriel Kolko, *Main Currents in Modern American History, 274.*

19: *"Another effect of Bukowski's . . ."* Bukowski has viewed the hiatus in his career positively, as a time when he acquired experience, though his view of experience is not a simplistic one: "This diffusion of talent usually occurs among writers in their twenties who don't have enough experience, who don't have enough meat to pick off the bone. YOU CAN'T WRITE WITHOUT LIVING AND WRITING ALL THE TIME IS NOT LIVING. Nor does drinking create a writer or brawling create a writer, and although I've done plenty of both, it's merely a fallacy and a sick romanticism to assume that these actions will make a better writer of one." Charles Bukowski, "Upon the Mathematics of the Breath and the Way," in *Glazer,* 84.

19: *"Yet to me,* Factotum *. . ."* The fact that it took him four years to finish *Factotum,* his second novel, whereas *Post Office* was written in a matter of months seems evidence of the radical change his conception of writing was undergoing. See "Bukowski—Interview" with Thomas Kettner, 141.

19: *"The first was the prospect . ."* "'He used to call me late at night from the Post Office,' says John Martin, 'and say "I am going to die if I don't get out of here."'" Paul Ciotti, "Bukowski," 18.

19: *"The significance of this offer . . ."* Martin serves as Bukowski's editor and hence, for a writer who doesn't revise his poetry much ("I revise, but not much. The next day I retype the poem and automatically make a change or two, drop out a line, or make two lines into one or one line into two, that sort of thing to make the poem have more balls, more balance." William Packard, 318), plays a significant role. Cp. also: "Bukowski's writing was also 'freed up' by his refusal to serve as his own editor or critic. He feels it is his job to write, and leaves the selection and evaluation to others. Thus he is free to write *a lot.*" Gerald Locklin,

"Setting Free the Buk," in *The Review of Contemporary Fiction* 5.3 (1985): 29. Finally, again, Cherkovski: "He [John Martin] became friend, editor, and agent, literally shaping the poet's career and book projects while promising him a secure future (*Whitman's*, 23)

Chapter 1: Poetry and Class

29: *"In light of his popular success . . ."* German figure from "'Harter Junge' Bukowski wird 70. *Lübecker Nachrichten* 8 Aug. 1990.

30: *"freedom . . . earlier poets did not have."* Nor, in fact, do all contemporary writers. For an interesting analysis of what he characterizes as "what may be the greatest freedom enjoyed by any published writer in American literary history," see Gerald Locklin, "Setting Free The Buk," *The Review of Contemporary Fiction* 5.3 (Fall 1985): 28.

30: *"Indeed, the amount of poetry . . ."* The comparison with high modernism is not unwarranted, even at this late date. In the first place, such modernists had an unusually long "shelf life." Commenting on "the fifties revival of the twenties," James Breslin writes: "The prestige and influence of Eliot, as reinvented by the New Critics, were enormous by the mid-fifties." In the second place Bukowski, though achieving real fame only in the 1980s was born in 1920 and began publishing poetry in the mid-1950s. Breslin's discussion of the staying power of the moderns is interesting. See James E. B. Breslin, *From Modern to Contemporary: American Poetry, 1945–1965*, 14.

30: *"The major Black Sparrow publications . . ."* Astounding as it may seem, this represents only the (rather substantial) tip of the iceberg. In a review of two collections of the mid-1980s totalling 314 pages and comprising 129 poems, Gerald Locklin wrote that "[Bukowski] has written me that these poems represent only about a sixth of his poems composed during this time period." Gerald Locklin, rev. of *War All the Time* and *Horses Don't Bet on People and Neither Do I*, *The Review of Contemporary Fiction* 5.3 (Fall 1985): 36.

31: *"This variety has contributed . . ."* More than a century after Whitman, the question of form was still, for some, an issue. Cp. a 1975 review by Hayden Carruth: "Whether or not Charles Bukowski's 'poems' are actually poems is open to legitimate debate, even after the loosening up of our ideas about poetic form that has occurred in the past ten or fifteen years." Hayden Carruth, "Images," in *Harper's Magazine*, 31 Mar. 1975: 4, in "Bukowski." *Contemporary Literary Criticism* 81, Carolyn Riley and Phyllis Carmel Mendelson, eds.

32: "*As he told Packard . . .*" Cp. the poems "immortal wino" in *Septu-agenarian Stew* and "slow night" in *Dangling in the Tournefortia*. Brecht, too, a poet with whom Bukowski shows a number of affinities, did not see poetic composition as an "irrevocable farewell to life." Cp. the poem, posted in Brecht's study in Buckow, beginning "*In consideration of the fact that I have only a few weeks of the year / to work for myself . . .*" in which he lists his reasons for needing privacy in order to write, only to end: "I ask, that this rule not be too strictly ob- / served. Principles survive through their / infringement." In W. Hecht, ed. *Brecht: Sein Leben in Bildern und Texten* 276. Cp., also, Brecht's having drafted his famous poem, "Of Poor B.B." returning to Augsburg on the night train from Berlin ("nachts 1/2 10 im Dezug"). See Philip Thomson, *The Poetry of Brecht*, 87–89.

32: "*You get a bit dramatic . . .*" Bukowski continues: "I don't always write drunk. I write sober, drunk, feeling good, feeling bad. There's no special way for me to be" (49).

32: "*scenic poem*" For an enlightening discussion of the latter (and of more than the poetry of the 70s), see "The dominant poetic mode of the late seventies" in Charles Altieri, *Self and sensibility* in *Contemporary American Poetry*, 32–51.

33: "*Bukowski, some 1200 years after Tu Fu . . .*" Charles Bukowski, "Introduction" to Douglas Blazek, *Skull Juices* (1970). This point, too, had been made by Williams, who wrote to Marianne Moore in 1935 of his "rebellion against stereotyped poetic process—that too meticulous choice among other things. In too much refinement there lurks a sterility that wishes to pass too often for purity when it is anything but that." *The Selected Letters of William Carlos Williams*, 155–156. Indeed, such a reaction is a recurring phenomenon in poetic history. Cp. Hugh Kenner: "Even Augustan poets had occasional moments of vertigo, when the whole inherited corpus of poetry seemed a set of effects, like fireworks or neon signs, all potentially affecting, all potentially a little absurd." Hugh Kenner, *A Homemade World: The American Modernist Writers*, 69.

34: "*There are no* personae . . ." In most of his poems Bukowski uses one of two quite similar personae. The first is Henry Chinaski, the second is "Charles Bukowski." The second I take to be the persona not only of the poems in which through internal evidence we can identify the narrator as Charles Bukowski but also those narrated in the first person with no mention of Henry Chinaski. When it is helpful to the discussion, in both these latter instances I refer to the narrator as "Bukowski." Although this use of quotation marks may seem mannered, I feel they are necessary in order to preserve that distance between first-person narrator and historical individual, the bridging of which is always so tempting in an author like Bukowski, who seems to rely in so unmediated a fashion on the events of his life for the subject matter of his writings.

35: *"But the issue of 'appropriate' material . . ."* The example of Ginsberg would seem to contradict this statement. But while Bukowski's freedom owes a lot to the trailblazing Ginsberg, the latter is given to a kind of sensationalism (resting on the *assumption*—thus acceptance—of tabus) which makes for a significant difference in their treatment of formerly tabu subject matter, a point discussed later in this essay. With respect to Ginsberg, it is worth nothing that he is one of the few contemporaries for whom Bukowski has consistently expressed approval and admiration. See letters of 3 and 24 January and 2 March 1965 in *The Bukowski/Purdy Letters: 1964–1974*, ed. Seamus Cooney. Cp. also: "I've never said this before but I am now high enough as I write this to perhaps say that Ginsberg has been the most awakening force in American poetry since Walt W. . . ." "A Rambling Essay," 14. For a less positive response to Ginsberg see Wennersten, 43.

36: *"extreme individualization . . ."* Georg Lukács, "The Intellectual Physiognomy of Literary Characters," in *Radical Perspectives in the Arts*, 115.

40: *"The attempt to marginalize the experience . . ."* A different tack was to acknowledge the working-class experience described and then somehow see *that* as extreme: "If a writer must sample life at its most elemental, then surely Bukowski qualifies as a laureate of poetic preparedness, an unskilled laborer at jobs that include dishwasher, stock boy, and elevator operator; he also has hung posters in New York subways and worked in dog-biscuit factories, slaughterhouses, and bakeries." "Charles Bukowski." *Dictionary of Literary Biography* (Gale, 1980), 113.

41: *"While formally indebted to the Beats . . ."* For someone as published as Bukowski (Al Fogel estimated 1500 periodical publications as of 1983), who over many years struggled to a position of eminence exclusively through little magazines, small presses and alternative publications and who was beginning to be translated into a number of languages and to achieve recognition in Europe as an important new American writer in the early 1970s (by the end of the decade he had become in Germany a "Klassiker" of American underground literature), it must have been a little galling to see the apparent ease with which others received grants and comfortable teaching positions, while he continued to work evenings as a postal clerk until the age of fifty.

41: *"Confessional poetry paved the way . . ."* Cp. Ekbert Faas "Due to the influence of T. S. Eliot, to whom poetry was 'an escape from personality' rather than an expression of it . . . prudishness continued to dominate Anglo-American poetry in our century, and it is only since [Robert Lowell's] *Life Studies* that the portrayal of one's private agonies and neuroses has ceased to be considered a breach of poetic decorum." Ekbert Faas, *Towards a New American Poetics: Essays and Interviews*, 17.

41: *"[a]bove all . . . the willingness . . ."* Steven K. Hoffman, "Impersonal Personalism: The Making of a Confessional Poetic," *ELH* 45 (1978): 691.

42: *"Lowell claimed . . ."* This false aspect of Lowell was recognized by Rosenthal. Commenting on "Walking in the Blue," he wrote: "Lowell is not free of the illusion of superiority deriving from his family background . . . Though assimilating to himself, through the identification of private with public suffering, the problems of the age, he pays little attention to the lives of ordinary men and women who may either experience the same things with as much meaning but in different form, or possibly, offer alternative possibilities if regarded with sufficient empathy. As a result, he also arrogates to himself the embodying through experience of our cultural direction and destiny" (54). This is not to deny, though, the value in the demystification that Lowell performs on the assorted Lowells, Winslows and St. Mark's classmates. The Beats, too were operating from a privileged position, outside the system of commodified labor-power.

43–44: *"The sin in Lowell . . ."* Both Lowell and Bukowski respond to the norm for class. It should be noted that Lowell's not reproducing himself as upper-class, his not conserving and developing his capital, is also a form of refusal.

45: *"What they achieved . . ."* An analogous transformation is evident in Bukowski's vulgarity. Rosenthal notes that "the initial excitement over Ginsberg's *Howl and Other Poems* when it appeared . . . seemed to come first of all from the gross vocabulary of vulgar speech." He goes on to make an important point: "but actually Ginsberg never gives us the unadulteratedly elemental speech of the streets, the farm, and the factory . . . he uses some words that in this context are almost euphemisms—'copulated,' for instance—and in any case engulfs the more elemental language in deliberately intellectual phrasing ('the last gyzym of consciousness,' 'solipsisms of johns') or rhapsodic lyricism ('sweetened the snatches of a million girls trembling in the sunset')" (91–92). It is just this that Bukowski does *not* do. It is the very casualness of Bukowski's vulgarity that bring readers up short and in some cases offends them.

Chapter 2: The Individual and the Social in Bukowski's Poetry of the 80s

52:*"Indeed, a striking feature . . ."* While this is not new in American poetry (Williams was something of a precursor in this regard), Bukowski has pushed this refusal of metaphor and of any kind of symbolism to a new level. In this, Bukowski was part of what Marjorie Perloff saw as a larger trend in American poetry. See her "Realism and the Confessional Mode of Robert Lowell" in *Contemporary Literature* 11.4 (1970): 470–487.

60: *"Bukowski's position is a not uncommon . . ."* It has been aptly characterized by Raymond Williams as the "personal revolt" in his analysis of the phenomenon: "It is no accident, but an element of this structure of thinking, that the terms of the personal revolt so often include contempt for other persons: the crowd, the herd, the benighted masses. A point can be reached when the only reality is 'I and the crowd,' and the vacuum this leaves is filled by acceptance of the 'impersonal' system . . ."(111).

63: *"One can see why Bukowski . . ."* In a letter to Jory Sherman he wrote: "Jeffers, I suppose, is my god—the only man since Shakey to write the long narrative poem that does not put one to sleep. . . . Jeffers is stronger, darker, more exploratively modern and mad." (Cherkovski, *Hank*, 118.)

65: *"I should have loved her more . . ."* One bit of linguistic confusion illustrates the narrator's dilemma. Bukowski writes: "the best thing I liked about / her was" when what we would expect is either "the best thing about her was" or "what I liked best about her was." It is the ultimate testimony to the problematic of unmediated refusal because it results in objectifying everything.

66: *"This becomes the ultimate objectification . . ."* For Bukowski's poetry this dilemma has consequences beyond its content. His penchant for objectification has led, in his poetry, to a reliance on metonymy and an avoidance of metaphor. Bukowski shies away from language that is not concrete, objectified. Much safer are the metonymies which can never be completely divorced from the object itself.

Chapter 3: Poetry and the Working Class

69–70: *"Moreover, the extent . . ."* Bukowski originally began as a short-story writer, publishing five stories between 1944 and 1948. When he resumed writing in the mid-1950s, coincidental with beginning his career as a postal clerk, it was as a poet. Towards the end of that career he began publishing short prose again and on leaving the Post Office, he began writing novels. Work as the content of his writing became more prominent after he left the jobs behind him. (See *Post Office, Factotum, Dangling in the Tournefortia, War All the Time*.)

76: *"Thus the winner needs the losers . . ."* The mechanism whereby Chinaski/"Bukowski" "realizes" his superiority to the "common herd" appears in a number of contexts. Cp. the poem, "fire station," where the unemployed, humiliated narrator engages in and wins the games of "twenty-one" with the firemen because, "they were bad players really . . . basically they hit too high, / didn't hold low / enough" (P 40–41) and the incident in *Factotum*, where Chinaski and Manny take their co-workers' money (but don't wager it): "they didn't know how to bet; they bet too short or too long" (107).

80: *"The lack of explicitness . . ."* Contrast, for example, the scene in *Factotum*, where the recently fired Henry Chinaski wants to get his last check "and get drunk." "That may not sound noble," he acknowledges, "but it's my choice" (158). It is the very acknowledgement of the irrationality that assures the passage its success. The self manifested hero may or may not be admirable, but it is more in control of its manifestations.

88: *"In the absence of any kind . . ."* Though, by the time Bukowski left the Post Office, this was clearly not true for many postal workers. Cp. Aronowitz: "The 1970 postal walkout was remarkable both for its militancy and for the break with the old traditions of postal unionism . . ." (311).

92: *"As it is, though . . ."* Still, it represents a quantum leap forward from the early Post Office poem, "the workers," first collected in *Crucifix in a Death Hand* (1965 [B 58]).

Chapter 4: Metonymy

96: *"In an earlier essay . . ."* Roman Jakobsen, "Marginal Notes of the Poet Pasternak," 310.

96: *"We need a literary term . . ."* Charles Altieri, "Objective Image and Act of Mind in Modern Poetry" in *PMLA* 91.1 (1976): 103.

96: *"Bukowski's early poetry had shown . . ."* Jory Sherman, *Bukowski: Friendship, Fame & Bestial Myth*, 22. Bukowski does admire Neruda: "Outside of myself I don't know anyone with such a clean line. When he says 'blue' he means blue." Neeli Cherkovski, *Whitman's*, 13. See also

Fox, 15. For Bukowski's negative reaction to these early interpretations see his letter to Carl Weissner of 1. Aug. 1969 (?) in Charles Bukowski, *Gedichte die einer schrieb bevor er in S. Stockwerk aus dem Fenster sprang*, 93. For Williams, see Jimmy Cain, "Bukowski's Imagist Roots," in *West Georgia College Review* 20 (1987): 10.

102: *"Altieri feared that '[m]etonymy' . . ."* Such a reductive view would seem to accept the possibility of a "value-free" depiction of the world. Sartre's response (in *What Is Literature?*) seems convincing: "The error of realism has been to believe that the real reveals itself to contemplation, and that consequently one could draw an impartial picture of it. How could that be possible, since the very perception is partial, since by itself the naming is already a modification?" (66).

110: *"A rough count . . . yielded . . ."* By comparison, in Lowell's "Sailing Home from Rapallo" (also an extended narrative) roughly 20% of the words are adjectives.

111: *"As a stylistic device . . ."* Cp. "They had hammers with which they pounded objects in front of them"; "Men sat at desks under reading lamps working at copy"; "Firemen in large metal helmets. Firemen dressed in asbestos. Firemen with axes" (F 13, 18, 101). Articles are, grammatically, "a subclass of determiners, the class of words that specifies, points, counts or ascribes possession and by this specification implies some kind of relationship between the article and the subject determining them." (I owe this formulation to Prof. Carey McIntosh.) Bukowski's omission of this subclass in these and similar passages throughout his writing reflects, it seems to me, an innate distaste for effecting any kind of relationship (let alone identification) between humans and work. It is the grammatical registration of alienate labor that often informs his descriptions of work.

Excursus: Brecht

116: *"In what houses / Of gold-glittering Lima . . ."* Bertolt Brecht, *Poems*
1913–1956 ed. John Willett, 252. (All the Brecht poems quoted are from this edition, unless otherwise noted.)
116: *"This accounts for the power . . ."* Bertolt Brecht, *Arbeitsjournal*, 780. (Referred to as AJ hereafter.)
118: *"We hold the curve like tape . . ."* Bertolt Brecht, "Singende Steyrwägen," in *Gesammelte Werke IV Gedichte*, 318. (My translation.)

119: *"The 'sentimentality, lack of authenticity'. . ."* See Bertolt Brecht, "Kurzer Bericht über 400 (vierhundert) Junge Lyriker" in *Über Lyrik*, 9.

Chapter 5: Work, Refusal of Work and the Job in *Post Office* and *Factotum*

123: *"The only human essence . . ."* A. Negri, "Archaeology and Project: The Mass Worker and the Social Worker," 226.

126: *"But with Roosevelt's opting for full employment . . ."* The turning point was Roosevelt's refusal to fully back the Black–Connery thirty-hours bill of 1933. See Benjamin Hunnicutt, *Work Without End: Abandoning Shorter Hours for the Right to Work*, Chapter 6, "FDR Counters Shorter Hours."

127: *"Taylor is in fact expressing . . ."* He is referring to Taylor's famous characterization of the pig-iron handler: "This work is so crude and elementary in its nature that the writer firmly believes that it would be possible to train an intelligent gorilla so as to become a more efficient pig-iron handler than any man can be." Frederick Winslow Taylor, *The Principles of Scientific Management*, 40.

127: *" 'Womanizing' demands too much leisure . . ."* For a contemporary expression of this "ethic" compare GM assembly-line worker Ben Hamper on a womanizing auto-worker who thinks a switch to the first shift will allow him time "to prowl for chicks the rest of the night.

'It doesn't work like that,' I told him. 'First shift only works for the married guys. They have a very rigid system—rush home, drink three beers, eat supper, watch *Wheel of Fortune*, hop the old lady and be sound asleep by 9:00. Clean, decent American living. A bar hound like you will never beat the clock. You'll miss so much work, your ass will be out on Van Slyke within a month.' " Ben Hamper, *Rivethead: Tales from the Assembly Line*, 186. (Gramsci's Latin quotation translates as "easy and available love.")

128: *". . . and those who worked them . . ."* Another factor was that the work week had not only stopped getting shorter, it had begun to get longer: "a comparison of 1949 and 1978 shows a 1.3 hour *increase* in average weekly working time." (Roediger and Foner, 257. Emphasis in original.) It gets worse according to Juliet B. Schor, who examined the period 1969–1987: "the average employed person is now on the job an additional 163 hours, or the equivalent of an extra month a year" (29). For the increased technological efficiency, cp. Harry Braverman: "Thus in the United States between 1947 and 1964 . . . the output of the textile industries grew by more than 40 percent but employment was cut by one third. Other industries, such as iron and steel foundries, lumber and wood products, malt liquors and footwear, showed production increases of from 15 percent to 40 percent in the same period, accompanied by employment drops of ten percent to 25 percent. The petroleum industry poured out five sixths more product at the end of the period than at the beginning, but its employment was one fourth lower." "The Degradation of Work in the Twentieth Century," in *Monthly Review* 34.1 (1982): 10.

128–129: *"Work and the 'work ethic'..."* I use quotation marks around the phrase because there is some doubt as to how strong such an ethic ever was, at least in some areas of Western capitalism. As one example, see E. P. Thompson's discussion of "Saint Monday" in his essay, "Time, Work-Discipline, and Industrial Capitalism," in *Past & Present* 38 (December 1967): 73–74. It is not an accident that a number of the texts that I discuss in this essay were all published at roughly the same time, between 1971 and 1975, the beginning of capitalism's long crisis whose now notorious symptom, the decline in the real wage, is usually seen to have commenced in 1973.

130: *"For the world of human freedom..."* Herbert Marcuse, *An Essay On Liberation,* 6. Here Marcuse openly follows the Marx of the *Grundrisse.* Marcuse also saw the issue in concrete terms: "Since the length of the working day is itself one of the principal repressive factors imposed upon the pleasure principle by the reality principle, the reduction of the working day ... is the first prerequisite for freedom." Quoted in Roediger and Foner, vii. Marcuse's prescription is idealist in that he would seem here to be saying that "values" are the cause of the " 'voluntary' servitude." His suggestions for how change may come about, "disengagement and refusal," seem passive, rather than engaged.

132: *"damn near anybody..." [9/13]" Post Office* was reset with new pagination in 1992 for the 26th and subsequent printings. Citations therefore give two page numbers, to the earlier and later printings respectively.

138: *"This bit of Fordist..."* Ford himself put it this way: "When first we raised the wage to five dollars a day, we had to exercise some supervision over the living of the men because so many of them, being foreign born, did not raise their standards of living in accord with their higher incomes." Henry Ford in collaboration with Samuel Crowther, *Today and Tomorrow,* 159.

138: *"Since the Post Office..."* Such threats were even endorsed by unions. Cp. Roediger and Foner: "Moreover, unions repeatedly connected their acceptance of long hours with Cold War preparedness, as *The Machinist* [a union paper] did in 1957 when it headlined the question: 'Will Soviets Cut Their Overtime?' " (269).

139: *"This is a book about the working class . . ."* Harry Braverman, *Labor and Monopoly Capital: The Degradation of Work in the Twentieth Century*, 26–27. Much of what Braverman says here is relevant to what makes Bukowski's writing about the American working class as important and powerful as it is, especially his remark that "what is needed first of all is a picture of the working class as it exists, as the shape given to the working population by the capital accumulation process."

139: *"This does not mean . . ."* Just how limited is seen, for example, in Studs Terkel's interview with a mail carrier in *Working* (361–364). This man feels quite differently about the job than Chinaski does. Subjectively, it would appear that he is not an alienated worker, though any but the most superficial reading of the interview leaves one with an impression of a worker who is, objectively, alienated.

140: *"In the course of the decade . . ."* Twenty-two, I think. The uncertainty is owing to certain problems of categorization, e.g., should his cleaning the venetian blinds of the Philadelphia bar for five dollars and free drinks, be counted as gainful employment? Should the trackman and cab driver positions where he receives no money (and no payment of any kind by the cab company) and never makes it beyond a kind of pre-trainee or trainee status, be counted as jobs? The jobs are: packing magazines at a magazine publishers distributing house, compositor's helper at a newspaper, trackman, stock boy in an auto parts warehouse, subway advertisement installer, oven operator in a dog-biscuit factory, shipping clerk in a ladies' dresswear shop, stock/shipping clerk in a bicycle warehouse, receiving clerk at an auto parts warehouse, "extra ball-bearing" at a clothing store, delivery man at a clothes manufacturer, shipping clerk at a fluorescent light fixture company, maintenance man/janitor at the Los Angeles *Times*, stock clerk in an auto brake supply house, truck driver with the Red Cross, cab driver trainee at Yellow Cab, shipping clerk in an art supply store, warehouseman at a "company specializing in Christmas items," "Coconut Man" at National Bakery Goods, loading dock worker and Sunday manager of the employment office at the Hotel Sans. *Factotum* thus realizes what we could call, borrowing a term from Negri, the social-service "mass worker," i.e., a semi-skilled worker whose skills are well on the road to being completely abstracted. See "Archaeology and Project," 217–18.

141: *"I remember how my father . . ."* Cp. *Ham on Rye* where, in the Depression-era family of Henry Chinaski's youth, to be without a job, or rather to be known to be without a job, was viewed as the worst of fates: "My mother went to her low-paying job each morning and my father, who didn't have a job, left each morning too. Although most of the neighbors were unemployed he didn't want them to think he was jobless. so he got into his car each morning at the same time and drove off as if he were going to work. Then in the evening he would return at exactly the same time" (113).

145: "*In* Factotum *Bukowski . . .*" This is in clear contrast to *Post Office* where Chinaski had at first rebelled against the work load, "I took my time" (42/69); "I just stood there in my fancy new clothes. Stood there with my hands in my pockets" (47/78), but by the end of the novel has been beaten down into a state beyond caring. On being "counseled" for low productivity, he says, "The clerks grab what they call the 'fat' trays. I don't bother. Somebody has to stick with the tough mail" (105/180).

149: "*The working class strategy . . .*" Emphasis in original. This is sensible in any event since full employment under capitalism, outside of a war economy, has never been anything but an illusion, for reasons demonstrated in a seminal essay by Michal Kalecki a half century ago: "The assumption that a Government will maintain full employment in a capitalist economy if it only knows how to do it is fallacious. In this connection the misgivings of big business about maintenance of full employment are of paramount importance This attitude was shown clearly in the great depression in the thirties, when big business opposed consistently experiments for increasing employment by Government spending in all countries, except Nazi Germany." See "Political Aspects of Full Employment," in Michal Kalecki, *Selected Essays on the Dynamics of the Capitalist Economy: 1933–1970*, 138. The ZEROWORK group (some of whose articles have been collected in *Midnight Oil*) was the most significant American representative of the Italian New Left Autonomy Movement, one of the most influential European marxist groups unallied to the Communist Party.

149: "*In the Tendency . . .*" Mario Montano, "Notes on the International Crisis," in *Midnight Oil*, 139.

149: "*The idea that the worker . . .*" Here a comparison with Jack London is illuminating. In London, the worker takes a perverse kind of pride in his capacity to suffer prodigies of exploitation. No matter how difficult the work may be, as in the steam laundry in *Martin Eden*, nor how duplicitously exploited the worker is, as when, in *John Barleycorn*, the young London—unbeknownst to himself—is given the work of two men to do and nearly works himself into physical collapse (the physical effects of the overwork remaining with him for a year after he quits the job), the relationship between production and the wage is never questioned. In spite of these trials London's workers pride themselves on staying the course and on doing a good job, encouraged, in part, by the Horatio Alger myth of unlimited opportunity for advancement:

"A canal boy could become a president. Any boy, who took employ-ment with any firm, could, by thrift, energy, and sobriety, learn the business and rise from position to position until he was taken in as a junior partner. After that the senior partnership was only a matter of time." *John Barleycorn*, in Jack London, *Novels and Social Writings*, (1032). It should be noted, though, that London is being somewhat iron-ical in this reference to the rags-to-riches myth.

150: "*The latter phenomenon* . . ." The New Left viewed these forms of refusal positively. As Negri wrote: such phenomena "gradually unco-vered, in increasingly socialized forms, an attitude of struggle against work, a desire for liberation from work . . . as conceded to the capitalist in exchange for a wage" (205).

151: "*It is no accident* . . ." "For my second novel, which is just out (FAC-TOTUM), on the other hand, I needed four years. That was an entire-ly different piece of work." See "Bukowski Interview" with Thomas Kettner, in *Kaputt in Hollywood*, 141 (my translation).

Excursus: Miller

153: "*I held the job for almost five years* . . ." Henry Miller, *The Cosmo-logical Eye*, 368.

155: "*On the other hand* . . ." There were similarities in this area, though. Nin comments that "in all the stories he tells me, it is the woman who has taken the initiative. He even admits that this is what he likes about the prostitutes" (125).

156: "*After working as a journeyman* . . ." Mary V. Dearborn, *The Hap-piest Man Alive: A Biography of Henry Miller* (New York: Simon and Schuster, 1991), 51. Cp. "The Tailor Shop": "A joint corporation of father and son, with mother holding the boodle" (79).

156: "*Yet in a perverse* . . ." Robert Ferguson, *Henry Miller: A Life*, 103. Miller also tried to start a speakeasy by borrowing money from his Uncle Dave and his mother, "whom he wilfully misled about the pur-pose of the loan" (111).

156: "*Whether it is as a* . . ." Henry Miller, *Gliding into the Everglades*, 44.
157–158: "*For Miller, borrowing* . . ." *Sexus*, 10, 24, 44.

Chapter 6: Politics, Class
and the Plebeian Tradition

163: "*I had also read somewhere . . .*" This echoes Harry in Hemingway's story, "The Snows of Kilimanjaro": ". . . when your affections are not too involved you give much better value for the money." Bukowski had used this sentiment earlier in the short story "Politics" (in *South of No North*), an earlier version of the L.A. City College episode. A significant difference between the two versions is that in "Politics," Bukowski ties Chinaski's activism to the College's decision to charge a two-dollar enrollment fee.

164: "*(Indeed as one German critic . . .*" Karl Corino rev. of *Fast eine Jugend* in *Stuttgarter Zeitung* 10 Nov. 1983. (Schmidt, 105.)

168–169: "*experiences its exploitation . . .*" Nicos Poulantzas, *Classes in Contemporary Capitalism*, 290. Cp., also: "Afraid of proletarianization below, attracted to the bourgeoisie above, the new petty bourgeoisie often aspires to 'promotion,' to a 'career,' to 'upward social mobility,' i.e. to becoming bourgeois . . . by way of the 'individual' transfer of the 'best' and 'most capable' . . . this is particularly focused on the educational apparatus, given the role that the latter plays in this respect" (292).

169: "*They stop at a grove.*" According to Carey McWilliams, orange groves had a special connotation in Southern California that help us understand why Chinaski, Sr., directs his anger toward this target: "The aristocrat of the orchards, it has, by a natural affinity, drawn to it the rich and the well-born, creating a unique type of rural-urban aristocracy. There is no crop in the whole range of American agriculture the growing of which confers quite the same status that is associated with ownership of an orange grove" (207). He notes that "The grove . . . is not a farm, but a kind of outdoor hothouse guarded as jealously as a scottish lord's hunting park. (If you doubt this statement, try to pick an orange sometime in Southern California.)" Carey McWilliams, *Southern California: An Island on the Land*, 208.

171: "*He still thought about being rich.*" Bukowski is emphasizing class differences, as is clear from *Hank*, where Cherkovski writes: "In *Ham on Rye*, Hank tends to portray himself as a lower-class kid thrown in with those from rich families. The reality, according to his class-mates, was that plenty of children from poorer families attended Los Angeles High School. The school was a cross-section of the city's economic makeup, and by no means an enclave of the rich" (30).

172: "*In any event, the sacrifices . . .*" Nor did Bukowski himself find the "deal" attractive: "And having watched my father . . . I realized that a man could work a lifetime and still remain poor; his wages were taken in buying things he needed, small things like automobiles and beds and radios and food and clothing, which . . . demanded a price far beyond their worth and kept him poor. . . ." ("A Rambling Essay on Poetics and the Bleeding Life Written While Drinking a Six-Pack [Tall]," in Douglas Blazek, ed. *A Bukowski Sampler*, 9.)

175: *"The crux of the conflict . . ."* McWilliams wrote: "From 1890 to 1910, wages were from twenty to thirty, and in some categories even forty percent lower than in San Francisco. It was precisely this margin that enabled Los Angeles to grow as an industrial center. Thus the maintenance of a cheap labor pool became an indispensable cog in the curious economics of the region. For the system to work, however, the labor movement had to remain unorganized; otherwise it would become impossible to exploit the homeseeker element. The system required—it absolutely demanded—a non-union open-shop setup. . . . Once lured to the region and saddled with an equity in a cheap home, most of the homeowners had no means of escape. Just as the open-shop principle was essential to the functioning of the cheap labor market, so the continued influx of homeseekers made possible the retention of the open shop" (277).

175–176: *"Homeownership growth in the 1920s . . ."* Mike Davis, *City of Quartz*, 28.

178: *"There was something wrong . . ."* Bukowski's analysis of the varying degrees of patriotism among the rich and the poor, and the reasons for that variation is remarkably similar to Noam Chomsky's in *Power and Ideology*: "the educated classes are not only the main targets of the system of indoctrination but also its practitioners; their self-interest dictates that they adopt and believe its doctrines . . ." (118–19).

179: *"The alternative plebeian reaction . . ."* It is this rational utopian strain that in the end comes closest to expressing the ideology of the novels. It is the line of thought that gives the lie to the occasional existentialist utterances of that Chinaski who claims the narrator of Dostoyevsky's *Notes from Underground* as his spiritual progenitor. For after all, is not the view Chinaski expresses here at the end of *Factotum* diametrically opposed to that of the underground man who states: "I will not accept as my crowning wish a block of flats for poor tenants on thousand-year leases and, in any case, with 'Wagenheim Dental Surgeon' as the signboard" (42)?

181: *"On the other hand, the declining . . ."* Cp.: ". . . the supply of college graduates will increase by 12 or 13 million during the decade [the

1990s], probably a quarter of whom will be assigned to the burgeoning ranks of 'overeducated' clerical or service workers. (Between 1970 and 1982 the percentage of college graduates attaining entry to technical and professional occupations declined from 65 per cent to 54 percent—despite the much-vaunted rise of new 'high-tech' industries.)" Mike Davis, *Prisoners of the American Dream*, 217. See Bukowski's recent poem, "Dinosauria, We": "as the supermarket bag boy holds a college degree" (R, 9).

Chapter 7: Sex, Women and Irony

183: *"Bukowski's antics with women . . ."* Len Fulton, "See Bukowski Run," *Small Press Review* 4. April 1973 [1972]: 31.

184: *"In his novels Bukowski . . ."* Karin Huffzky, "Big Daddy Is Watching You," in *literatur konkret* (Fall 1979): 22. Hence, it becomes important to recognize the distance between the author and his protagonist because this leads to the realization that traditional male chauvinist attitudes are being undermined. As Millet noted of Henry Miller: "the major flaw in his oeuvre—too close an identification with the persona, 'Henry Miller'—always operates insidiously against the likelihood of persuading us that Miller the man is any wiser than Miller the character" (413–14). The problem is present in Norman Mailer, too, but in a more subtle way: "Mailer, of course, makes a fetish of being male; but what gives his fetishism its unique quality is the fact that it is impossible to determine to what degree it is parody and to what degree it is endorsement." Judith Fetterly, *The Resisting Reader: A Feminist Approach to American Fiction*, 155.

186: *"although she cries 'rape!' . . ."* A woman clawing both sides of a man's (usually Chinaski's) face is something that happens a number of times in Bukowski. In fact, it achieves an almost formulaic quality in his descriptions. See, for example, *Factotum*, 29 and 85 and *Notes*, 241.

191: *"It is the loss of control . . ."* One might also note the developing oedipal relationship with Wilbur as the father and the women somewhere between mothers and sisters to Chinaski. More significant, though, is the reversal of the situation Chinaski normally sets up: he is not paying (for) them; hence they cannot be whores (to him). However he does his best to objectify them in the scene in the boat mentioned above.

193–194: *"Given his unwillingness . . ."* Unresolved neurotic conflicts are undoubtedly at work. Without entering into a psychoanalytic discussion, one might note that while Chinaski's relationship with his father is presented in some depth (in *Ham On Rye*), that with his mother is barely touched upon. Her absence from the fiction is significant. For the classic psychoanalytic view of the desire for women who will be unfaithful, see Sigmund Freud, "A Special Type of Object Choice made by Men." Freud connects such a choice to early feelings for the mother and states that the need to compulsively repeat such choices exists because "[I]f the love objects chosen by our type are above everything mother-surrogates, then the formation of a long series of them . . . becomes comprehensible as well. We learn . . . that the pressing desire in the unconscious for some irreplaceable thing often resolves itself into an endless series in actuality—endless for the very reason that the satisfaction longed for is never found in any surrogate" (53).

195: "*It is, presumably* . . ." An interesting difference between the dream scene and the one in the bar is that here, Chinaski takes out his anger on the man, rather than on Jan, as he did in the bar. The suggestion of a homoerotic component present in such triangular constellations is underlined at the end of the novel when Chinaski, concealed, watches Jan kissing her new lover. It was given vivid expression in Bukowski's poem "fire station," a poem that also seems to be about Jane Cooney, Bukowski's lover of those years. See the author's "An Analysis of Charles Bukowski's 'fire station,' " where such behavior is analyzed in detail, in *Concerning Poetry* 18 (1985): 67–83.

196: "*Men are shown as 'helpless'* . . ." Chinaski, contrary to Huffzky's interpretation, is no narcissist. In Freud's terms, Chinaski loves according to the anaclitic, rather than the narcissistic type, choosing "women who tend." Cp. Chinaski's statement, a few pages along, after he has left Jan: "I have followed so many women up stairways like that, always thinking, if only some nice lady like this one would offer to take care of me and feed me warm tasty food and lay out clean stockings and shorts for me to wear, I would accept" (123). See Freud, "On Narcissism: An Introduction," 71.

197: "*In the course of* Women . . ." Jimmy E. Cain, Jr. "Women: The Siren Calls of Boredom" in *The Review of Contemporary Fiction* 5.3 (1985): 12. (I counted 20.)

198: "Women *is both an attempt* . . ." Fulton, 31.

198: "*Although the book is entitled* Women . . ." The original title was not *Women*. It is partially preserved in the German edition, which is also not identical in other respects to the American. The original working title was: *Love Tale of the Hyena*, clearly a more ironic title. See Charles Bukowski, *Das Liebesleben der Hyäne* (Köln: Kiepenhauer &

Witsch, 1986 [1980]). In addition there are slight differences between the first and second printings of the American edition. See *Hank*, 262.

198: *"At moments like these . . ."* Cp. Fulton: "Bukowski offers us a fishbowl view of the base and brutal repertoire of the American male's hangup on 'being a man' . . ." (30).

203: *"But whatever we finally decide . . ."* Bukowski greatly admires Thurber, especially for his portrayal of male-female relationships. He told Penn: "About the last best humorist was a guy called James Thurber. But his humor was so great, they had to overlook it. Now this guy was what you call a psychologist/psychiatrist of the ages. He had the man/woman thing—you know, people seeing things" (96). Bukowski's drawings also bear a striking resemblance to Thurber's.

203: *"he has begun to deconstruct . . ."* Cp. one critic who, in just this context, wrote: "in the age of women's liberation, his poems and stories read like a tragi-comic swansong to the last man." Hans Christoph Buch, in *Süddeutsche Zeitung* 18 May 1977, in Schmidt, 44.

211: *"I wasn't quite sure of anything."* It is worth noting that Chinaski's imagined family does not include children. While he is consistently shown as loving, affectionate and supportive of his illegitimate child, the traditional nuclear family has always been anathema to him, a result, probably, of his own unfortunate experience in that institution.

213: *" 'O.K.,' I said, . . ."* It should be noted that with the topic of clitoral orgasm, a major issue of the 1960s and 1970s is here broached. See the whole discussion of female sexuality, including the issue of clitoral vs. vaginal orgasms in Millet, 162–169, as well as in Norman Mailer's *The Prisoner of Sex*, 71–90.

Chapter 8: Connections:
Fante—Hamsun—Mahler

219: *"Indeed, the revival of interest . . ."* Cp. *Hank*: "Bukowski had shown John Martin Fante's work, most of which had gone out of print, and . . . Black Sparrow Press was now reissuing all of it, and . . . it was selling well" (304). For an account of the Fante renaissance, especially as it affects the film industry, see Frank Spotnitz, "The Hottest Dead Man in Hollywood," *American Film* July/August 1989.

219: *"Although everyone may not . . ."* See the characterization of Fante as "a fellow ham that Black Sparrow Press has rescued from obscurity." in Ken Tucker, rev. of Charles Bukowski, *Dangling in the Tournefortia*, the *Village Voice* 23 Mar. 1982: 42.

220: "*(For thirty years . . .*" That Fante valued financial success highly is clear in a letter to H. L. Mencken (an early admirer of Fante's and instrumental in launching his career): "It has taken me four years to realize that what I want most from art is money. I'll get it, too, and plenty of it, if my kidneys and liver hold out." Letter of 11 Jan. 1937 in *Fante/Mencken: John Fante & H.L. Mencken: A Personal Correspondence 1930-1952*, ed., by Michael Moreau, 110. Cp., also, Cherkovski in *Hank*: "My uncle and Fante had been best friends back in the early thirties. 'He wanted to be the great American writer,' Uncle Herman told me. 'Somehow he got sidetracked into Hollywood' " (304). This is also Bukowski's view: "Bukowski is unequivocal in condemning Fante's screenwriting. 'I think it was utterly destructive,' he says. 'I asked him, "Why in the hell did you ever go to Hollywood?" "Times were hard," he said, "and Mencken told me to go for it—go take 'em." And I think this was very bad advice.' " Spotnitz, 44. Yet, according to Joyce Fante, when he had achieved financial success, had time and was in his prime, he still didn't write, "spen[ding] literally years of his life at the golf course and the gambling table." See *John Fante: Selected Letters 1932–1981*, ed., Seamus Cooney, 214.

220: "*like a man who had found gold . . .*" Bukowski mentions two other books as influencing him, *Wait Until Spring, Bandini* (1938) and *Dago Red* (1940). Thus it is the early fiction that is important for its influence on Bukowski.

222: "*The acceptance of his . . .*" This issue is a good example of Fante's refusal to confront his own ambivalence on a subject. It is especially evident in *Full of Life* where Fante has written a veritable paean to marriage and reproduction. (Indeed, a good part of the novel is taken up with the preparations for the trip to the hospital for the birth.) *Full of Life* is so relentlessly good-natured, so like a fairy-tale (or at least the conventional image of a fairy tale) in its optimistic way of looking at its world that it comes to seem over-determined and to be purposely avoiding any conflicts that the protagonist may have felt in the situation. For a description of just how false the novel was to the actual situation see *Selected Letters*, 225.

222: "*In the subsequent novels . . .*" This attitude perhaps accounts for Bukowski's positive reaction to *Eraserhead,* an anti-nuclear family movie, and, given Bukowski's general dislike of films, not an especially propitious candidate for his approval. See "Charles Bukowski interviewed by Chris Hodenfeld," in *Film Comment* 23.4 (1987): 54.

222: "*In Bukowski's work . . .*" Cp. "we've got to communicate": " 'but no / you don't *like* Lance, do you? / he wears a necktie and he's into real estate . . .' " (D 93).

224: *"In several ways . . ."* Cp. Moreau on the circumstances surrounding the rejection of Fante's first novel: *"The Road to Los Angeles* had been rejected by Knopf and . . . half a dozen other publishers, most likely because of the explicit language and subject matter and the unconscionable character of the protagonist, the young Arturo Bandini" (*Fante/Mencken*, 116). (It was first published by Black Sparrow Press in 1985, two years after Fante's death.)

224: *"Like the young Bukowski . . ."* Norman Mailer, in an essay published a quarter century after *Ask the Dust*, generalizes well about this situation: "The people who were most American by birth, and who had the most to do with managing America, gave themselves a literature which had the least to say about the real phenomena of American life, most particularly the accelerated rate, the awful rate, of growth and anomaly through all of society. That sort of literature and that kind of attempt to explain America was left to the sons of immigrants. . . ." Norman Mailer, "The Argument Reinvigorated" in Marcus Klein, ed., *The American Novel Since World War II*, 70.

225–226: *"Himself a poor . . ."* Fante's racism is even more striking than his misogyny. His profound ambivalence towards race and its intimate connection (for him) with sexuality become clear on reading the passages in his letters and the journal entry on his projected Filipino novel. The novel was to be called *The Little Brown Brothers* and Fante "got one third of it written . . . before abandoning it in 1944." (SL, 98.) In a 1935 letter to Carey McWilliams he wrote: "I have come to the conclusion that the Filipino is a pathetic species hopelessly out of the American pale. There are not many of them, perhaps not more than 125,000 in the United States, but their outcast existence, their diversions, labors and loves, are so curious that they form a mountain of grotesque Americana. Fundamentally, of course, they are no better or worse than any people. . . . And then there is that most marvelous folk lore the American workingman has built up for the Filipino. Nine out of ten Americans who work side by side with the Filipino in canneries and lettuce-field—the hundred-percenter—believe the Filipino is 'queer,' is successful with American women because he is a cunt-licker, because he 'lavishes' money on them; in fact a score of reasons false, without once mentioning that perhaps American girls simply like Filipinos for what they are: clean, primitive, sensual, soft-hearted little guys who need a woman even as you or I . . ." (SL, 100). It is hard not to see something of Fante's own prejudices behind his "sociological" presentation of the "nine out of ten Americans' " beliefs. According to Joyce Fante, "Covici himself detested the work. He said he had a very strong sense that John was 'off the track.' Fante felt that Covici detected an implied racism" (SL, 207). Covici rejected the novel. The issues of race and sex combine in *Ask the Dust* to produce the odd and intense relationship between Arturo Bandini and Camilla Lopez.

227: *"It should also be noted . . ."* For a detailed discussion of Bukowski's efforts to avoid even a hint of racism, see the author's "The Blue Suit: An Episode from Charles Bukowski's *Factotum*" in *Germanica Olomucensia* VIII (1989): 85–92 (Olomouc, Czechoslovakia).

230: *"Vera, who virtually assaults . . ."* Cp. his letter of 17 Oct. 1951 to Carey McWilliams in New York: "How can you stand it in that filthy bedlam, niggers to the right, dagos to the left, and Hebes everywhere. . . ." Although the tone suggests that the writer thinks he is making such comments in quotation marks, the final impression is that of someone who is expressing his own (ambivalent) feelings without wanting to assume responsibility for them. In the same letter he remarks (in what seems a clear instance of projection), apropos of a witness in the HUAC hearings on Communist influence in the film industry: "I caught that serial in a bar on Western Avenue, with service men looking on, and it was acutely painful because they hated the sight of her, of her Jewishness. . . ." *Selected Letters*, 227, 229.

231: *"I was not Hamsun . . ."* Charles Bukowski, "Forward" to *The Roominghouse Madrigals: Early Selected poems 1946–1966*, 6. Cp. also: "I think much of the work of Knut Hamsun as a man who grew and widened . . . his first book HUNGER was the most interesting. . . ." Charles Bukowski, "He Beats his Women."

237: *"Readers of Bukowski. . . ."* For a detailed survey of the mentions of composers in Bukowski's work see Robert Sandarg, "The Classical Buk," in *Sure, the charles bukowski newsletter* (Ojai: Edward L. Smith) 3 (1991): 22–32.

238: *"Hence, unlike in . . ."* In fact, in those novels which are most indebted to specific predecessors, as *Factotum* is to *Hunger* and *Women* is to Boccaccio's *Decameron*, there is no suggestion in the text of such a relationship.

238: *"They are peripheral . . ."* Cp. Bukowski's own listening habits: "I have a radio—no records—and I turn that classical music station on and hope it brings me something I can align with while I'm writing. I don't listen deliberately. . . . I don't. I use it like the modern person uses a television set: they turn it on and walk around and kind of ignore it, but it's there. It's a fireplace full of coals that does something for them" (Wennersten, 50).

239: *"This is another expression . . ."* See the poem "the soldier, his wife and the bum," in *Run with the Hunted*, ed. John Martin (New York: HarperCollins, 1993), to my knowledge the only mention in his poetry of attending a concert: "and the music was good but something about the / audience was not" (171). He expresses his dislike for the movies as an art form a number of times, going so far as to call them a "con" and one can't help thinking that this is in part owing to the collective nature of their reception. (Perhaps this has changed with the advent of the VCR.) Cp. his comments to Chris Hodenfeld: "It's embarrassing to see a movie. I feel gypped, sitting there with all these people. . . . I feel mobbed, I feel diluted, I feel mugged by watching a movie. I feel they take something away from me. They've chewed up my auras and mutilated me. I want to mutilate my own auras at my own behest, I don't want to sit in front of a screen and do it." Chris Hodenfeld, 55–56.

239: *"In Bukowski's writings . . ."* "Classical Buk." According to Sandarg "his oeuvre contains nearly 300 references to no less than 50 different composers" (22).

239: *"Mahler's reputation . . ."* Cp. "Although Mahler was not in popular or critical favor before the 1950's, performances of his music were by no means rare on the Continent. But recordings were exceedingly rare; this was largely due to the dominance of the English and American recordings industries of the commercial market which meant that outside Europe very few records of Mahler appeared." Burnett James, *The Music of Gustav Mahler*, 204.

240: *"Adorno suggested that . . ."* Mahler, 29, 216. Cp. also: "his strong ego helped the weak, the speechless to express themselves and saved their aesthetic image." "Wiener Gedenkrede," 137.

240: *"While it is hard to imagine . . ."* Cp., for example, the poem "classical music and me" (R, 52–56) as well as Henry Chinaski's possession of the two-volume *Lives of the Classical and Modern Composers* in *Post Office*.

241: *". . . instrumental voices that . . ."* The posthorn solo at the beginning of the third movement of the *Third Symphony* is often cited as an instance of such prominence.

241: *"Mahler substituted . . ."* "Gedenkrede," 117.

241: *"Both these devices . . ."* Indeed, it is just when Bukowski attempts a "reconciliation" of this split, as in *Post Office* and *Women* that he fails artistically; when he acknowledges the split, as in *Factotum*, *Ham on Rye* and "Sparks" he is most successful.

242: "*Mahler, the complex composer . . .*" See Lea, chapter IV, "A Musical Ironist": "Mahler's symphonies differ from the nineteenth-century symphony as derived from Beethoven in two essential respects: they abandon the idea of a single basic key and they make abundant use of irony. I am using irony here in the meaning of incongruousness, paradox, contradiction, incompatibility and also as an unmasking or disillusioning device" (67). Irony would almost seem to demand abandoning "the idea of a single basic key," an indication of an identity Mahler rejected.

Excursus: Gleason

243: "*On more than one occasion . . .*" See his letter to Loss Glazier of 16 Feb. 1983 (quoted at the beginning of the previous chapter). Although he doesn't list W. C. Fields as one of these influences, I think there are similarities here too. Henry Chinaski does bear a resemblance to the opinionated, iconoclastic, anti-familial (not to mention alcoholic) Fields.

243: "*I always liked Gleason's comedy . . .*" Whitman's, 12.

Chapter 9: The Fascination of the (Extra)Ordinary: The Short Stories of Charles Bukowski

249: "*I started with . . .*" Letter to Douglas Blazek, 4 Nov. 1964.

249: "*He began almost compulsively . . .*" In *Hank*, Bukowski gives the following account (similar to the one in *Ham on Rye*): "In the fall of 1935, when his acne was at its worst, Hank wrote his first short story, basing his main character on Baron Manfred von Richthofen, the World War I flying ace. 'His hand was shot off, and he kept fighting guys out of the sky. This is all psychologically impossible. I understand. But remember, my face was breaking out in boils while everybody else was making love to their fellow students and all that. I was the ugly boy of the neighborhood, so I wrote this long story. It was a little yellow notebook. It cost me six cents. I wrote with a pencil, how this guy with the iron hand shot down this guy and that guy' " (34). The first published story was "Aftermath of a Lengthy Rejection Slip," *Story* (New York, March–April, 1944) 2, 4, 5, 97–99. For a more precise chronology of the early short story publications, see David Barker, "Charles Bukowski: The *First* Quarter Century" in *Sure*, 5 & 6 (1992): 53–54.

249: "*Although he returned . . .*" For the some of the details surrounding this event, and the experience of writing for *Open City* generally, see the "Foreword" in Charles Bukowski, *Notes of a Dirty Old Man*, 5–8 and the story "The Birth, Life and Death of an Underground Newspaper," in Charles Bukowski, *Erections, Ejaculations, Exhibitions and General Tales of Ordinary Madness*, 109–29. According to Cherkovski, the column, which began in May of 1967, resulted in some minor harassment of Bukowski by the postal authorities (*Hank*, 187–93).

249: *"These columns subsequently included . . ."* Julian Smith, "Charles Bukowski and the Avant-Garde" in *The Review of Contemporary Fiction* 5.3 (1985): 56.

249–250: *"The fiction was of two sorts . . ."* The content of many of his stories would later appear in his novels. This is especially true of the *Notes* collection where roughly half of the columns contain incidents later used in the novels.

250: *"Although his serious short story production . . ."* See letter of 16 February 1983 to Loss Glazer. A propos of Saroyan, Bukowski told Cherkovski: "A tough daddy. You should read *The Daring Young Man on the Flying Trapeze*. It was revolutionary in its day" (*Whitman's*, 30). For a discussion of the relationship to Saroyan, see, David Stephen Calonne, "Two on the Trapeze: Charles Bukowski & William Saroyan," in *Sure*, 5 & 6 (1992): 26–35.

250: *"In terms of his contemporaries . . ."* As Thomas McGonigle put it "no university is gonna save this guy with a chair in creative writing like they did for Raymond Carver, the academy's favorite rewrite man of the low-life experience." Thomas McGonigle, "A Bottle Stain," in *The Review of Contemporary Fiction* 5.3 (1985): 37. Carver was an admirer of Bukowski's. See the poem, "You Don't know what Love is (an evening with Charles Bukowski)," in Raymond Carver, *Fires: Essays Poems Stories*, 57.

250: *"indeed, in the most recent collection . . ."* The extent to which Bukowski has moved away from the use of the first person and the subjectivity that it lends a text is striking. The statistics are as follows, with the percent indicating the number of stories in each collection written in the third person:

Notes of a Dirty Old Man:	21%
Erections, Ejaculations, Exhibitions and General Tales of Ordinary Madness:	19%
South Of No North:	44%
Hot Water Music:	56%
Septuagenarian Stew:	76%

251: *"Not surprisingly . . ."* James Michael Cooke's masters thesis, *The Grotesque Tradition in the Short Stories of Charles Bukowski* (University of North Texas, 1988) is interesting but focuses on one aspect of the earlier stories. (It is also, to my knowledge, the first and only M.A. thesis or Ph.D. dissertation in English on Bukowski.)

255: *"Sexual arousal . . ."* Some of the stories collected in *Hot Water Music* first appeared in "girlie" magazines and one sometimes feels that the more explicit sexual passages were inserted in the stories for extra-artistic reasons, as a function of the place of their first publication. There is some support for this suspicion. Queried about writing for "porno" magazines, Bukowski told an interviewer: "I would write a good story that I liked, but I would find an excuse to throw in a sex scene right in the middle of the story. It seemed to work. It was okay." See Hodenfeld, 59.

255: *"It would be hard to imagine . . ."* Bukowski was aware of the problem of distance: "Giovanni Boccaccio wrote it [about sex] much better. he had the distance and the style. I am still too near the target to effect total grace. people simply think I'm dirty" (N 165).

256: *"Such writing calls . . ."* Roland Barthes, *Writing Degree Zero*, 67–68.

258: *"One reviewer perceptively . . ."* In Schmidt, 111.

259: *"As Bukowski remarked . . ."* Charles Bukowski, "He Beats His Women."

260: *"In 'Decline and Fall' . . ."* One sign of increasing mediation is the number of stories which are, so to speak, told second hand: one character telling another what happened to him, or even something that has been told to him. Moreover, 17 of the 36 stories in *Hot Water Music* involve the telephone, a materialization of the increased distance in the stories.

263: *"What strains credulity . . ."* But that this, too, is clearly within the realm of possibility is corroborated by the 1991 Dahmer case in Milwaukee where the killer was not overly concerned with hiding his tracks.

264: *"Here the situation . . ."* It is also less sensational and brutal than in "The Fiend," a story in *Erections* with a similar theme. The differences are instructive and typical of the differences between the early and late stories. Kevin's alleged abuse in "Some Hangover" is of having taken two girls into a closet, removed their panties and "sniffed their peepees." In "The Fiend," Martin Blanchard is shown brutally raping a little girl. It is a powerful story (also not without humor) and a serious attempt to examine the causes of such behavior. But the literal description of the act and the description of the policemen's brutality at the end work against the humor. "Some Hangover" profits from the fact that the abuse itself is of a relatively mild sort, isn't described at any length and is not conclusively proven and that it is the aftereffects that provide the content of the story and allow the humor. Another factor that "normalizes" the later stories is that they frequently involve couples whereas the early stories often had to do with loners.

267: *"The tone throughout is objective . . ."* Roger Fowler's description of how Hemingway achieved his objectivity in *Linguistic Criticism*, 57.

268: *"Yet the stories . . ."* And certainly of content to life. A number of the stories in *Hot Water Music* and *Septuagenarian Stew* reflect the filming of *Barfly* and the increased fame which came to Bukowski in the 1980s after its release. See "Less Delicate than the Locust," and "Scum Grief" in *Hot Water Music* and "Action," "Fame," and "Mad Enough" in *Septuagenarian Stew*.

278–279: *"Generally speaking . . ."* Thomas M. Leitch, "The Debunking Rhythm of the American Short Story," in Susan Lohafer and Jo Ellyn Clarey, eds. *Short-Story Theory at the Crossroads*, 133.

WORKS CITED

PRIMARY SOURCES

Works by Charles Bukowski (all published by Black Sparrow Press unless otherwise noted):

Burning in Water Drowning in Flame: Selected Poems 1955–1973 (1974)

Dangling in the Tournefortia (1981)

Erections, Ejaculations, Exhibitions and General Tales of Ordinary Madness (San Francisco: City Lights Books, 1975)

Factotum (1975)

Ham on Rye (1982)

Hot Water Music (1983)

In the Shadow of the Rose (1991)

Love Is a Dog from Hell: Poems 1974–1977 (1977)

Notes of a Dirty Old Man (City Lights, 1969)

Play The Piano Drunk Like A Percussion Instrument Until The Fingers Begin To Bleed A Bit (1979)

Post Office (1971, reset 1992 for 26th and later printings)

Roominghouse Madrigals (1988)

Septuagenarian Stew: Stories & Poems (1990)

Sometimes You Get So Alone That It Just Makes Sense (1986)

South of No North: Stories of the Buried Life (1973)

War All the Time Poems 1981–1984 (1984)

Women (1978)

Horses Don't Bet On People & Neither Do I, The Wormwood Review: 95, Vol. 24, No. 3.

"He Beats His Women," in *Second Coming: Special Charles Bukowski Issue*, Vol. 2, No. 3 (1974).

"Aftermath of a Lengthy Rejection Slip," *Story* (March–April, 1944).

"Preface" to John Fante, *Ask the Dust*. Santa Barbara: Black Sparrow, 1980.

"Introduction" Douglas Blazek, *Skull Juices*. San Francisco: Twowindows Press, 1970.

"A Rambling Essay on Poetics and the Bleeding Life Written While Drinking a Six-Pack Tall." *A Bukowski Sampler*. Ed. Douglas Blazek. Madison: Quixote Press, 1969. 9–15.

"Upon the Mathematics of the Breath and the Way." *Alt's Normal Here: A Charles Bukowski Primer*. Fremont: Ruddy Duck, 1985. 81–85.

Das Liebesleben der Hyäne Köln: Kiepenhauer & Witsch, 1986.

Letters:

————. "To Al Purdy." 2 March 1965. *The Bukowski/Purdy Letters: 1964–1974*. Ed. Seamus Cooney. Sutton West and Santa Barbara: The Pagel Press, 1983. 43–44.

————. "To Douglas Blazek." 4 Nov. 1964. *A Bukowski Sampler*. Madison: Quixote Press, 1969. 3–5.

————. "To Carl Weissner." 1 Aug. 1969. *Gedichte die einer Schrieb bevor er im 8. Stockwerk aus dem Fenster Sprang*. Augsburg: MaroVerlag, 1974. 92–93.

————. "To Loss Glazier." 16 Feb. 1983. *Alt's Normal Here: A Charles Bukowski Primer*. Fremont: Ruddy Duck, 1985. 108–110.

Interviews:

Bukowski, Charles. *Paying for Horses: an interview with Charles Bukowski*. *London Magazine* (Dec. 1974–Jan. 1975): 35–54.

————. "Bukowski-Interview." *Kaputt in Hollywood*. Augsburg: Maro-Verlag, 1976, 2 Nov. 1975. 134–42.

————. "Rolling with Life's Punches." with Silvia Bizo. *Los Angeles Times* 1 Jan. 1981.

————. "Charles Bukowski." *The Poet's Craft: Interviews from the New York Quarterly*. Ed. William Packard. New York: Paragon, 1987. 318–323.

————. "Charles Bukowski interviewed by Chris Hodenfeld." *Film Comment* 23 (1987): 53–59.

————. "Tough Guys Write Poetry: Charles Bukowski by Sean Penn." *Interview* (Sept. 1987): 94–100.

SECONDARY SOURCES

Abrams, M.L. *The Mirror and the Lamp: Romantic Theory and the Critical Tradition*. Oxford: Oxford U. Press, 1953.

Adorno, Theodor. *Mahler: Eine Musikalische Physiognomik*. Frankfurt: Suhrkamp, 1960.

—————. "Mahler: Wiener Gedenkrede." *Quasi Una Fantasia: Musikalische Schriften II*, 115–54. Frankfurt: Suhrkamp, 1963.

Altieri, Charles. *Self and Sensibility in Contemporary American Poetry*. Cambridge: Cambridge U. Press, 1984.

—————. "Objective Image and Act of Mind." *PMLA* 91 (1976).

Anon. Rev. of *Burning in Water Drowning in Flame: Selected Poems 1955–1973*. *Virginia Quarterly Review* 51 (1975): lv–lvi.

Aronowitz, Stanley. *False Promises: The Shaping of the American Working Class Consciousness*. New York: McGraw-Hill, 1973.

Barker, David. "Charles Bukowski: The First Quarter Century." *Sure, The Charles Bukowski Newsletter* 5 & 6. Ojai. 51–61.

Barthes, Roland. *Writing Degree Zero*. New York: Noonday, 1968.

—————. "Flaubert and the Sentence." *A Barthes Reader*. Ed. Susan Sontag. New York: Hill and Wang, 1982. 296–304.

Beckett, Samuel. *Three Novels*. New York, Grove, 1958.

Benjamin, Walter. "The Storyteller." In *Illuminations*. New York: Schocken, 1969.

Bloom, Harold. *The Anxiety of Influence*. New York, Oxford, 1973.

Braverman, Harry. *Labor and Monopoly Capital: The Degradation of Work in the Twentieth Century*. New York: Monthly Review Press, 1974.

—————. "The Degradation of Work in the Twentieth Century." *Monthly Review* 34 (1982): 1–13.

Brecht, Bertolt. *Arbeitsjournal*. 2 vols. Ed. W. Hecht. Frankfurt, 1973.

—————. "A Dialogue About acting." *Brecht on Theatre*, Ed. John Willett. New York: Hill and Wang, 1964. 26–28.

—————. "Kurzer Bericht über 400 (vierbundert) junge Lyriker." *Über Lyrik*. Frankfurt: Suhrkamp, 1964. 7–10.

—————. *Mother Courage and Her Children*, English version by Eric Bentley. New York: Grove Weidenfeld, 1966.

—————. *Poems 1913–1956*. Ed. John Willett. New York: Methuen, 1979.

————. "Singende Steyrwägen." *Gesammelte Werke IV Gedichte.* Frankfurt: Suhrkamp, 1967, 318.

Breslin, James E. B. *From Modern to Contemporary: American Poetry, 1945–1965.* Chicago: U. of Chicago Press, 1984.

Brooks, Cleanth. "Irony as a Principle of Structure." *The Critical Tradition.* Ed. David H. Richter. New York: Bedford/St. Martins, 1989. 799–806.

Cain, Jimmy E. "Bukowski's Imagist Roots." *West Georgia College Review* 19 (1987): 10–17.

————. "*Women*: The Siren Calls of Boredom." *The Review of Contemporary Fiction* 5 (1985): 9–14.

Calonne, David Stephen. "Two on the Trapeeze: Charles Bukowski & William Saroyan." *Sure, The Charles Bukowski Newsletter* 5 & 6 (19923): 26–35.

Cherkovski, Neeli. *Hank: The Life of Charles Bukowski.* New York: Random House, 1991.

————. "Notes on a Dirty Old Man: Charles Bukowski." In *Whitman's Wild Children.* Venice: Lapis, 1988. 3–37.

Chomsky, Noam, *On Power and Ideology: The Managna Lectures.* Boston: South End Press, 1987.

Ciotti, Paul. "Bukowski." *Los Angeles Times Magazine.* 22 March 1987, 18.

Conroy, Jack. Rev. of "Crucifix in a Deathhand" and "Cold Dogs in the Courtyard." In *American Book Collector* (Feb., 1966): 5.

Cooke, James Michael. "The Grotesque Tradition in the Short Stories of Charles Bukowski." University of North Texas, 1988.

Dauzat, A., Dubois, J., and Mitterand, H. *Nouveau Dictionnaire Etymologique et Historique* art. "banal." Paris: Librairie Larousse, 1964.

Davis, Mike. *Prisoners of the American Dream: Politics and Economy in the History of the US Working Class.* London: Verso, 1986.

————. *City of Quartz: Excavating the Future in Los Angeles.* London: Verso, 1990.

Dictionary of Literary Biography. "Charles Bukowski." Detroit: Gale, 1980. 112–116.

Dearborn, Mary V. *The Happiest Man Alive: A Biography of Henry Miller.* New York: Simon and Schuster, 1991.

Dostoyevsky, Fyodor. *Notes from Underground/The Double* trans. and introduced by Jesse Coulson. London: Penguin, 1972.

Engels, Friedrich. "Letter to Minna Kautsky." *Marxists on Literature:*

An Anthology. Ed. David Craig. Harmondsworth: Penguin, 1975. 267–268.

Esterly, Glen. "Buk: The Pock-marked Poetry of Charles Bukowski: Notes of a Dirty Old Mankind." *Rolling Stone*, 17 June 1976: 28–34.

Faas, Ekbert. *Towards a New American Poetics: Essays and Interviews*. Santa Barbara: Black Sparrow, 1978.

Fante, John. *Ask the Dust*. Santa Barbara: Black Sparrow, 1980.

—————. *The Wine of Youth: Selected Stories*. Santa Barbara: Black Sparrow, 1985.

—————. *Selected Letters 1932–1981*. Ed. Seamus Cooney. Santa Rosa: Black Sparrow, 1991.

—————. *Fante/Mencken: John Fante & H.L. Mencken A Personal Correspondence 1930–1952*, Ed. Michael Moreau. Santa Rosa: Black Sparrow, 1989.

Ferguson, Robert. *Engima: The Life of Knut Hamsun*. New York: Farrar, Strauss & Giroux, 1987.

—————. *Henry Miller: A Life*. New York: Norton, 1991.

Fetterley, Judith. *The Resisting Reader: A Feminist Approach to American Fiction*. Bloomington: Indian U. Press, 1978.

Fogel, Al. "I Collect Charles Bukowski." In *Under the Influence: A Collection of Works by Charles Bukowski*. Sudbury, MA: Jeffrey H. Weinberg, 1984.

Ford, Henry, in collaboration with Samuel Crowther. *Today and Tomorrow*. Garden City: Doubleday, Page & Company, 1926.

Fowler, Roger. *Linguistic Criticism*. Oxford: Oxford U. Press, 1986.

Fox, Hugh. *Charles Bukowski: A Critical and Bibliographical Study*. Somerville, MA: Abyss, 1969, 1971.

Freud, Sigmund. "On Narcissism: An Introduction." *General Psychological Theory*. New York: Collier, 1963. 56–82.

—————. "A Special Type of Object Choice Made by Men." *Sexuality and the Psychology of Love*. New York: Collier, 1963. 49–58.

Fulton, Len. "See Bukowski Run." *Small Press Review*, 4 Apr. 1973: 26–31.

Geraths, Armin and Herget, Kurt. "Paradoxate Trivialität—Die Kurzprosa-Künste des Underground-Poeten Charles Bukowski." *anglistik & englischunterricht*. 2 (1977): 173–195.

Gramsci, Antonio. *Selections from the Prison Notebooks*. Ed. and trans. Quintin Hoare and Geoffrey Nowell Smith. New York: International Publishers, 1971.

Harrison, Russell T. "The Blue Suit: An episode from Charles Bukowski's Factotum." *Germanica Olomucensia* 8 (1989): 85–92.

————. "An Analysis of Charles Bukowski's 'fire station.'" *Concerning Poetry* 18 (1985): 67–83.

Hallberg, Robert von. *American Poetry and Culture, 1945–1980.* Cambridge: Harvard U. Press, 1985.

Hamper, Ben. *Rivethead: Tales from the Assembly Line.* New York: Warner, 1991.

Hamsun, Knut. *Hunger.* New York: Farrar, Straus & Giroux, 1967.

————. *The Cultural Life of Modern America.* Ed. and tr. Barbara Gordon Morgridge. Cambridge: Harvard U. Press, 1969.

Hecht, Werner, ed. *Brecht: Sein Leben in Bildern und Texten.* Frankfurt: Insel, 1988.

Hinton, David. "Introduction." *The Selected Poems of Tu Fu.* New York: New Directions, 1989. vii–xvi.

Hoffman, Steven K. "Impersonal Personalism: The Making of a Confessional Poetic." *ELH* 45 (1978): 687–709.

Huffzky, Karin. "Big Daddy Is Watching You." *Literatur Konkret* (Fall, 1979): 22–23.

Hunnicutt, Benjamin. *Work Without End: Abandoning Shorter Hours for the Right to Work.* Philadelphia: Temple U. Press, 1988.

Jakobsen, Roman. "Two Aspects of Language and Two Types of Aphasic Disturbance." *Language and Literature.* Eds. Krystyna Pomorska and Stephen Rudy. Cambridge: Harvard U. Press, 1987. 95–114.

————. "Marginal Notes on the Prose of the Poet Pasternak." *Language and Literature.* 301–17.

James, Burnett. *The Music of Gustav Mahler.* Rutherford: Fairleigh Dickinson, 1985.

Kalecki, Michal. "Political Aspects of Full Employment." *Selected Essays on the Dynamics of the Capitalist Economy: 1933–1970.* Cambridge: Cambridge U. Press, 1971. 138–145.

Kenner, Hugh. *A Homemade World: The American Modernist Writers.* Baltimore: Johns Hopkins, 1975.

Kinsman, Clare D., ed. *Contemporary Authors.* Detroit: Gale Research Co., 1976.

Kolko, Gabriel. *Main Currents in Modern American History.* New York: Pantheon, 1976.

Lacan, Jacques. "The Agency of the Letter in the Unconscious or Reason since Freud." *Écrits: A Selection.* New York: Norton, 1977.

Langbaum, Robert. *The Poetry of Experience: The Dramatic Mono-logue in Modern Literary Tradition.* Chicago: U. of Chicago Press, 1957.

Lea, Henry A. *Gustav Mahler: Man on the Margin.* Bonn: Bouvier, 1985.

Leitch, Thomas A. "The Debunking Rhythm of the American Short Story." *Short-Story Theory at the Crossroads.* Eds. Susan Lohafer and Jo Ellyn Clarey. Baton Rouge: LSU Press, 1989.

Lemay, J. A. Leo. "Franklin's Autobiography and the American Dream." *Benjamin Franklin's Autobiography.* Eds. J. A. Leo Lemay and P. M. Zall. New York: Norton, 1986. 349–360.

Locklin, Gerald. "Bukowski's *War All the Time* and 'Horses Don't Bet on People and Neither do I.'" *The Review of Contemporary Fiction* 5 (1985): 34–36.

—————. "Setting Free the Buk." *The Review of Contemporary Fiction* 5 (1985): 27–31.

—————. Rev. of *Dangling in the Tournefortia. The American Book Review* 4 (1982): 6

Lodge, David. *The Modes of Modern Writing.* Chicago: U. of Chicago, 1977.

London, Jack. *John Barleycorn. Novels and Social Writings,* New York: The Library of America, 1982.

—————. *Martin Eden.* Harmondsworth: Penguin, 1967.

Lowell, Robert. *Life Studies.* New York: Noonday, 1964. 73–74.

Lübecker Nachrichten. "'Harter Junge' Bukowski wird 70." 8 Aug. 1990.

Lukács, Georg. *History and Class Consciousness: Studies in Marxist Dialectics.* Cambridge: MIT Press, 1971.

—————. "The Intellectual Physiognomy of Literary Characters." *Radical Perspectives in the Arts.* Ed. Lee Baxandall. Harmondsworth: Penguin, 1972. 89–141.

—————. Marcuse, Herbert. *Eros and Civilization.* New York: Vintage, 1962.

—————. An Essay on Liberation. Boston: Beacon, 1969.

Mayer, Hans. "Bertolt Brecht oder die plebejische Traditon." *Anmerkungen zu Brecht.* Frankfurt: Suhrkamp, 1965. 7–23.

McGonigle, Thomas. "A Bottle Stain." *The Review of Contemporary Fiction* 5 (1985): 37–38.

McWilliams, Cary. *Southern California: An Island on the Land.* Salt Lake City: Gibbs Smith, 1973.

Mailer, Norman. "The Argument Reinvigorated." *The American Novel Since World War II*. Ed. Marcus Klein. New York: Fawcett. 1969.

—————. "Narcissism." *Critical Essays on Henry Miller*. Ed. Ronald Goltesman. New York: G. K. Hall, 1992. 131–144.

—————. *The Prisoner of Sex*. New York: Primus, 1985.

Marx, Karl. *Grundrisse*. New York: Vintage, 1973.

Miller, Henry. *The Cosmological Eye* New York: New Directions, 1939.

—————. *Gliding into the Everglades*. Lake Oswego, OR: Lost Pleiade Press. 1977.

—————. "The Tailor Shop" in *Black Spring* (New York: Grove, 1963): 77–147.

—————. *Sexus*. New York: Grove, 1965.

—————. *Tropic of Capricorn*. New York: Grove, 1961.

Millet, Kate. *Sexual Politics*. New York: Ballantine, 1978.

Mitchell, Roger. Rev. of *Love is a Dog from Hell: Poems 1974–1977*. *Library Journal* 103 (1978): 465.

Montano, Mario. "Notes on the International Crisis." *Midnight Oil: Work. Energy. War. 1973–1992* ([New York]: Autonomedia, 1992): 115–142.

Negri, Antonio. "Archaeology and Project: The Mass Worker and the Social Worker," in A. Negri: *Revolution Retrieved: Selected Writings on Marx, Keynes, Capitalist Crisis & New Social Subjects 1967–1983*. London: Red Notes, 1988.

Nin, Anaïs. *The Diary of Anaïs Nin 1931–1934*. Ed. Gunther Stuhlmann. New York: Harcourt Brace Jovanovich, 1966.

Orwell, George. *Down and Out in Paris and London*. New York: Berkeley, 1959.

Paz, Octavio. *The Labyrinth of Solitude*. New York: Grove Weidenfeld, 1985.

Perloff, Marjorie. "Realism and the Confessional Mode of Robert Lowell." *Contemporary Literature* 11 (1970): 470–487.

Poulantzas, Nicos. *Classes in Contemporary Capitalism*. London: Verso, 1978.

Riley, Carolyn and Phyllis Carmel Mendelson. Eds. *Contermporary Literary Criticism*. (Detroit: Gale, 1981).

Rimbaud, Arthur. *Oeuvres Complètes* Ed. Antoine Adam. Bibliotheque de la Pléiade. Paris: Gallimard, 1972.

Roediger, David R. and Philip Foner. *Our Own Time: A History of*

American Labor and the Working Day. London: Verso, 1989.

Rosenthal, M. L. *The New Poets: American and British Poetry Since World War II* New York: Oxford U. Press, 1967.

Sandarg, Robert. "The Classical Buk." *Sure, the Charles Bukowski Newsletter* 3 (1991): 22–32.

Schmidt, Horst. *"It's Good to be Back": Ein Outsider und seine deutschen Leser: Die Rezeption Charles Bukowskis im deutschen Sprachgebiet (1968–1986).* Augsburg: MaroVerlag, 1988.

Schor, Juliet B. *The Overworked American.* New York: Basic Books, 1991.

Sherman, Jory. *Bukowski: Friendship, Fame & Bestial Myth.* Augusta, GA: Blue Horse, 1981.

Smith, Julian. "Charles Bukowski and the Avant-Garde." *The Review of Contemporary Fiction* 5 (1985): 56–59.

Spotnitz, Frank. "The Hottest Dead Man in Hollywood." *American Film* (July/August 1989): 40–44, 54.

Swados, Harvey. *On the Line.* Urbana: U. of Illinois Press. rpt. 1989.

Taylor, Frederick Winslow. *The Principles of Scientific Management.* Easton: Hive, 1985.

Terkel, Studs. *Working People Talk About What They Do All Day and How They Feel About What They Do All Day.* New York: Ballantine, 1974.

Thompson, E.P. "Time, Work-Discipline, and Industrial Capitalism." *Past & Present* 38 (1967): 56–97.

Thomson, Philip. *The Poetry of Brecht.* Chapel Hill: U. of N. Carolina Press, 1989.

Tucker, Ken. Rev. of *Dangling in the Tournefortia. The Village Voice* 23 Mar. 1982: 42.

Watt, Ian. *The Rise of the Novel: Studies in Defoe, Richardson and Fielding.* Berkeley: U. of California Press, 1957.

Weinstein, Norman. "South of No North: Bukowski in Deadly Ernest." *The Review of Contemporary Fiction* 5 (1985): 52–55.

Williams, Raymond. *The Long Revolution: An Analysis of the Democratic Industrial and Cultural Changes Transforming Our Society.* New York: Columbian U. Press, 1961.

Williams, William Carlos. *The Selected Letters of William Carlos Williams.* Ed. by John C. Thirlwall. New York: New Directions, 1957.

Work in America: Report of a Special Task Force to the Secretary of Health Education and Welfare. Cambridge: MIT Press, 1973.

Zerowork Collective. "Introduction" to *Zerowork* 1. *Midnight Oil: Work, Energy, War. 1973–1992*. ([New York]: Autonomedia, 1992): 108–114.

Zinn, Howard. *A People's History of the United States*. New York: Harper, 1980.

Index to the Text

Abbott, Bud, 244
Abrams, M. H., 21, 95, 113
Adorno, Theodor, 240–241
"Aftermath of a Lengthy Rejection Slip" (Bukowski), 237
Alger, Horatio, 129, 154
"All the Assholes in the World and Mine" (Bukowski), 269
"All the Pussy We Want" (Bukowski), 250
Altieri, Charles, 80, 92, 96, 101–103, 106
American Dream, 13, 153, 177, 219, 222
An American Tragedy (Dreiser), 124
Anderson, Sherwood, 217, 218, 250, 251
The Anxiety of Influence (Bloom), 217
Aristotle, 95
Aronowitz, Stanley, 87, 128, 151
Ask the Dust (Fante), 219–230
Autobiography (Franklin), 13–14

Bach, 217, 237
Barthes, Roland, 31, 256
Beat poets, 29, 41
Beckett, Samuel, 269
"Beer at the Corner Bar" (Bukowski), 268
Beethoven, 237, 238, 239, 241
Benjamin, Walter, 99
"The Birth, Life and Death of an Underground Newspaper" (Bukowski), 269
Bloom, Harold, 217
Bottom Dogs (Dahlberg), 124
Brahms, 237
Braverman, Harry, 139
Brecht, Bertolt, 31, 33, 115–120, 174, 215
Breslin, James E. B., 32, 33

Brooks, Cleanth, 33, 95
Bryan, John, 249
Buddenbrooks (Mann), 168
Burroughs, William, 35
Butler, Samuel, 168

Cantwell, Robert, 124
Carver, Raymond, 250
The Castle (Kafka), 235
Céline, Louis-Ferdinand, 217, 218
Chaplin, Charlie, 218
Cherkovski, Neeli, 20, 243
City of Quartz (Davis), 176
Clark, Tom, 47
Coates, Eric, 217
Confessional poets, 29–30, 41–45
"Confessions of a Man Insane Enough to Live with Beasts" (Bukowski), 20, 269
Conroy, Jack, 40, 124
Costello, Lou, 244
"A Couple of Winos" (Bukowski), 256–258
Couples (Updike), 197
Cultural Life of Modern America (Hamsun), 233–234
Cummings, E. E., 217

Dahlberg, Edward, 124
Dangling in the Tournefortia (Bukowski), 219
Davis, Bette, 218
Davis, Mike, 176
"The Day We Talked about James Thurber" (Bukowski), 253, 263
Death and Transfiguration (Strauss), 86
"The Death of the Father II" (Bukowski), 265–268
"Decline and Fall" (Bukowski), 259–265, 279
The Disinherited (Conroy), 124

"Doing Time with Public Enemy No. 1" (Bukowski), 250

"$$$$$$ (Bukowski), 18, 70–77, 78, 80

Dostoyevsky, 217, 218, 235

Down and Out in Paris and London (Orwell), 157, 236–237

Dreiser, Theodore, 124

"eating my senior citizen's dinner at the Sizzler" (Bukowski), 53–57

"education" (Bukowski), 61

Eliot, T.S., 30, 33

Engels, Friedrich, 124

Erections, Ejaculations, Exhibitions, and General Tales of Ordinary Madness (Bukowski), 250, 252, 253, 255, 259

Eros and Civilization (Marcuse), 129

An Essay on Liberation (Marcuse), 129, 135

"everybody talks too much" (Bukowski), 64

Factotum (Bukowski), 14, 15, 17, 18, 20, 21, 123, 124, 131, 140–151, 158, 161, 179–180, 186–196, 202, 204, 207, 213, 222, 223, 227, 230, 231–239, 244–247, 256

Fante, John, 7, 21, 217, 218–230, 250

Flaubert, Gustave, 30, 31, 32, 96

Ford, Henry, 131, 137

Franklin, Benjamin, 13–14

"The Fuck Machine" (Bukowski), 259

Full of Life (Fante), 220

Fulton, Len, 183

Galileo (Brecht), 118

"the gentleman and the bastard" (Bukowski), 117–118

Geraths, Armin, 251, 255, 259

Germany, Bukowski's acceptance in, 16, 29

Ginsberg, Allen, 30

Glazier, Loss, 217

Gleason, Jackie, 116, 218, 243–247

Gramsci, Antonio, 126–128, 137

Grundrisse (Marx), 128–129

"guava tree" (Bukowski), 116

Gustav Mahler: Man on the Margin (Lea), 240

Hall, Donald, 100

Hallberg, Rovert von, 29

Ham on Rye (Bukowski), 17, 18, 20, 160, 162–182, 198, 222

Hamsun, Knut, 21, 217, 218, 224, 231–235

"Have You Read Pirandello?" (Bukowski), 254–255

Haydn, 241

"Head Job" (Bukowski), 258–259

Hegel, 37, 47, 63

Hemingway, Ernest, 210, 217, 218, 250, 251

Hepburn, Katharine, 204

Herget, Kurt, 251, 255, 259

Hinton, David, 32

History and Class Consciousness (Lukács), 85

Hitler, Adolf, 218

"horse & fist" (Bukowski), 60

Hot Water Music (Bukowski), 250, 253, 259, 264, 265, 268

Howard, Leslie, 218

Huffzky, Karin, 214

Hunger (Hamsun), 224, 231–237

Huxley, Aldous, 218

"I didn't want to" (Bukowski), 30, 60–66

In Dubious Battle (Steinbeck), 124

The Iron Heel (London), 123

"It's a Dirty World" (Bukowski), 268

Jakobson, Roman, 95–96, 101, 102

James, Burnett, 241
James, Henry, 31
Jerrers, Robinson, 63, 217, 218
John Barleycorn (London), 15, 123
Joyce, James, 35
The Jungle (Sinclair), 123

"*Kenyon Review*, After the Sandstorm" (Bukowski), 34
Kolko, Gabriel, 126, 150–151, 175
Kuhle Wampe (Brecht), 116–117

Labor and Monopoly Capitalism (Braverman), 139
Lacan, Jacques, 111
The Land of Plenty (Cantwell), 124
Langbaum, Robert, 41, 48, 52, 59
Lawrence, D. H., 30, 210, 218
Lea, Henry A., 240
Leaves of Grass (Whitman), 33
"let nothing ever happen" (Bukowski), 36
Lévi-Strauss, Claude, 96
"The Life of a Bum" (Bukowski), 15, 265, 270–279
Life Studies (Lowell), 44, 98, 102
Lodge, David, 95
London, Jack, 15, 123
"looking for a job" (Bukowski), 107–114
Los Angeles Times, 145, 159, 175
Love Is a Dog from Hell (Bukowski), 19
Lowell, Robert, 42–45, 98–102, 110
Lukács, Georg, 85
Lyrical Ballads (Wordsworth), 33

Mahler, Gustav, 13, 237–242
Mailer, Norman, 154–155, 188
"Maja Thurup" (Bukowski), 259
Mann, Thomas, 168
Marcuse, Herbert, 129–130, 135
Martin Eden (London), 15, 123
Marx, Groucho and Chico, 244
Marx, Karl, 128–129

Mayer, Hans, 174, 178, 180
McCullers, Carson, 217, 218, 250
McWilliams, Carey, 175
Midnight Oil, 149
Miller, Henry, 35, 153–158, 188, 207, 210, 223, 229
Millett, Kate, 184
Mitchell, Roger, 40
Molloy (Beckett) 269
Mondrian, Piet, 217
Moore, Marianne, 35
"The Most Beautiful Woman in Town" (Bukowski), 253–254
Mother Courage (Brecht), 115, 173–174
Mozart, 217, 237, 238, 239, 241

Negri, Antonio, 123
Neruda, Pablo, 96
Nicholson, Jack, 218
Nietzsche, 217, 218
Notebooks of Malte Laurids Brigge (Rilke), 235
Notes from Underground (Dostoyevsky), 235
Notes of a Dirty Old Man (Bukowski), 250, 255

On the Line (Swados), 124, 125
One-Dimensional Man (Marcuse), 129
Open City (newspaper), 249
Orwell, George, 21, 157, 236–237
"out of the mainstream" (Bukowski), 37–39
"overhead mirrors" (Bukowski), 43–45, 102–107

Packard, William, 30, 32, 159, 218
Paterson (Williams), 251
Paz, Octavio, 197–198
Penn, Sean, 69
Perloff, Marjorie, 102
Phenomenology (Hegel), 47
Poetics (Aristotle), 95
Portnoy's Complaint (Roth), 197

Post Office (Bukowski), 7, 14, 17, 19, 21, 123, 124, 131–141, 150–151, 160–161, 181, 183, 184–186, 193, 207, 222, 223
Poulantzas, Nicos, 168–169
Pound, Ezra, 30, 31

"A Rambling Essay on Poetics and the Bleeding Life . . ." (Bukowski), 33
"retired" (Bukowski), 97–102
Richthofen, Baron von, 218
Rilke, Rainer Maria, 235
Rimbaud, Arthur, 176
Roosevelt, Franklin Delano, 128, 167
Rosenthal, M. L., 42
Roth, Philip, 197

"Sailing Home from Rapallo" (Lowell), 110
Saroyan, William, 217, 250, 251
Schmeling, Max, 218
Schopenhauer, 217, 218
Scientific Management (Taylor), 17
A Season in Hell (Rimbaud), 176
Septuagenarian Stew (Bukowski), 31, 250, 265, 268
Sexual Politics (Millett), 184
Sexus (Miller), 153, 156–158
Shostakovich, Dimitri, 13, 237
Sinclair, Upton, 123
Sister Carrie (Dreiser), 124
"Skunk Hour" (Lowell), 42–44
Smith, Julian, 255–256
Snodgrass, William, 32
"Some Hangover" (Bukowski), 264–265, 279
"sometimes it's hard to know what to do" (Bukowski), 18
South of No North (Bukowski), 250, 251, 256, 259
"Sparks" (Bukowski), 18, 70, 78, 80–87, 110, 116
Steinbeck, John, 124
"The Storyteller" Benjamin), 99

Strauss, Richard, 86
Swados, Harvey, 124
"sweater" (Bukowski), 48–53, 56, 57

Taylor, Frederick, 17, 33, 126, 131, 137, 139
Tchaikowsky, 238
"Terminal Days at Beverly Farms" (Lowell), 98–101
"There are So Many Houses and Dark Streets Without Help" (Bukowski), 57–59
"transformation and disfiguration" (Bukowski), 18, 70, 82, 87–93, 110, 113, 116
Tropic of Capricorn (Miller), 153, 157
Tu Fu, 32–33
Turgenev, 217, 218
"Two Aspects of Language and Two Types of Aphasic Disturbances" (Jakobson), 96

Updike, John, 197

"The Vengeance of the Damned" (Bukowski), 268
Vergil, 114

Wagner, Richard, 217, 237
"Waking in the Blue" (Lowell), 43
War All the Time (Bukowski), 18
The Way of All Flesh (Butler), 168
Wennersten, Robert, 32, 237
"we've got to communicate" (Bukowski), 66–68
Whitman, Walt, 30, 32, 35, 60, 102
Williams, Raymond, 70
Williams, William Carlos, 30, 32, 35, 41, 96, 251
Women (Bukowski), 19, 161, 193, 194, 197–215, 227, 238, 253
Wordsworth, William, 33, 95
"the workers" (Bukowski), 18
Work in America, 140

"Yankee Doodle" (Bukowski), 18,
70, 77–80, 82, 83, 86
"Yes" (Bukowski), 119
*You Get So Alone at Times That It
Just Makes Sense* (Bukowski), 31,
97

Zerowork Collective, 7
Zinn, Howard, 161